Lectures on Rhetoric and Belles Lettres

*The Author of the Wealth of Nations*

Adam Smith

Reproduced from *A Series of Original Portraits* by John Kay

# Lectures
## on
# Rhetoric and Belles Lettres

Delivered in the University of Glasgow by

### ADAM SMITH

Reported by a Student in 1762-63

Edited with an Introduction and Notes

by

### JOHN M. LOTHIAN

Thomas Nelson and Sons Ltd

London Edinburgh Paris Melbourne Johannesburg
Toronto and New York

THOMAS NELSON AND SONS LTD
Parkside Works Edinburgh 9
36 Park Street London W1
117 Latrobe Street Melbourne C1

THOMAS NELSON AND SONS (AFRICA) (Pty) LTD
P.O. Box 9881 Johannesburg

THOMAS NELSON AND SONS (CANADA) LTD
91-93 Wellington Street West   Toronto 1

THOMAS NELSON AND SONS
18 East 41st Street New York 17, N.Y.

SOCIÉTÉ FRANÇAISE D'ÉDITIONS NELSON
97 rue Monge Paris 5

Printed in Great Britain by
Robert Cunningham and Sons Ltd, Alva

# Preface
## and acknowledgments

I HAVE tried to make a continuous text from the three parts of the manuscript as indicated in the section of my Introduction which deals with Method of Treatment. As a result I am well aware that much depended on my sense of the natural sequence of Adam Smith's thought, and occasionally something on a hazardous guess. I have thought it proper, on this account, to indicate in every case the particular part of the manuscript from which inserted passages are drawn. A list of the *sigla* used to indicate the sources of the text will be found at the end of the Introduction.

I did not think it necessary, in these days of photostats, to give, like Cannan in his edition of Smith's *Lectures on Jurisprudence*, a long, detailed description of the manuscript. I am indebted to Dr Rae, of the National Library of Scotland, for the succinct technical description to be found in the Appendix.

I am deeply grateful to two of my University colleagues, Professor Alexander Macdonald, of the Chair of Bacteriology, for his help in the negotiations leading to the purchase of the manuscript, and Professor W. S. Watt, of the Chair of Humanity, for his most generous assistance in the deciphering of difficult passages in the manuscript, in supplementing my meagre acquaintance with the classics from his expert knowledge, and in suggesting or supplying or checking many notes. My thanks are also due to Dr W. Douglas Simpson, C.B.E., Librarian to the University of Aberdeen, and his assistants, for invaluable help in securing books and photostats necessary to my work as editor; to the Aberdeen University authorities for securing typing services, and to Miss Hay, secretary to the English Department, for her patience in rendering them; and to the Carnegie Trust for the Universities of Scotland for travelling and maintenance grants in aid of the necessary research. The untimely death of Principal Sir Thomas Taylor of the

University of Aberdeen has deprived the editor of the opportunity of renewing in public the thanks for help and encouragement which he previously offered in private. I received very great assistance from Mr Colin Finlayson, of Edinburgh University Library, who directed me to much relevant material still in manuscript; and Mr Weir rendered similar assistance with the Buchan and other manuscripts in Glasgow University Library; for the service of books from both these libraries, and at the National Library of Scotland, I am grateful. The editor of *The Scotsman* has readily granted permission to use in the Introduction certain phrases and paragraphs which appeared originally in that newspaper.

I wish, finally, to thank the printing and editorial staff of Messrs Thomas Nelson & Sons for their meticulous care and indispensable help most cheerfully and generously given.

JOHN M. LOTHIAN

*King's College*
*University of Aberdeen*

# Contents

## Introduction

The Manuscript xi-xiii—Lectures on Rhetoric, 1748-51 xiii-xiv
—Adam Smith's Literary Interests xiv-xv—Smith's Early
Lectures at Glasgow xv-xvii—Contents of the Lectures xvii-xix
—Characteristics and Influence xix-xxiii—Aims of Literary
Societies xxiii-xxv—Professor Stevenson's Methods and In-
fluence xxv-xxix—Logic and Belles Lettres xxix-xxxi—The
Eighteenth Century Transition xxxi-xxxiii—Pulpit Rhetoric
xxxiii-xxxiv—Thomas Sheridan and the Scots xxxiv-xxxv—
The Desire for Self-Improvement xxxv-xxxvii—Periodicals
and Courses in Culture xxxvii-xxxix—Method of Editing the
Text xxxix-xl.

## Adam Smith's Lectures

CONTENTS

## Appendix

## Index

# Introduction

At various dates in the autumn of 1958 remnants of what had once been the considerable country-house library of Whitehaugh were dispersed by auction in Aberdeen. The collection had been begun by William Forbes of Tolquhoun in the late sixteenth century. In a list of his effects, he mentions 'my haill silver-work, buikis, bedding,' etc. Tolquhoun Castle[1] was sold by an order of the Court of Session in November 1716, and taken over on behalf of the creditors in 1718, in spite of the stout resistance of the owner, William Forbes. That some, at least, of the books had been removed seems certain, for his second son, John,[2] wrote in 1779 to James Beattie, the poet and professor, concerning 'old Musick Books which had belonged to my predecessors, and were found by me among some small remains of a valuable Library, which my Gt. Gt. Grandfather, Wm. Forbes of Tolquhoun, possessed about 200 years ago. I find many of his books marked in 1588, etc. . . . Whenever I can recover any bearing his name . . . I think it an acquisition.'[3]

It would appear that John's nephew, Colonel John James Forbes-Leith, took an interest in the library and put it in order, for many of the books sold at the Aberdeen sales already mentioned contained the elaborate book-plates of himself and his wife, and in addition many contained the book-plate designed for his wife, when she became a widow. Three catalogues of the library, one made apparently in the late eighteenth, and the others in the middle of the nineteenth century, exist,[4] showing the repeated efforts of the owners to 'take stock' and to note the whereabouts on particular shelves of some of the rarer items. When, about the middle of the nineteenth century, financial difficulties again beset the family, part of the library, probably the more valuable part, was sold. A writer in *Notes and Queries* for 10 September 1859,[5]

[1] W. D. Simpson, 'Tolquhoun Castle and its Builder', *P.S.A.S.* LXXII (1938), pp. 248-74.
[2] John by right of his mother, Anne Leith, daughter and heiress of John Leith of Whitehaugh, had become laird of that estate and taken the name Forbes-Leith.
[3] Simpson, *art. cit.*, p. 252.    [4] Now in the Library of King's College, Aberdeen.
[5] 2nd Series, VIII, pp. 203-04.

J. M. [James Maidment], records the finding of an edition of Erasmus's *Apophthegmata*, 1533, with a letter from Florence Wilson to John Ogilvie on the fly-leaf. The volume was inscribed 'Williame Forbes of Tolquhoun, 1588.' 'This gentleman,' says Maidment, 'was a great book-collector, and the very rare and curious volumes which recently came from the North, and were disposed of in detached portions by Mr Nisbet in Edinburgh at various times, make it a matter of regret that the library was not sold in its entire state with a proper descriptive catalogue.' Maidment's sentiments might well be echoed a century later, for in spite of its many vicissitudes, the library at its ultimate dispersal still contained many valuable volumes—first editions of Thomas Hobbes, of Hume, Adam Smith, Thomas Reid, and others, in addition to several seventeenth-century poetical, scientific, and legal manuscripts, the records of a baronial court for something like a hundred years, estate records, and family papers.

Among the numerous Whitehaugh books and papers purchased by me at different dates at the Aberdeen sales, were two sets of lecture notes made by students. One set, in five octavo volumes, lacking the first and numbered 2 to 6, was a course of lectures on Jurisprudence, with no indication as to who delivered them. On closer examination they proved to be a variant version of Adam Smith's Lectures on Jurisprudence. About seventy years ago, Professor Edwin Cannan discovered the existence of a version of these lectures and in 1896 produced a scholarly edition of them. In the neatly-bound octavo volumes of my purchase there was a version differently arranged and often more fully illustrated and explained, but obviously emanating from the same learned source. After an exciting three weeks' search, I eventually recovered the missing first volume.

The second set of manuscripts, in two volumes,[1] similarly bound but with leather tips to protect the corners, carried on the spine of each volume in neat hand-writing the inscription, 'Notes of Dr. Smith's Rhetorick Lectures.' These manuscripts proved to be an almost complete set of a student's notes on part of Smith's course on Moral Philosophy given in 1762-3, his last unbroken academic session as Professor at the University of Glasgow. Evidence provided from other sources makes it clear that these lectures, given late in his career as a University teacher, were an elaboration of the public discourses on Rhetoric and Belles Lettres that he had given in Edinburgh during the years 1748-51.

[1] For a description of the manuscript by Dr T. I. Rae, see Appendix, p. 194.

After his appointment in 1751 to the chair of Logic at Glasgow, Smith included these discourses as part of his professorial lectures. When in 1752 he succeeded Thomas Craigie in the Chair of Moral Philosophy, he repeated them again as part of that discipline.

## LECTURES ON RHETORIC, 1748-51

Little has hitherto been known about this early course of lectures. 'There is a certain amount of mystery,' says Professor W. R. Scott,[1] the greatest authority on the matter, 'about the circumstances and the subject-matter of the lectures which Adam Smith delivered at Edinburgh during the three years 1748-1751.' He proceeds to explain Smith's need to find a post of some kind after his return in 1746 from his six years in Oxford. Although as Snell Exhibitioner in Oxford he was expected to take orders in the Church of England, Smith was reluctant to do so. Moreover, he had failed to secure a tutorship to some young nobleman. Scott thinks, therefore, though on what evidence he does not state, that after Smith returned to Edinburgh three of his friends, Lord Kames, James Oswald and Robert Craigie suggested that he might earn some money by lecturing and 'outlined the project for a series of public lectures which would be different from any that were available at that time in Edinburgh.' The most influential of those friends was probably Lord Kames. 'It was by [Kames's] persuasion,' says A. F. Tytler the historian, in his *Memoirs of the Life and Writings of Henry Home of Kames*,[2] 'that Mr Adam Smith, soon after his return from Oxford, and when he had abandoned all views towards the Church, for which he had been originally destined, was induced to turn his early studies to the benefit of the public, by reading a course of Lectures on Rhetoric and *Belles Lettres*. He delivered those lectures at Edinburgh in 1748, and the following two years, to a respectable auditory, chiefly composed of students in law and theology.' Scott does not give his reasons for linking the other two friends with Kames in promoting the project; but James Oswald of Dunnikier, M.P. for Fife, was a friend of Smith's boyhood, and Craigie, who in 1754 became President of the Court of Session, was related to Smith's mother.

The course given by Smith was a success and brought him about £100 a year, as Hume reminded him some eight years later.[3] When he

---

[1] W. R. Scott, *Adam Smith as Student and Professor*, Glasgow 1937, p. 46.
[2] Vol. I, Edinburgh 1814, p. 266. It was presumably from this source that W. R. Scott derived his information.   [3] W. R. Scott, *op. cit.*, p. 62.

moved to Glasgow in 1751, another similar course was given at Edinburgh by Robert Watson. In 1756, Watson was chosen to fill the Chair of Logic at St Andrews.[1] He was followed at Edinburgh in December 1759 by the Reverend Hugh Blair, who, from June, 1760, was allowed by the Town Council to use the title Professor (but without stipend). Blair's success in turn led to the creation of the Regius Chair of Rhetoric and Belles Lettres—the first of its kind in Britain—on 27 April 1762.

## Adam Smith's Literary Interests

It has not hitherto been sufficiently realised how easily Adam Smith might himself have been the first Professor to occupy the new Chair of Rhetoric. His studies at Oxford had been mainly of Greek and Latin literature, history and philosophy. All through life, says Rae,[2] he showed a knowledge of Greek and Latin literature not only uncommonly extensive but uncommonly exact. Dalzel, Professor of Greek at Edinburgh, and an intimate friend of Smith's later years, used often to find him reading one of the classical authors, 'in conformity with his theory that the best amusement of age was to renew acquaintance with the writers who were the delight of one's youth.' Dalzel admired the readiness and accuracy with which Smith called to mind the Greek authors, and also his skill in handling niceties of Greek grammar. In addition to his constant reading of the classics, Smith had always been in the habit of studying French authors, and of translating passages from their works in order to improve his own style; in Italian poetic literature he was also well read. In July 1755 the first *Edinburgh Review* was started by Smith in collaboration with Wedderburn, as editor, Robertson the historian, Blair, and the Reverend John Jardine. Before the magazine died after the second number Smith made two contributions to it, both literary. The first was a lengthy review of Johnson's Dictionary. After commenting on the defects of the dictionary, Smith showed how he thought it ought to have been compiled by writing two articles on the words 'wit' and 'humour'. The second took the form of a letter to the editor in which he set out how he thought the *Review* might be improved by the introduction of articles of wider scope and by accounts of foreign literature of all kinds. This, he maintained, would make the journal less provincial and at the same time more acceptable to a cultivated public.

[1] In 1777 Watson became Principal of St Salvator's, St Andrews.
[2] J. Rae, *Life of Adam Smith*, London 1895, p. 23.
[3] E. Cannan, *Adam Smith's Lectures on Jurisprudence*, Oxford 1896, pp. xxxiii-iv.

It would give it a wider appeal than the rather provincial magazines then in vogue. He made a cursory survey of the contemporary scene in European literature, especially in France, and gave an account of the *Encyclopédie*, of the scientific works of Buffon and Réaumur, and of Rousseau's discourse on the Inequality of Mankind.

Smith's interests in literature in general and in literary characters continued throughout his life. On 1 November 1785 he wrote to the Duc de la Rochefoucauld to tell him of the works he then had in hand: 'the one is a philosophical history of all the different branches of literature, of philosophy, poetry and eloquence; the other is a sort of theory and history of law and government. . . . The materials of both are in great measure collected, and some part of both is put into tolerable order.' In 1791, the Earl of Buchan, in an article in the *Bee*,[1] wrote of the free and confident opinions expressed by Smith to him on many figures of the contemporary literary world—Shaftesbury, Swift, Pope, Johnson, Goldsmith and others.

It is not surprising, therefore, to find that in all his lectures Smith showed a distinct fondness for digressing into literary topics. Even into his more strictly philosophical or economic lectures, literature was allowed to intrude. 'Those who received instruction from Dr Smith,' says Richardson,[2] 'will recollect with much satisfaction many of those incidental and digressive illustrations and discussions, not only in morality but in criticism, which were delivered by him with animated and extemporaneous eloquence as they were suggested in the course of question and answer. They occurred likewise, with much display of learning and knowledge, in his occasional explanations of those philosophical works, which were also a very useful and important subject of examination in the class of moral philosophy.'

It seems likely, then, that his friends considered that by his native bias of taste and his prolonged literary studies pursued at Oxford, and, probably, at home, he was a natural choice for those who thought the time was ripe for a course of lectures on Belles Lettres in Edinburgh. The time, it may also appear presently, was auspicious for the launching of such a course.

## SMITH'S EARLY LECTURES AT GLASGOW

Two reports on Smith's Lectures on Rhetoric and Belles Lettres given in Glasgow confirm the opinion that the manuscript notes now in

[1] Vol. III, pp. 1-8.     [2] J. Rae, *op. cit.*, p. 56.

our possession, are, in effect, an expanded version of the course of lectures given originally in Edinburgh. The first report comes from Professor John Millar, the second from James Wodrow.

John Millar was one of the most brilliant of Smith's students. He had attended Smith's lectures on Jurisprudence in Edinburgh, and had followed him to Glasgow, where he was a member of the professor's Logic class in Smith's first year. According to Rae, he was influenced 'by the high reputation the new professor brought with him from Edinburgh, to take out the class a second time, although he had already completed his University curriculum.' It was Millar who supplied Dugald Stewart with the information for his *Memoir of Adam Smith*. According to this:

In the Professorship of Logic, to which Mr Smith was appointed on his first introduction into this University, he soon saw the necessity of departing widely from the plan that had been followed by his predecessors, and of directing the attention of his pupils to studies of a more interesting and useful nature than the logic and metaphysics of the schools. Accordingly, after exhibiting a general view of the powers of the mind, and explaining so much of the ancient logic as was requisite to gratify curiosity with respect to an artificial method of reasoning, which had once occupied the universal attention of the learned, he dedicated all the rest of his time to the delivery of a system of rhetoric and belles lettres. The best method of explaining and illustrating the various powers of the human mind, the most useful part of metaphysics, arises from an examination of the several ways of communicating our thoughts by speech, and from an attention to the principles of those literary compositions which contribute to persuasion or entertainment. By these arts, everything that we perceive or feel, every operation of our minds, is expressed in such a manner, that it may be clearly distinguished and remembered. There is, at the same time, no branch of literature more suited to youth at their first entrance upon philosophy than this, which lays hold of their taste and their feelings.[1]

It is clear from this that Smith deliberately proposed to make an emotional rather than an intellectual appeal to the interest of the students, to stimulate their feelings and their aesthetic sense, rather than their powers of reasoning. This inference with regard to the lectures is confirmed by the report of James Wodrow, Library Keeper to the University of Glasgow, during Smith's early years as professor. It is contained in a letter to the Earl of Buchan:

Adam Smith delivered a set of admirable lectures on language (not as a grammarian, but as a rhetorician), on the different kinds and characteristics

[1] A. Smith, *Theory of Moral Sentiments*, London 1853, with a Biographical and Critical Memoir of the Author, by Dugald Stewart, p. xvi.

of style suited to the different subjects, simple, nervous, etc., the structure, the natural order, the proper arrangement of the different members of the sentence, etc. He characterised the style and genius of some of the best of the ancient writers and poets, but especially historians, Thucydides, Polybius, etc. translating long passages of them; also the style of the best English classics, Lord Clarendon, Addison, Swift, Pope, etc. . . . his remarks and rules given in the lectures I speak of were the result of a fine taste and sound judgement, well calculated to be exceedingly useful to young composers, so that I have often regretted that some part of them has never been published.[1]

Wodrow graduated at Glasgow in 1750, and left the University's service in 1755. His letter was written after 1776, when Smith had become famous. Doubtless a golden glow of idealisation suffuses these memories, but doubtless too they record Smith's first happy impact on his Glasgow listeners. In any case, it is clear from Wodrow's account, brief as it is, that the general sequence of topics followed by Smith in his earliest years at Glasgow is the same as that followed in the manuscripts which we now possess. That for his lectures in Glasgow Smith should use his original lectures on Rhetoric and Belles Lettres, is in keeping with what we know of his careful and conservative methods in the preparation of his materials for lecture or publication. Moreover, since in his very first year as Professor of Logic at Glasgow he had been called upon to lecture on jurisprudence and politics for the sick and absent Professor of Moral Philosophy, Thomas Craigie, it is not surprising that he should use the lectures which he had already delivered in Edinburgh, for he would have had but little time to prepare anything new.

## CONTENTS OF THE LECTURES

Wodrow's bare outline of the course in Rhetoric has been quoted: it will be useful and convenient to follow the sequence of topics as given in the manuscript.

As might be expected from his plainly practical mind, Smith was not interested in the innumerable figures of rhetoric distinguished by the writers on the subject. His object was to teach his students to write a simple and direct style, without ornament, and when he had analysed and expounded the best method of achieving such a style, he dismissed any further elaboration of the subject with a shrug of contempt. Towards the end of the lectures directly concerned with style, he comments:

[1] W. R. Scott, *op. cit.*, p. 52.

INTRODUCTION

The result of all which, as well as the rules we have laid down, is that the perfection of style consists in expressing in the most concise, proper, and precise manner the thought of the author, and that in the manner which best conveys the sentiment, passion, or affection with which it affects—or he pretends it does affect—him, and which he designs to communicate to his reader. This, you'll say, is no more than common sense: and indeed it is no more.[1]

The first section of the lectures, then, is devoted to a simple exposition, with numerous illustrations, of the principles of good composition, dealing especially with narrative and descriptive prose. It is eminently practical in spirit. Smith is concerned that words should say exactly what the writer thinks or feels, and nothing more.

After this general discourse, Smith turns to narrative writing and particularly to the method of describing events, characters and speeches in historical writing. He discusses the principles guiding the selection of the events to be included, the treatment of their causes, proximate and remote; he then touches on the methods employed by Thucydides, Xenophon, Tacitus and Livy; he discusses the relation of the order of events as they occurred to that to be observed in the narrating of them; the links provided by time, and place, and cause; the impersonality of the historian, and his avoidance of dissertations and digressions woven into the narrative. (At this point the tired recorder of Smith's prolonged lucubrations observes 'not a word more can I remember,' and abruptly ends the lecture!)

Having discussed and illustrated the points he considers to be most important in prose composition, Smith turns to a review of the historians in some detail—Herodotus, Thucydides, Xenophon, Polybius, Livy, Tacitus, Machiavelli, Guicciardini, Clarendon, Burnet and even Rapin. Some he dismisses briefly; others, like Tacitus, he considers at some length. He is fond of comparison, finds it a great help in analysis, and enlivens his discourses with some very effective contrasts.

From the historians he proceeds to expository writing, and analyses in some detail the elements that contribute to unity, to variety, to decorum. Then he completes a brief analysis of *didactic* discourses, which he divides into the Socratic and the Aristotelian, according to whether one draws one's audience gently on to a conclusion, or boldly states one's proposition and deduces the consequences directly. From this point he reviews the *deliberative* orations of Demosthenes and Cicero, the orations of a similar type introduced into their histories by

[1] Lecture 11, p. 51.

xviii

Thucydides, Livy, and Tacitus, with many incidental digressions on the state of Athens or of Rome. Finally, he turns to *judicial* oratory, explains its nature, analyses the methods appropriate to it in Greece and in Rome, accounts for the stability of the Roman commonwealth from the superior nature of its law-courts, and engages in a lengthy comparison of Demosthenes and Cicero. He rounds off his course with a brief account of English oratory, and an appreciation of the methods and style appropriate to the English race.

## Characteristics and Influence

Smith's views on the historians and orators of ancient and modern times show his strong analytical mind working from first principles clearly articulated in a typical neo-classical fashion. He is simple and direct rather than subtle and refined, and depends more upon accurate application of well-reasoned principles than on a delicate and cultivated sensitivity. He ranges at ease in the world of scholarship, of literature and literary principles. He is obviously at home among the great historians and orators both of antiquity and of modern times. 'In the groves of Eden he walks familiar as in his native paths,' and is on easy terms with the poets and pleaders, the character writers and narrators of events. He is able to assure us confidently that a certain device occurs not once, 'no, not once, in the whole of Demosthenes,' or that Aristotle never deviates from a certain style 'in his whole works.' He can tell us that exclamations by the author are used very sparingly by Tacitus and the Elder Pliny: 'besides these two there is no historian who has used them, unless it be Valerius Maximus and Florus.' He speaks his mind freely on them, and when he differs from the received opinion, he has his principles clearly formulated for the support of what he has said.

But it is not only on Smith's opinions that these lectures throw a great deal of new light: in many ways they are revealing about his personality. Twice the 'scribbler' who took down (or copied) the professor's words records that he lectured without notes, or without book 'save what he read from Livy.' Repeatedly, Smith's delight in character-analysis and character-sketching—a delight easily inferred from his first book, *The Theory of Moral Sentiments*—reveals itself in his keenly differentiated sketches of 'the plain man' and 'the simple man,' exemplified in Swift and Temple, or in his contrasted 'characters' of Demosthenes and Cicero. In the midst of his comments on La Bruyère's sketch of 'the absent-minded man,' the 'scribbler' here noted Smith's own reputation in that kind. '*Mutato nomine*,' he records, '*de te fabula narratur*, said Mr Herbert of Mr Smith,' change but the name, and what was true of La Bruyère's Menalcas was true of Adam Smith. And Mr Herbert had every opportunity to know, for he (who afterwards became Lord Porchester, and later Earl of Caernarvon), spent most of the academic session 1762-3 as a gentleman-boarder in Adam Smith's house.

Here and there we smile at the engaging pedantries and solemn didactic intention of the professor, as he reminds his hearers of what is expected—or not expected—'of one in the character of a gentleman.' The exercise of their minds on questions of literature was obviously not the *only* purpose of this unusual class, but the cultivation, in addition, of their taste and feelings on all aspects and problems of human life. It was no narrow view of his professorial functions that Adam Smith took. Professor John Millar speaks of the debt they all owed to him for stimulus and enlightenment in things not usually associated with a university class-room. Whatever the 'professed' subject of discourse— rhetoric, belles lettres, moral philosophy, jurisprudence, political eco- nomy—to accompany that strong mind in its review of human history and thought, moving with ease from long familiar study through the historians, philosophers, and poets of antiquity and modern times, analysing the causes of events and seeking to sketch a philosophy of progress, must indeed in itself have been a liberal education for those young men in the Scotland of his time who had the good fortune to hear him.

Professor Cannan, in his Introduction to the newly-discovered and edited *Lectures on Jurisprudence*, inclined to think that the loss of the companion Lectures on Rhetoric was no serious matter. 'It would doubtless be extremely interesting,' he said,[1] 'to have before us the text or a full report of Adam Smith's lectures on rhetoric, belles lettres, and natural theology,' but these would not be of any historical importance. 'However excellent any of them may have been,' he went on, 'they had not the opportunity of exercising a very wide influence in their own time,' and he added that of course they could have little in ours.

Cannan's estimate of the historical importance of the Lectures on Rhetoric was based apparently on the fact that they were never printed, and so could not reach a very wide audience, and it was probably affected by his sense of the great value of the *Lectures on Jurisprudence* in throwing light on *The Wealth of Nations*. He was writing at a time

[1] p. xiv.

(1896) when books were still cheap, plentiful, and influential, and the radio had not come to restore and emphasise the power of the spoken word. Many students came long distances to sit at the feet of Adam Smith, and the sons of English noblemen were sent to live in his house and listen to his lectures, long before the book for which he is now famous was written. 'His lectures,' says the learned and exact David Murray,[1] 'attracted students from all quarters at home and abroad, and were attended by many young men, or private students as they were termed, who were engaged in business in Glasgow and did not take a full academical course, so that his views on various questions of Political Economy must have been well known in Glasgow [and elsewhere?] before they were given to the world in *The Wealth of Nations*.' A claim to comparable influence could reasonably be made for his views on literature. When they were first given these lectures were attended by men whose reputations were already established, or who were soon to become known for their ability—Kames; Wedderburn, who became Lord Chancellor; William Johnstone (later Sir William Pulteney, M.P.); Robertson, the historian, who became Principal of Edinburgh University; and James Oswald of Dunnikeir, M.P. for Fife. The Reverend Hugh Blair, who was later to give the course and to become the first Regius Professor of Rhetoric and Belles Lettres in Edinburgh, also attended Smith's lectures. He indeed borrowed part of Smith's manuscript for his own lectures and, as he admits, took over some of his ideas. 'On this head,' he writes,[2] 'of the general characters of style, particularly the plain and the simple, and the characters of those English authors who are classed under them, in this and the following lecture, several ideas have been taken from a manuscript treatise on rhetoric, part of which was shown to me many years ago by the learned and ingenious author, Dr Adam Smith; and which it is hoped will be given by him to the public.' Rae, Smith's biographer, thinks Blair 'does not seem to have borrowed anything but what was the commonest of property already.' He took only what his superficial mind had the power of taking, and the pith of Smith's thinking must have been left behind. 'To borrow even a hat to any purpose, the two heads must be something of a size.'[3] With the discovery of Smith's lectures, it will now be possible to measure the two heads.

---

[1] *Early Burgh Organisation in Scotland*, Glasgow 1924, Vol. I, pp. 436-7.
[2] *Lectures on Rhetoric and Belles Lettres*, Edinburgh 1820, Vol. I, p. 381.
[3] Rae, *Life of Adam Smith*, p. 33.

Another who was prepared to borrow from the same source was Smith's successor in the Chair of Moral Philosophy at Glasgow, Thomas Reid, as we learn from A. Campbell Fraser's biography of him. There he quotes verbatim from Reid's inaugural lecture:

I shall be much obliged to any of you gentlemen, or to any others, who can furnish me with notes of his [i.e. Adam Smith's] prelections, whether in morals, jurisprudence, politics, or rhetoric. I shall always be desirous to borrow light from every quarter, and to adopt what appears to me to be sound and solid in every system, and ready to change my opinions upon conviction, or to change my method and materials, where I can do it to advantage. I desire to live no longer than this candour and ingenuity, this openness of mind to education and information, live with me.[1]

Reid's attitude to his predecessor is illuminating, and confirms what is said below regarding the willingness of the Scottish intellectual leaders to learn from one another.

The contemporary influence of the literary lectures was thus probably much greater than Cannan was prepared to admit. They were attended by hundreds of young Scots, James Boswell among them, and Professor George Jardine, and a fair number of English, some of whom, like Henry Herbert, Lord Porchester, later became influential in the affairs of their countries. Moreover, as Professor Millar informed Dugald Stewart, the influence of Smith was not limited to what his hearers carried away in their memories: the written word, in the form of students' notes, remained frequently to recall and reinforce what had been heard, and to act, in effect, like a book. 'From the permission given to students of taking notes,' says Millar, 'many observations and opinions contained in these lectures have either been detailed in separate dissertations or engrossed in general collections, which have been given to the public.'[2] The 'borrowings' did not grow less as Smith's reputation increased. Indeed, Smith himself seems to have become aware of the way in which his generosity had come to be abused. A writer in the Edinburgh *Oracle* for 9 August 1791 tells us that 'the Doctor was in general extremely jealous of the property of his lectures and, fearful lest they should be transcribed and published, used often to repeat, when he saw anyone taking notes, that he hated scribblers.' This clearly marks a change from the earlier, more generous Adam of Millar's description.

It was a misjudgment on Cannan's part to imagine that this course

---

[1] A. C. Fraser, *Thomas Reid*, Edinburgh 1898, p. 76.
[2] Stewart's Biographical Memoir in A. Smith, *Theory of Moral Sentiments*, p. xvii.

on Rhetoric and Belles Lettres, even though it can now be read only in the form of students' notes, had little influence on 'the shape of things to come.'[1] These lectures mark quite clearly the transition from the earlier, long-established and traditional study of formal rhetoric in the University to that of Belles Lettres or polite literature. They show the study of literature rather than of language to be the important concern of the student, and they admit the 'moderns' in the vernacular on terms of equality with the 'ancients' in the classical tongues. They were the first of their kind, as far as we know, to be given in Great Britain, though something similar had been given by Rollin in the University of Paris. One of the early obvious fruits of their success, and a not unimportant one for the history of literature, was as has already been said the creation of the Regius Chair of Rhetoric and Belles Lettres in Edinburgh University. A later and less obvious, but equally important though sometimes bitter fruit, might be considered to be the flourishing of the *Edinburgh* and *Blackwood's* Reviews, which dominated critical opinion for at least a quarter of a century. Perhaps the most certain and yet least measurable outcome was the creation in Scotland of an interested and informed audience for both what was creative and what was critical in literature. This change, though difficult to perceive in action, is quite evident if a comparison be made between the Reviews mentioned and those which were current at the time when Smith's lectures were first given.

## AIMS OF LITERARY SOCIETIES

At the time when Smith's Lectures on Rhetoric were first delivered, the interest in Belles Lettres was undoubtedly in the air. The cultivation of literary study by the educated classes had become fashionable, and there was an obvious desire to see this study given university status. We find Charles Mackie, the first Professor of History at Edinburgh, being addressed by one of his students as 'Professor of History and

[1] An interesting parallel instance of the influence of lectures is to be found in Bernard Weinberg's *A History of Literary Criticism in the Italian Renaissance*, Chicago 1961, Vol. II, p. 810:—

'The critical tradition does grow from year to year, ideas are cumulative and depend on their predecessors. In many cases, the tradition grew orally, and works which had not yet been published in print—and some of them never were—nevertheless exercised a strong influence on later theorists; Maggi's lectures on Aristotle beginning in 1541 and Segni's Platonic lectures of 1573 are cases of "works" which became immediately famous and which were carefully studied by younger critics. Professors affected the thinking of their students, academicians of their colleagues, writers of their readers.'

Belles Lettres.'[1] A Hague bookseller, Thomas Johnson, wrote letters to him as 'Professor of History and Literature at Edinburgh.' The need felt by many for authoritative instruction in English and encouragement in literary effort, is expressed in a letter to Mackie by his friend John Mitchell, who congratulates him on the prospect of a revival of letters in Scotland. 'Give me leave to say that I wish some method might be fallen upon to teach Young Gentlemen the English, our chief Tongue, and that whereby any can make a figure in affairs at home, and the want of it is a very great loss to all who come, or are sent here.'

That this need was widely felt can be seen from the avowed purpose of many of the literary and other societies formed in Scotland at this time. The Fair Intellectual Club, which was responsible for the publication of *The Edinburgh Miscellany* (only Vol. 1 appeared), proposed to pay attention, among other things, to English composition[2]; and the much more famous Select Society, started in 1754, of which Adam Smith was an original member, had as its purposes 'philosophical inquiry, and the improvement of the members in the art of speaking.'[3] In the following year, 1755, this same society offered a prize for the best essay on Taste. Much of the self-improving spirit of the time is shown by the fact that an Aberdeen Professor, Gerard, did not think it beneath his dignity to enter an essay, (and incidentally, to accept the prize), and that David Hume did not find it beneath him to act as one of the judges. In Scotland at this time many able men were prepared to sink their pride in order to profit from one another's criticism. Adam Smith and his fellow club-members submitted papers for discussion which were afterwards incorporated in their published works.[4] A digest of Dugald Stewart's account of Thomas Reid, in the *Scots Magazine* for January 1802,[5] records that soon after Dr Reid's appointment as Professor at Aberdeen,

he projected (in conjunction with his friend, Dr John Gregory) a literary society, which subsisted for many years and which seems to have had the happiest effects in awakening and directing that spirit of philosophical research which has since reflected so much lustre on the North of Scotland. The meetings of this society were held weekly; and afforded the members . . . an opportunity of submitting their intended publications to the test of friendly criticism. The number of valuable works which issued nearly about the same

[1] L. W. Sharp, 'Charles Mackie, the First Professor of History at Edinburgh University', *S.H.R.* XLI (1962), pp. 23-45.

[2] D. D. McElroy, *The Literary Clubs and Societies in Eighteenth-Century Scotland.* (Unpublished Ph.D. Thesis, 1951-2, Edinburgh University Library), p. 62.

[3] *Ibid*, p. 138.  [4] Rae, *op. cit.*, p. 95.  [5] Vol. LXV.

time, from individuals connected with this institution, more particularly the writings of Reid, Gregory, Campbell, Beattie, and Gerard, furnish the best panegyric on the enlightened views of those under whose direction it was originally formed.

George Campbell, a professor of Divinity and later Principal of the College, submitted practically the whole of his *Philosophy of Rhetoric* (1776; begun 1750) to this body.

In the year 1757 [the first outline] was read to a private literary society, of which the author had the honour to be a member. It was a difference in his situation at that time, and his connection with the gentlemen of that society, some of whom have since honourably distinguished themselves in the republic of letters, that induced him to resume a subject that he had so long laid aside. The three following years all the other chapters of that book, except the third, the sixth, and tenth, . . . were composed, and submitted to the judgement of the same ingenious friends. All that follows on the subject of Elocution . . . has undergone the same review.[1]

Campbell also sent his essay on miracles via Blair to David Hume for criticism, the writer against whose opinions it was chiefly directed, and received compliments on its excellence. Robertson and Blair performed similar services for each other. 'I will read with the utmost attention, and put down on paper,' wrote Robertson[2] to Andrew Dalzel who had sent him the manuscript of a volume of sermons, 'every observation, great and small, which occurs to me, while you have full liberty to adopt or to reject them as you think best. This is what Dr Blair and I have always done for one another in every work we have published.' A contributor to the *Scots Magazine* of 1802 said, in an article on the student days of Dr John Erskine, that 'A spirit for literature and philosophy had lately begun to appear in Scotland, and the professors in the University of Edinburgh contributed much to promote it.' Two of these professors he selects for special consideration, and certainly as to the influence of one of them, John Stevenson, Professor of Logic in Edinburgh from 1730 to 1775, there is overwhelming evidence.

### PROFESSOR STEVENSON'S METHODS AND INFLUENCE

In any account of the transition in University teaching from emphasis on the 'bare bones' of ancient logic and rhetoric to the cultivation

---

[1] G. Campbell, *The Philosophy of Rhetoric*, London, 2nd ed., 1801, Vol. I, pp. v-vi.
[2] A. Dalzel, *History of the University of Edinburgh* (edited by D. Laing), Edinburgh 1862, Vol. I, p. 96.

of literary taste and style, Stevenson's name must rank high. Not all his students felt that his lectures on Logic were sufficiently free from scholastic taint. 'The matter of Dr Stevenson's lectures on Logic,' said Dr Thomas Somerville,[1] after a protest against lectures being given in Latin, 'was in great part hardly less antiquated than the form. In particular, the doctrine of syllogisms was too largely insisted upon, and a paramount respect to the authority of that mode of argument recommended in the investigation of truth.' But the general opinion of his more purely philosophical lectures is more justly expressed by a writer in the *Scots Magazine*:

The science that he taught was not that scholastic jargon, which for ages had usurped the name and place of logic, but the philosophy of Bacon and Locke. He was the first public teacher in this country that ascribed its due importance to their mode of philosophizing, at the same time that he did not discard what was useful in the Aristotelian system. Not satisfied, however, with explaining the principles of Logic and Metaphysics, he endeavoured, by prelections on the most esteemed classics, ancient and modern, to instil into the minds of his pupils, a relish for works of taste, and a love of elegant composition.[2]

It was his habit, we learn elsewhere,[3] in his eight-o'clock lectures, to have his students 'read and translate in his hearing, the Greek text of Aristotle's *Poetics* and of Longinus' essay,' and he 'commented critically on what they read, so copiously, from the critical works then known, such as the prose discourses and prefaces of Dryden, Addison's papers in the *Spectator*, Bossu, Dacier, and Pope's notes on Homer, as greatly to delight and instruct his hearers, whom he thus initiated into those pleasing studies, which, at that period of life, were quite new to them.'

Stevenson's lectures, says Grant,[4] 'had really an extraordinary effect: they were delivered just at a period when a certain aspiration after literature was beginning to be felt in Edinburgh, when an intellectual revival, after the Covenanting dark age, was in the air.' 'I derived more substantial benefit,' says Somerville,[5] 'from these exercises and lectures, than from all the public classes which I attended at the University.' 'Jupiter' Carlyle and Principal Robertson both pay tribute to the deep impression left by the lectures, and there is a touching story of Robertson's first visit to Stevenson's class, as Principal, and his public com-

---

[1] Thomas Somerville, D.D., *My Own Life and Times, 1741-1814*, Edinburgh 1861, p. 13.　　　　　　　　　　　[2] *Scots Magazine* (Feb. 1803), LXV, p. 76.

[3] *Scots Magazine* (Jan. 1802), LXIV, p. 21.

[4] Sir Alexander Grant, *Story of the University of Edinburgh*, Edinburgh 1884, Vol. I, p. 329.　　　　　　　　　　　[5] T. Somerville, *op. cit.*, p. 14.

mendation of the lectures, which he had attended as an undergraduate, to the students of a later day.

Robertson, in presenting himself in Stevenson's class-room to listen to student discourses, was following in the footsteps of his penultimate predecessor, Dr William Wishart. Wishart, an enthusiast for the classical literatures and for moral and political science, in an attempt to raise the level of Arts studies in the University, made it necessary for graduands in Arts to present theses, which were read as discourses to the other members of the class, and to members of the staff and students of other classes. We know that he 'often honoured these discourses with his presence, listened to them with attention, criticised them with candour; and when he observed indications of good dispositions, and discerned the blossoms of genius, on these occasions, and afterwards as he had opportunity, testified his esteem and regard.'[1]

A considerable collection of these exercises or theses, delivered in Stevenson's Logic Class, is preserved in the library of the University of Edinburgh.[2] Some of them bear evidence of having been intended for public academic presentation; the listeners are addressed as 'Doctissimi hujus Academiae praefecte professores eruditissimi,' or the speaker may apologise to them as he ends his discourse: 'Denique ne aures vostras nimia hujus oratiunculae prolixitate fatigem, finem ei imponam.' The handwriting is sometimes the same for several successive theses, and sometimes a new thesis is begun on the verso of the last page of the previous one; the handwriting in one instance changes half-way through an essay: it would appear that someone, possibly a scrivener, had made a fair copy of the essays for the students; but each thesis is signed, with the date, by the author. The dates run from 16 April 1737 to 27 April 1750; probably Principal Wishart's emphasis on theses—he was elected in March 1736, inducted a year later—had already begun to bring results. Most of the theses are on subjects strictly philosophical, but some deal with aesthetic and literary matters. John Gibson presented one περὶ τοῦ καλοῦ, sive de Pulchro, on 16 April 1737, and the subject was taken up again by Gilbert Elliot, two years later. Essays on Taste by David Clark in May 1740, and by Thomas Young[3] in May 1742, show that the subject which was to be prescribed by the Select Society in 1755 for the prize essay was already being debated in academic circles and

---

[1] Scots Magazine (Feb. 1803), LXV, p. 76.    [2] MS DC.4.54.

[3] Probably the same Thomas Young who was selected by Adam Smith to continue to read his lectures to the students for the remainder of the Session, after his departure in January 1764, and who contested the succession to the Chair with Thomas Reid.

teaching. In May 1740, Robert Clark presented a dissertation 'On the Nature and Origin of Poetry,' in which the argument was conducted in quasi-logical fashion. The influence of Longinus, or of Stevenson's teaching on Longinus, is plainly evident in this essay, and it is filled with recollections of Horace. Part of it is worth quoting as an example of the matter and style of these student exercises.

Since poetry is an art, it must have an end and means proper for attaining it. The end of poetry is to satisfy and improve and delight and reform the mind: from which it appears that poetry has two ends, a subordinate and a final one. The subordinate end of poetry is to please, for that pleasure is the business and design of poetry is evident, because unless it pleases, nay, and please to a height, it is the most contemptible thing in the world. Other things may be borne with if they are indifferent, but poetry unless it is transporting is abominable.

But the final end of poetry is to reform mankind, for since poetry is an art, instruction must be its final end. Now the proper means to obtain these ends is by exciting passion, because everyone who is pleased is moved, and either desires, rejoices, admires, or the like.

There is ample evidence that Stevenson's lectures exercised a great influence on the minds of the young men who heard him. Bower, in his *History of the University of Edinburgh*,[1] thought that no professor in Edinburgh ever 'had the honour of training up so many young men to a love of letters, who afterwards made a distinguished figure in the literary world, as Stevenson.' Dr Carlyle, Dr Robertson and Dr Somerville, all acknowledged a debt of pleasure and of profit to his teaching; and a quarter of a century after his death, Professor Dalzel, writing in the *Scots Magazine*,[2] claimed that though Stevenson published no work of his own,

it cannot be doubted that his instructions promoted the success of many of those who have since so highly exalted the celebrity of Scottish Literature. His critical lectures, it must be owned, contributed a large share towards the production of the more polished and refined, but not more useful, academical discourses of the late Dr Blair; . . . it was not without reason that the institution of a separate chair for a Professor of Rhetoric and Belles Lettres was complained of, by the respectable veteran, as an encroachment upon his province.

That Stevenson's influence continued to be felt and remembered, is evident from the curious circumstance that when the Commissioners

---

[1] A. Bower, *History of the University of Edinburgh*, Edinburgh 1817, Vol. II, p. 280.
[2] *Scots Magazine* (Jan. 1802), LXIV, p. 22.

investigated the affairs of the University 1825-30, it was because of what they had heard of the success of Stevenson's Rhetoric class, that they 'recommended that Rhetoric should again be joined with Logic, and the Chair of Rhetoric and Belles Lettres be abolished.'[1]

## LOGIC AND BELLES LETTRES

Stevenson's lectures on literary criticism are far from being the only part of the historical background of Smith's courses which merits our attention. Logic and rhetoric had long been associated in academic teaching. In the ordinary text-books of Logic in the first half of the eighteenth century a considerable section was usually devoted to Form or Method. One of these text-books, which ran to several editions, was written by Isaac Watts. Nearly a quarter of his book is an elaborate discussion of how, having found the truth by means of the system of logic propounded in the earlier pages, it was to be presented most effectively. In the numerous *compendia* of Professors' lectures which have survived, the same interest in form and method is often manifested. One of these compendia was transcribed by John Campbell and is now in Edinburgh University Library.[2] It contains digests of the lectures in logic given by Stevenson at Edinburgh, Reid at Aberdeen and Watson at St Andrews, and it mentions those of Clow at Glasgow, which Campbell had collected in another volume. In the summary of Watson's lectures there is a chapter on words, and a whole section on the Means of Improvement. These means were to be concentration, the development of one's memory, and reading. Watson's rules of interpretation deserve to be quoted.

The first is, that if any passage of an author admit of two senses, we should choose that which is most agreeable to the Author's end, character, and general Principles, or to the occasion and circumstances in which he wrote. The second is . . . that of different meanings we should study that which is attended by the fewest absurdities. The third is, to take words always in their common and proper sense, unless it be accompanied with some absurdity; but if it be, then to give the words a meaning as consistent as possible with the context and parallel passages.

In the same compendium of lectures it is recorded[3] that in 1763, Reid informed his students at Aberdeen that

a true knowledge of criticism and an acquaintance with the manners of the times of which you read will be of much service this way. If the art of com-

---

[1] Sir A. Grant, *op. cit.*, Vol. I, p. 330.    [2] MS DK.3.2.    [3] *Ibid.* ff. 97-101.

posing be reduced to rules, so that a man could be taught to be a composer, they might be of great use; but instead of this they many times lead those that use them in composition to very strange and trifling forms or reasoning. 'Tis by far too great an attempt to lay down general rules of analysis and synthesis proper for all subjects and occasions. . . . As to general methods of composition on all subjects, I know not any of much importance, and the best I know is to be well acquainted with the ablest masters in the different subjects we treat of. . . . Taste and Judgment joined together are above all rules whatever. A man will be more profited and succeed better by endeavouring to copy exactly the most eminent and noble examples, than by paying the strictest attention to any rules.

A like reaction against the emphasis on and multiplication of rules, is voiced in the manuscript digest of the lectures of Professor James Clow of Glasgow,[1] transcribed by John Campbell in 1773. 'These' Clow exclaims, after a lengthy exposition of the handling of complex themes, and particularly of an exegesis, 'these are the rules of an exegesis, but Sense and Wit are more necessary to a composer than any rules that can be prescribed, for if anyone understands his subject he will be at no loss for a method to illustrate it, and without this, Rules will be of little avail.'

In 1797, George Jardine, who had succeeded Clow as Professor of Logic at Glasgow in 1787, and who conducted his classes, we are told,[2] on lines originally laid down by Adam Smith, published for the use of his students a *Synopsis of Lectures on Logic and Belles Lettres*. In 1802, Watson's successor in the Chair of Logic, Rhetoric and Metaphysics at St Andrews, William Barron, published his lectures as *Lectures on Belles Lettres and Logic*. The substitution of Belles Lettres for Rhetoric, of Sense and Taste for rules learned by rote, had been carried out. That it began with Adam Smith, Millar's and Wodrow's accounts, already quoted, make clear; that it was continued by his successors is evident from Thomas Reid's statements in his account of the University of Glasgow prepared for the first Statistical Account of Scotland, and probably written in 1794, where he sums up the change and the reasons for it in his remarks on the teaching of Logic by Professor Jardine.

Logic has, in general, preceded the other two in the order of teaching, and has been considered as a necessary preparation for them. Before the student entered upon the subjects of moral and natural philosophy, it was thought proper to instruct him in the art of reasoning and disputation; and the syllogistic art, taken from the Analytics of Aristotle, was, for many ages, considered as the most effectual and infallible instrument for that purpose. It was sup-

---

[1] Edinburgh University Library MS DC.8.13. f. 252.
[2] D. Murray, *Early Burgh Organisation in Scotland*, Vol. I, p. 437n.

posed to afford a mechanical mode of reasoning, by which, in all cases, a truth and falsehood might be accurately distinguished. But the change of opinions on the subjects of literature, and on the means of comprehending them, has occasioned a correspondent alteration in the manner of treating this part of the academical course. The present Professor, after a short analysis of the powers of the understanding, and an explanation of the terms necessary to comprehend the subjects of his course, gives a historical view of the rise and progress of the art of reasoning, and particularly of the syllogistic method, which is rendered a matter of curiosity by the universal influence which for a long time it obtained over the learned world; and then dedicates the greater part of his time to an illustration of the various mental operations, as they are expressed by the several modifications of speech and writing; which leads him to deliver a system of lectures on general grammar, rhetoric, and belles lettres. This course, accompanied with suitable exercises and specimens, on the part of the students, is properly placed at the entrance to philosophy: no subjects are likely to be more interesting to young minds, at a time when their taste and feelings are beginning to open, and have naturally disposed them to the reading of such authors as are necessary to supply them with facts and materials for beginning and carrying on the important habits of reflection and in-vestigation.[1]

## THE EIGHTEENTH CENTURY TRANSITION

The reaction against the more formal part of rhetoric had indeed begun long before Smith's time. In 1693, the writer of a rather lively *Select Essays Tending to the Universal Reformation of Learning*, William Freke, after he has listed the 'Topics Intrinsic' and 'Topics Extrinsic,' the 'Figures of Words' and 'Figures of Sentences,' and the classical 'five parts' of a discourse, sums up in the following words: 'But indeed, after all, as I have said, no Rhetoric is like honesty, and no speech like reason, if we have truth on our side, that's all, and enough, if we take but care to illustrate that sufficiently; only this we ought to remember in prudence, to let our last words be most forcible, as they are likely to be the most lasting impression; and indeed, to leave the truth and follow colours too much, is like Æsop's dog, by catching at the shadow to lose the substance.'[2] A somewhat later writer, Thomas Baker, of St John's College, Cambridge, in his *Reflections Upon Learning* (1708), after listing 'the tumults and concussions of state' roused by oratory among the Greeks, and the 'continual brawls and internal commotions' occasioned in Rome when it had got a footing there, till there was 'no more peace in that state', reflects that 'our common eloquence is usually a cheat

[1] T. Reid, *Works*, ed. Hamilton, Edinburgh 1846, p. 735.
[2] William Freke, *Select Essays*, London 1693, p. 132.

upon the understanding, it deceives us with appearances, instead of things; and makes us think we see reason, whilst it is tickling our sense: its strongest proofs do often consist in an artificial turn of words, and beautiful expressions, which if unravelled, its strength is gone and the reason is destroyed'.[1]

The tradition of division and sub-division and endless classification of the figures of rhetoric was hard to break. I have seen an *Art of Rhetoric* prepared by a headmaster for the use of his scholars, in which upwards of two hundred and fifty devices and figures of rhetoric were named.[2] It was probably against such absurdities that Anthony Black-wall, the writer of a popular and well-written *Introduction to the Classics* —the eighteenth-century equivalent of the classical primers of Jebb and Mahaffy—was protesting in his Preface.

My Design was to reform *Rhetoric* from the Rubbish and Barbarism which it lies under in the common Books; and to reduce it to a liberal and rational Science. As we have it in those dry and trifling Systems of it in some Schools, it is little better than a Heap of hard Words of ill Sound, of Definitions without Meaning, and Divisions without any Distinctions. I have thrown aside all little Alterations and Figures purely Grammatical, and struck out of the List of beautiful Schemes of Speech all Puns and Quibbles, all childish Jingle of Sound, and vain Amusement of Words; and have selected only the noblest *Tropes* and *Figures*, which give real Strength and Grace to Language; which heighten and improve our Notions: and are of excellent Use to persuade and please.[3]

Adam Smith was entirely in accord with this more modern way of thinking.

It is, however, from the consideration of these figures [i.e. of rhetoric, of which he was speaking], and divisions and sub-divisions of them, that so many systems of rhetoric, both ancient and modern, have been formed. They are generally a very silly set of books, and not at all instructive. . . . The rhetoricians divide all these topics into many orders and classes. (These will be found in Quin-tilian by those who incline to read them. For my part, I'll be at no further trouble at present.)[4]

That Blackwall's sentiments probably found general support is to be inferred from an editorial footnote to Johnson's Preface to *The Pre-ceptor*. This was a compendium 'Containing A general Course of

---

[1] (Thomas Baker), *Reflections upon Learning*. By a Gentleman, p. 52.
[2] John Holmes, Master of the Holt (Norfolk) Summer School, *The Art of Rhetoric Made Easy*, 2nd Impression, 1755.
[3] Anthony Blackwall, *Introduction to the Classics*, 3rd edition, 1725, Preface, A3.
[4] Lecture no. 6, see below p. 23 and Lecture no. 28, p. 167.

Education, wherein The First Principles of Polite Learning are laid down in a way most suitable for trying the Genius and advancing the Instruction of Youth,' written in twelve parts, of which the fifth is entitled 'On Rhetoric and Poetry.' 'I found this subject,' says the editor, 'so concisely and sensibly handled by Mr Blackwall, . . . that despairing to get anything better, or more to my purpose, I prevailed with the printer to give me leave to make such use of it as should be thought proper.'[1]

## PULPIT RHETORIC

Another factor to be taken into account in the consideration of the background of Smith's lectures was the attention which was increasingly paid to oratory, particularly to that most influential kind of oratory practised in the pulpit. 'Whether the style of pulpit oratory be now better or worse than it was fifty years ago,' wrote Dr Thomas Somerville,[2] about 1814, 'no doubt, at least, can exist with regard to the rapid and substantial improvement which had been progressive for the thirty years preceding the last-mentioned period,' that is, from about 1740 to 1770. William Leechman, Professor of Divinity at Glasgow and later Principal, was in the habit of giving every other year a course of lectures to his students on the *Composition of Sermons*. This was essentially a practical course on how to present material to different types of audience.[3] Also at Glasgow, the Foulis brothers had published in 1750 Fénelon's *Dialogues Concerning Eloquence*, 'particularly that kind which is fit for the Pulpit'; his *Letter to the French Academy* concerning Rhetoric, Poetry, and History; his *Discourse* delivered on his admission to the French Academy; and two of his *Dialogues of the Dead*; in all of which an elegant simplicity was admirably advocated and practised. In his *Discourse* Fénelon wrote: "The use of learning, which was formerly affected with so much vain parade, is now rejected except in cafés, where it is indispensable; even wit itself receives a check, because the perfection of art consists in imitating the simplicity of nature so exactly, that it may be mistaken for her.'[4] In 1750, Campbell, as he himself says, first began his inquiry into the Nature and Foundations of Eloquence.[5] A desire to improve, if not excel, in oratory, was certainly characteristic of the period.

[1] *The Preceptor*, Vol. I, 1748, p. I.
[2] T. Somerville, D.D., *My Own Life and Times, 1741-1814*, Edinburgh 1861, p. 62.
[3] Wodrow's Life of Leechman, prefixed to Leechman's *Sermons* (1789).
[4] p. 6.        [5] G. Campbell, *Philosophy of Rhetoric*, Vol. I, p. v.

By contrasting the old-fashioned style of preaching with that which had developed in the late seventeenth and the first half of the eighteenth centuries, David Fordyce, formerly a Professor of Moral Philosophy in Marischal College, Aberdeen, made clear what was appreciated in the newer style of eloquence.

Instead of a tedious explication of the text, and giving a concordance of every word in it, as had been the way formerly, they plainly and briefly opened its connection and meaning, and then stated the propositions arising out of it, in their nature, truth, and reasonableness. Instead of discussing some nice and barren points of controversy, in a scholastic manner, they painted the beauty and advantages of substantial virtue, with great strength of reason and perspicuity of style; and instead of concluding their discourses coldly, with a few short *inferences* or uses, as they were called, they wound them up with a pathetic and manly address, in which they applied the whole to the consciences and lives of their hearers. Whether the strain of the former sermons was either flat or low, being wire-drawn with controversial disputes, and having the sense scattered by such spurious mixtures as did not enter into the body of the work, but rather stuck out like so many excrescences; or else the style swelled into a ridiculous kind of bombast, and sometimes an unintelligible jargon; the compositions of this new race of preachers were more according to the genuine simplicity and beauty of nature. Their diction was easy, clear, and nervous, pregnant with sentiment, adorned with apt metaphors, and splendid figures, and those not far-fetched, or high-strained, but such as grew out of the subjects, and were the most proper to enlighten and affect the auditory.[1]

Dr Hugh Blair profited from the instruction in Rhetoric of both Stevenson and Adam Smith. He was able to apply their principles not only to his Lectures on Belles Lettres but also to his sermons from the pulpit, and in this way he set the fashion for an elegant rather than for an earnest manner, for a fluent rather than for a fervid oratory. This oratorical manner was to stand the test of repeated publication and to bring its author the reward of being the first Presbyterian minister in Edinburgh to 'set up' a carriage!

### THOMAS SHERIDAN AND THE SCOTS

The strong interest that was being taken in the art of self-expression, especially in the art of speaking, was shown by the invitation extended by the Select Society of Edinburgh to Thomas Sheridan, the former director of the theatre at Dublin. Sheridan was an enthusiastic believer in the efficacy of elocution and of rhetoric as a means of improving the

---

[1] David Fordyce, *Theodorus, A Dialogue concerning the Art of Preaching*, London 1752, p. 64.

general level of education in Britain. It had, of course, to be taught by a professional! He had already delivered lectures at London, Oxford, and Cambridge, and had published, in 1756, a book expounding his views entitled *British Education*. The sub-title, which is as follows, makes plain his purpose: 'The source of the disorders of Great Britain; being an Essay towards proving that the immorality, ignorance, and false taste, which so generally prevail, are the natural and necessary consequences of the present defective system of education; with an attempt to show that a revival of the Art of Speaking, and the Study of our own Language, might contribute, in a great measure, to the cure of those evils.'

In June and July 1761, Sheridan delivered two courses of eight lectures each, one on Elocution, the other on The English Tongue (combined fee, one guinea), 'with considerable enlargements concerning those points with regard to which Scotsmen are most ignorant, and the dialect of this country most imperfect.' Towards the end of these lectures he announced a shortened course, to run from 'Tuesday, 28th July, and finishing the following Friday week, chiefly intended for the use of ladies.'[1] From these would be omitted the comparisons with the learned languages with which the first courses had been adorned. At the end of his first two courses, which were attended by more than 300 men, Sheridan promised to lay a plan before the Select Society 'for carrying on the study of the English tongue in a regular and proper manner.' This plan resulted in the formation of a branch of the Society 'for promoting the reading and speaking of the English language in Scotland.' Kames was one of the Extraordinary Directors of this group, and amongst the Ordinary were Lord Auchinleck, Blair, Robertson, Ferguson, and John Adam the architect. Sheridan's lectures were published in 1762.

### THE DESIRE FOR SELF-IMPROVEMENT

It is against this background of the desire for self-improvement in speech, in public-speaking generally and in preaching, in debate, in writing and in reading, that one must place Adam Smith's course of lectures, and those of Watson and Blair which followed them. The records of the literary clubs and associations of Scotland in the eighteenth century,[2] as has already been shown, reveal a society animated by an awareness of a need for culture and by an intense ambition to improve,

[1] *Scots Magazine* (July 1761), XXIII, pp. 389-90.
[2] McElroy, *Literary Clubs and Societies in Eighteenth-Century Scotland* (*ut supra*).

an ambition which was shared even by those who were the obvious intellectual leaders of the day. Smith's, Watson's, and Blair's lectures are full of practical suggestions for the bettering of style and taste, and it is constantly assumed on the part of the lecturers that those who listen to these analyses of metaphors or of methods in the writings of the masters of literature, will themselves apply what they learn from them in their own attempts at literary composition. Blair conducted a critical examination of a sermon by Atterbury, of an oration by Cicero, of four consecutive numbers of the *Spectator*, and set his students practical exercises in such analyses. In spite of the late Dr Meikle's statements[1] that Blair's lectures were given year by year 'apparently without change, every session for twenty-four years,' and that 'he set no essays nor exercises,' it is clear from a comparison of the printed text with the manuscript versions of students' notes of the lectures, that slight variations, omissions and re-arrangements were made from time to time, and that essays were set. 'Thus, gentlemen,' Blair said, according to one manuscript version,[2] 'have I finished my criticism on this paper [*Spectator*, no. 414] for which you have afforded me great store of materials. There was not one paper given in from which I did not draw some useful hints. Time did not allow me to go through them all. I could only consider the most material. But this convinces me more and more of the usefulness of such exercises.' According to this manuscript Blair was speaking in 1765, but Stevenson, as we have already seen, had made a practice of setting such exercises for his students, many years before. Evidently the practice had gained ground only gradually. In describing his method of instruction as Professor of Logic at Glasgow, George Jardine protested strongly against the notion common amongst university teachers that 'to lecture' was 'to teach.' 'It was reserved,' he said,[3] sarcastically,

for the times in which we live to make the singular discovery, that philosophy may be taught to any number of young persons and intellectual habits formed in their minds, by the simple act of pronouncing a lecture from a professorial chair; and agreeably to this view of things, no exertion is demanded on the part of the student; and no exercises are enjoined, whereby he might be led to arrange the knowledge communicated to him; to discover the connexion of its various parts; to compare opinions, principles, theories, and thus at once

[1] *University of Edinburgh Journal*, Vol. XIII, p. 93.
[2] Edinburgh University Library, MS DC.10.6.
[3] G. Jardine, *Outlines of Philosophical Education*, Glasgow 1818, p. 287.

to make that knowledge completely his own, by improving the faculties of his understanding.

Few of those who gave these courses, or published books on the subject, professed to be original. This general attitude is well expressed in one of Blair's manuscripts.[1] 'In these lectures I will not pass over anything that is useful because said by others; neither will I follow beaten paths; as I will make my observations freely, so I will not choose to differ from others for the sake of singularity; and as I will deliver my opinions with freedom, I expect to be heard with candour.'[2] 'These lectures,' he had earlier informed his audience, 'are addressed to Gentlemen supposed to be acquainted with all the Liberal arts, and Rhetoric takes all of them within its circle.' He took, it is clear, no narrow view of the scope of his subject. When announcing the distribution of a synopsis, he explained[3] that they were called Lectures on Rhetoric, 'as this is the staple word made use of at other Universities, though Composition, Oratory, or Criticism would convey the same idea.' He drew on a multitude of sources, classical and contemporary, philological, aesthetic, and literary, for his materials. Like Adam Smith, he favoured the French idea of eloquence, drew on Massillon or Fléchier (as did his more distinguished predecessor), and did honour to Fénelon's *Dialogues on Eloquence*. He commended Fénelon's preference for Demosthenes before Cicero. 'It is in his *Reflections on Rhetoric and Poetry*,' Blair wrote[4] 'that he gives this judgment, a small tract, commonly published along with his *Dialogues on Eloquence*. These dialogues and reflections are particularly worthy of perusal as containing I think the justest ideas on the subject that are to be met with in any modern critical writer.' Blair's purpose, like Smith's was eminently practical. 'The design of this course of lectures is to assist such as are to write, or speak in public, to speak or write in an accurate manner, or to enable such as intend neither, to read and hear the compositions of others with pleasure and satisfaction.'[5]

## PERIODICALS AND COURSES IN CULTURE

The importance of the English periodicals, such as the *Tatler*, *Spectator*, *Guardian*, *Rambler*, *World*, and so on, in spreading an interest in literary topics and setting a standard of enlightened taste in Scotland,

---

[1] Edinburgh University Library, MS DC.3.4.2. f. 7.       [2] *Ibid*. f. 4.
[3] *Ibid*. f. 7.                                    [4] Blair, *Lectures*, Vol. II, pp. 7-8.
[5] Edinburgh University Library, MS DC.3.4.2. f. 5.

was considerable. They were the popular ways by which the public sought to improve its understanding of letters and philosophy. The best edition of the *Rambler*, according to Boswell, was that which was printed by Elphinstone in Edinburgh and appeared in penny numbers simultaneously with the London edition. Before the *Spectator* had begun to appear in 1712, the *Tatler*, its predecessor, was being reprinted and imitated in Scotland.[1] The *Northern Tatler* appeared on 27 March 1710, 'to be continued every Monday and Friday.' Soon the *Spectator* papers were setting a new level for polite educated conversation in Scottish society. Smith constantly refers to them and assumes a knowledge of them, or easy access to them, on the part of his students. French writings on Belles Lettres and Eloquence also made a direct contribution to the popular desire for culture, and the methods of teaching these subjects advocated by them served as models for similar 'courses' in Scotland. Rollin's compendium, *De la Manière d'Enseigner et d'Étudier les Belles Lettres* was by far the most popular. The book appeared in several volumes between 1724 and 1731. An English translation in four volumes came out in 1737, and was reprinted, according to Lowndes, in 1742, 1749, 1759, 1770, 1804 and 1810. Rollin had served as Rector of the University of Paris for twice the usual period of one year, and was again elected as Rector-presumptive in 1719. His comprehensive treatise sketched a plan of a reformed system of education. The title-page of the English translation, long as it is, is worth transcribing. It reads: 'The Method of Teaching and Studying the Belles Lettres, or, An Introduction to Languages, Poetry, Rhetoric, History, Moral Philosophy, Physics, etc. with Reflections on Taste; and Instructions with regard to the Eloquence of the Pulpit, the Bar, and the Stage. The whole illustrated with Passages from the most famous Poets and Orators, Ancient and Modern, with Critical Remarks on them. Designed more particularly for Students in the Universities.'

Rollin's book doubtless proved invaluable to many a schoolmaster, and many a University Regent, harassed by the difficulty of showing himself 'well found' in a wide variety of subjects. Languages apart, Rollin provided a more or less complete education for a gentleman. That it soon found imitators we can see from the already-quoted *Preceptor* (1748), in twelve parts, including Reading, Speaking, and Writing Letters, Geometry, Geography and Astronomy, History, Rhetoric and

[1] McElroy, *op. cit.*, p. 251. Cf. also A. Andrew, *History of British Journalism*, London 1859, Vol. I, p. 287.

Poetry, Drawing, Logic, Natural History, Ethics, Trade and Commerce, Laws and Government, Human Life and Manners.[1] The repeated re-printing of the translation of Rollin's book does not seem to have dis-couraged the issue of a similar four-volume translation of *A Course of the Belles Lettres*, the work of the Abbé Batteux, published in London in 1761. The original had been printed in Paris in 1750. This book covers a less wide range of topics than Rollin's work, but it is arranged on more philosophical principles. It does not, however, appear to have been reprinted in English, though there were several French editions.

In Scotland the result of all these diverse activities was a wide-spread cultivation of the 'critical' spirit, which was in keeping with the national interest in political and economic philosophy, in history as a branch of literature, and in the discussion of philosophical and literary principles. It ultimately produced such notable results as the *Edinburgh Review* and *Blackwood's Magazine*. Adam Smith and his successors Watson, Blair, Campbell, Greenfield and the rest, had done their work of public education well.

## METHOD OF EDITING THE TEXT

The manuscript of these Lectures presents few difficulties in trans-cription: I have indicated all places where I have had to guess. The spelling and punctuation have been made modern, and occasional obvious errors or *lacunae* caused by mis-hearing or misunderstanding have been corrected. I have endeavoured to make a more-or-less con-tinuous text from the three sources available: (*a*) the great bulk of the lectures, written nearly always on the *recto* of the leaves of the manu-script, but sometimes continuing on to the *verso*; (*b*) very numerous additions in the same hand and ink as (*a*), written on the *verso* of the preceding leaf, occasionally marked for insertion at particular points in (*a*), but frequently not so marked; (*c*) occasional additions in a different ink, in what may be a different hand or the same hand at a later date, made either at the end of a lecture or on the *verso* of the leaves opposite the point where (presumably) they were meant to be inserted or used as additional comment. When not otherwise indicated, the text is from (*a*); all passages from (*b*) and (*c*) are so marked. The printed text is thus made to include the whole of the manuscript.

[1] Reprinted *seven* times by 1793. Professor W. S. Howell has shown that part of it, the Logic by Professor William Duncan of Aberdeen, frequently reprinted as a separate work, almost certainly influenced Jefferson in framing the Declaration of Independence. Cf. *William and Mary Quarterly* (October 1961) XVIII, No. 4.

Sources (*a*) and (*b*) are, to all appearance, contemporary, and (*b*) might have been additions or digressions by the lecturer or notes added by the student transcribed from another set of the same lectures, and added very soon after (*a*) was taken down. Source (*c*), it was at first imagined, might have been Adam Smith's own additions or comments for the benefit of a student living in his house; but since there were occasional failures to recognise names of persons or titles of books in those comments, this hypothesis had to be abandoned. In substance and expression source (*c*) seems to the editor to be as genuinely the work of Adam Smith as (*a*) and (*b*), and probably taken from the notes of another student. Dr Rae thinks it likely that the manuscript is that of a student's notes taken in the lecture-room. In a few lectures, however, there are traces of a copyist at work: these have been indicated in the notes. From Lecture 5 onwards an obvious slip in numbering the lectures has been corrected.

The following conventions have been used in editing the text:

(   )   Brackets in the manuscript.

⟨   ⟩   Passages on the verso pages of the manuscript written in the same hand and ink as the main text.

⟨ * ⟩   Passages on the verso pages, or at the end of the lectures, written in a different [?] hand and ink.

[   ]   Editorial brackets—emendations, or omissions supplied.

# 2

PERSPICUITY requires not only that the expressions we use should be free from all ambiguity proceeding from synonymous words, but that the words should be natives (if I may [say] so) of the language we speak in. Foreigners, though they may signify the same thing, never convey the idea with such strength as those we are acquainted with and whose origin we can trace. We may see an instance of this in the word 'unfold'—a good old English word derived from an English root, consequently its meaning must be easily received. This word, however, has within these ten years been most unaccountably thrust out of common use by a French word of not half the strength or significance, to wit, 'develop'. This word, though of the same signification with 'unfold', can never convey the idea so strongly to an English reader. ⟨In the same manner 'unravel' is thrown out to make room for [blank]¹.⟩ The words of another language may, however, be naturalized by time and be as familiar to us as those which are originally our own, and may then be used with as great freedom. But here likewise we may see the effect of the words being well known to us or not. For instance, the words 'insufferable'² and 'intolerable'², which are both borrowed of the Latin language and compounded of words of the same meaning, are of very unequal strength. The reason is that the word 'intolerable' had not been so long introduced amongst us and therefore does not carry the same power along with it. We say that the cruelty and oppression of a tyrant is 'insufferable', but the heat of a summer's day is 'intolerable'. 'Insufferable' expresses our emotion and indignation at the behaviour of the tyrant, whereas 'intolerable' means only that there is some difficulty and uneasiness in supporting the heat of the sun.

The English language perhaps needs our care in this respect more

¹ The [blank] has been filled up by a later hand with the word 'develop'; this in turn has been cancelled and 'perhaps "explicate"' substituted.
² The MS wavers between 'un-' and 'in-', with both words.

than any other. New words are continually pushing out our own original ones, so that the stock of our own is now become but very small and is still diminishing. This perhaps is owing to a defect which our language labours much under, of being compounded of a great number of others. ⟨No author has been more attentive to this point than Swift; we may say his language is more English than any other writer that we have.⟩ Most terms of art and most compounded words are borrowed from other languages, so that the lower sort of people, and those who are not acquainted with those languages from whence they are taken, can hardly understand many of the words of their own tongue. Hence it is that we see this sort of people are continually using these words in meanings altogether foreign to their proper ones. The Greeks used compounded words, but then they were formed from words of their own language. By this means their language was so plain that the meanest person would perfectly understand the terms of art and expressions of any artist or philosopher. The word 'triangle' would not be understood by an Englishman who had not learned Latin, but an Italian would at the first understand their 'triangolo', or a Dutchman their 'thriesnuik'.[1]

Our words must not only be English and agreeable to the custom of the country, but likewise to the custom of some particular part of the nation. This part undoubtedly is formed of the men of rank and breeding. The easiness of those persons' behaviour is so agreeable and taking that whatever is connected with it pleases us. (It is commonly said, also, that in France and England the conversation of the ladies is the best standard of language, as there is a certain delicacy and agreeableness in their behaviour and address, and in general we find that whatever is agreeable makes what accompanies it have the deeper impression and convey the notion of agreeableness along with [it]. For this reason we love both their dress and their manner of language.)

On the other hand many words, as well as gestures or peculiarities of dress, give us an idea of something mean and low in those in whom we find them. Hence it is that words equally expressive and more commonly used would appear very absurd if used in common conversation by one in the character of a gentleman. Thus perhaps nine-tenths of the people of England say 'I'se do't' instead of 'I will do it', but no gentleman would use that expression without the imputation of vulgarity. We may indeed naturally expect that the better sort will often

[1] *sic*: driehoek?

2

exceed the vulgar in the propriety of their language, but where there is no such excellence we are apt to prefer those in use amongst them, by the association we form betwixt their words and the behaviour we admire in them. It is the custom of the people that forms what we call propriety, and the custom of the better sort from whence the rules of purity of style are to be drawn. As those of the higher rank generally frequent the Court, the standard of our language is therefore to be met with there chiefly. In countries, therefore, which are divided into a number of sovereignties, we cannot expect to meet with any general standard, as the better sort are scattered into different places. Accordingly we find that in Greece and Modern Italy each state sticks by its own dialect, without yielding the preference to any other, even though superior in other respects, as the Athenians were.

Our words must also be put in such order that the meaning of the sentence shall be quite plain, and not depend upon the accuracy of the printer or of the reader in placing the points or laying the emphasis on any certain words. Mr Pope often errs in both these respects: as, first, in that line, 'Born but to die, and reasoning but to err'.[1] The sense of this line is very different in these two cases, when we put the accent in both members on *but*, or in the one on *born* and in the other on *reasoning*. The former I imagine was Mr Pope's own meaning, though Mr Warburton gives it a different turn.[2] But if that had been Mr Pope's meaning, Mr Pope had more properly have used *though* for *but*, and then there had been no ambiguity, though the line would not have been so strong as in the way it stands at present, if taken in the common apparent meaning. We have an example of the latter sort, when it is not easy to know what member of the sentence a word belongs to, in that line 'great master death and God adore'.[3] Here we will find the meaning altogether different if we place the pause before or after the word 'death'.

⟨We may here observe that it is almost always improper to place *and* in the beginning of a member of a sentence, though it may be sometimes, though rarely, proper to begin a sentence in that manner, and then there is no danger of ambiguity.⟩

Another ambiguity, also, to be avoided, is that where it is difficult

[1] *Essay on Man*, II, l. 10.
[2] Warton (ed.), *Works of Pope*, III, 57, gives a note by Warburton on l. 11 not relevant to l. 10.
[3] *Essay on Man*, I, l. 92. Pope has 'teacher', not 'master'.

to know what verb the nominative case belongs to, or what noun an adjective agrees with. The ancient languages were much more liable to this ambiguity than the modern ones, as they admitted of a greater freedom in the arrangement of the words. As an example of this we may take that line of Juvenal, *Nobilitas sola [est] atque unica Virtus*,[1] where the ambiguity is owing to the not distinguishing whether *sola* agrees with *virtus* or *nobilitas*.

This line may serve as an instance of the ambiguity proceeding from the verb not being ascertained to belong to one substantive more than another: 'In this alone beasts do the men excel', where one would be apt to think the author meant that the beasts excelled men in this alone, whereas the contrary is certainly the meaning.

The best authors very seldom fall into this error—Thucydides, Xenophon, and several others; nay, Dr Clarke[2] says he has found but one instance in all Homer. This, indeed, may be turned in very different ways, but as the rest is so exact this probably proceeds from the error of some transcriber. It is wonderful no more errors of this sort have crept in during so long a tract of time, and may serve to show the surprising accuracy of that writer.

Mr Waller, again, is a remarkable instance of the defect of this quality, and he pays very little regard to grammatical rules, his sense is sometimes hardly to be come at, though this method will often serve to discover the meaning of other obscure writers. The characterists[3] are extremely free from this, and would be the book most easily construed.

A natural order of expression, free of parentheses and superfluous words, is likewise a great help towards perspicuity. In this consists what we call easy writing, which makes the sense of the author flow naturally upon our mind without our being obliged to hunt backwards and forwards in order to find it. ⟨When there are no words that are superfluous, but all tend to express something by themselves which was not said before, and in a plain manner, we may call it precision, though this word is often taken to mean a stiff and affected style, such as that of Poim[4] and others of the Puritan writers.⟩ Bolingbroke especially, and Swift, have excelled most in this respect, and accordingly we find that their writings are so plain that one partly asleep may carry the sense along with him, ⟨even though the sentence be very long, as in that in the end of his essay

---

[1] Juvenal, *Satires*, VIII, l. 20.      [2] MS: *Clerk*.
[3] *sic*: *Characteristics*? Obviously Smith refers to one book, and Shaftesbury's *Characteristics* seems to be what he intended.      [4] *sic*: Pym?

on virtue.[1]⟩ Nay, if we happen to lose a word or two, the rest of the sentence is so naturally connected with it, as that it comes into our mind of its own accord.

On the other hand, writers who do not observe this rule often become so obscure that their meaning is not to be discovered without great attention and being altogether awake. Shaftesbury sometimes runs into this error by endeavouring to throw a great deal together before us.

Writings of this sort have a great deal of the air of translations from another language, where a certain stiffness of expression and repetition of synonymous words is very apt to be gone into.

Short sentences are generally more perspicuous than long ones, as they are more easily comprehended in one view; but when we intend to study conciseness we should avoid the unconnected way of writing which we are then very apt to run into and [which] at the same time is of all others the most obscure. The reason of this is that when we study short sentences we are apt also to throw out the connecting words and render our expressions concise as well as our sentences. But precision and a close adherence to a just expression are very consistent with a long sentence, and a short sentence may very possibly want both. Sallust, Tacitus, and Thucydides are the most remarkable in this way; and it is proper to observe that concise expressions and short-turned periods are proper only for historians who narrate facts barely as they are, or those who write in the didactic style. The three historians we mentioned are accordingly the chief who have followed this manner of writing. It is very improper for orators or public speakers, as their design is to rouse the passions, which are not affected by a plain simple style, but require attacks of strong and perhaps exaggerated expressions. No didactic writer has invariably adhered to this style, though it be proper to them, unless Aristotle, who never once deviates from it in his whole works, whereas others often run out into oratorical declamation.

What are generally called ornaments or flowers in language, as allegorical, metaphorical, and such-like expressions, are very apt to make one's style dark and perplexed. Studying much to vary the expression leads one also frequently into a dungeon of metaphorical obscurity. The Lord Shaftesbury is, of all authors I know, the most liable to this error. In the third volume of his works, talking of medi-

---

[1] I have found no essay on virtue by Bolingbroke. Smith probably refers to Shaftesbury's 'Inquiry Concerning Virtue', the penultimate sentence of which is very long.

tating and reflecting within oneself, he contrives an innumerable number of names for it, each more dark than another, as 'self-conversation', 'forming a plurality in the same person' etc. In another place he says that his head was the dupe of his heart, where another would have said that he was so intent on obtaining a certain [thing] that he could not help thinking he would obtain it. But it is plain this author had it greatly in view to go out of the common road in his writings, and to dignify his style by never using common phrases or even names for things, and we see hardly any expressions in his works but what would appear absurd in common conversation. To such a length does he carry this that he won't even call *men* by their own names. Moses is 'the Jewish lawgiver', Xenophon 'the young warrior', Plato 'the philosopher of noble birth'; and in his treatise written expressly to prove the being of God he never almost uses that word, but that of 'supreme being or mind', or 'he that knows all things',[1] etc.

The frequent use of pronouns is also not agreeable to perspicuity as it makes [us] look to what they refer to. They are, however, proper where the noun whose place they supply is not the chief or emphatical one in the sentence. But in that case the repetition of the word itself gives greater strength and energy to the sentence.

We might here insist on this, as well as proper variation of the form of a sentence, and how far our language could admit of it, but this, as well as many other grammatical parts, we must altogether pass over as tedious and unentertaining, and proceed to give an estimate of our own language compared with others. In order to do this it will be proper to premise somewhat with regard to the origin and design of language in general.

[1] Smith tends to overstate his case. The passage about Plato is: 'It is to some such catastrophe of this kind that we owe . . . the founder of the Academy, and others who were also noble in respect of their birth and fitted for the highest stations,' etc. *Characteristics*, Vol. II, pp. 131-2 (ed. 1757).

# 3

*Of the origin and progress of language.*[1]

IT seems probable that those words which denote certain substances which exist, and which we call substantives, would be *amongst* the first contrived by persons who were inventing a language. Two savages who met together and took up their dwelling in the same place would very soon endeavour to get signs to denote those objects which most frequently occurred and with which they were most concerned. The cave they lodged in, the tree from whence they got their food, or the fountain from whence they drank, would all soon be distinguished by particular names, as they would have frequent occasion to make their thoughts about them known to one another, and would by mutual consent agree on certain signs whereby this might be accomplished. Afterwards when they met with other trees, caves, and fountains, concerning which they would have occasion to converse, they would naturally give the same name to them as they had before given to other objects of the same kind. The association of ideas betwixt the caves, trees, etc. and the words they had denoted them by, would naturally suggest that those things which were of the same sort might be denoted by the same words. Thus it might perhaps be that those words which originally signified singular objects came to be special names to certain classes of things. As our savages made advances they would have occasion not only for names to the several substances near them, but also to express the relations betwixt those several objects.[2]

These names, however, as the objects multiplied, would not be sufficient to distinguish them accurately from one another: they would therefore be necessitated to have recourse to their peculiar relations or qualities. These are commonly expressed by prepositions or adjectives.

---

[1] This lecture was first published, in an expanded form, as an appendix to the *third* edition of Smith's *Theory of Moral Sentiments* (1767).
[2] This sentence has cancel strokes through it in the MS.

This is what chiefly difficults Mr Rousseau,[1] to wit, to explain how general names were first formed, as they require abstract thought and what is called generalization, before they can be formed, according to his way of thinking: which he thinks men at first hardly capable of. Thus they might express a certain tree by saying 'the tree above the cave', but those expressed by prepositions would not go any great length. They would then call in the [help] of the adjectives, and thus they might say 'the green tree' to denote one that was green from one that was not. The invention of adjectives would have required a much greater degree of exertion than that of substantives, for these following reasons. The quality denoted by an adjective is never seen in the abstract, but is always concreted with some substance or other; the word signifying such a quality must be formed from it by a good deal of abstract reflection. Besides, this quality is not seen in any general set of things, though it is a general quality, but must be at first formed from some singular object. For this reason we may imagine those adjectives would be formed before any of the substantives denoting the abstract qualities to those bodies to which the adjectives are applied. Thus *green* would be formed before *greenness*, as the quality, though abstract in itself, is seldom considered but when connected with some substances really existing and perceived in some singular one before us, whereas the quality abstracted from any body is never seen, but is only formed by abstraction and generalization from those bodies where they are found. It is also necessary before such adjectives be formed that those who form them have seen other things of the same kind which have them not. Thus the word *green*, if it was originally formed, e.g. the colour of a tree, would not have been formed if there were no trees of a different colour. But when there were other trees found of another colour, they might call such a tree a 'green' tree, and from thence other trees, and afterwards other things of that colour might get the appellation. From thence, too, the quality of *greenness* would at length be formed by farther abstraction.

When there is so much abstraction required to form those adjectives that denote colours, which are the most simple of all, it is plain there would be much greater in forming more complex and general ones. But whatever difficulty there might be in the formation of adjectives, there must be still more in forming prepositions. For that which is signified by them is not found in any one particular set of things, but is common

[1] See, for example, Rousseau, *Origin of Inequality*, published in 1755, pt. 1 (Everyman Library, p. 192).

to all those in a certain relation. Thus *above* denotes the relation of superiority, *below* that of inferiority, with regard to anything in that relation. It is not concreted with any other thing, but is of itself originally abstract. We may say a *green* tree, or anything else is *green*, but *above* is connected with the relation that two things bear to one another. It happens, too, that those prepositions which necessarily most frequently occur are those that are most abstracted and metaphysical. There is none of which such frequent use is made as of the preposition *of*, which at the same time is the most abstract of the whole number of them all. It denotes often no particular relation betwixt the things it connects, but barely signifies that there is a relation. And if we were to ask an ordinary man what he meant by the word *of* he might be allowed at least a week to consider of it. We may see the general signification of it from the various and contrary relations it is used to express as betwixt the whole and its parts. Thus we may say the *son of the father* or the *father of the son*, the *fir-trees of the forest* or the *forest of the fir-trees*. Other prepositions cannot be used so generally. We say the *tree above the cave* and the *cave above the tree*, but this cannot be said with regard to the same thing.

When such was the difficulty of forming these prepositions, which are so very requisite, it was natural for the contrivers of language, whom we are not to suppose very abstract philosophers, would contrive some method to answer these purposes by a more easy method. That which was most natural and obvious, and that which we find was the case in all the primitive and simple languages, is to express by various modification of the same word what would otherwise require a preposition. This they have done by varying the termination of the substantive; the different prepositions whose places were thus supplied gave occasion to the different cases, and according as fewer or more of them were thus supplied, the cases would be more or less in number in different languages, in some five, six, or, in others, ten.

The agreeableness of the same sound repeated, or love of rhyme,[1] made them suit their adjectives to the terminations of the suitable substantives, and hence it came to pass that all the adjectives were declined in the same manner as the substantives, though the signification is no way altered; as, *malus, mali, malorum, malis*, etc. all signify *evil* and are varied only to make them suit the substantives, as *equus, equi, equorum, equis*, etc.

[1] MS: *rythme*. From the printed essay *rhyme* would appear to be the correct reading.

As all animals are of some sex and other things of none, and it was requisite to have a distinction in this respect, and the quality in the abstract being not easily comprehended, they rectified this by making another sort of a change in the noun of one sex: hence *equus, equa*. And as those of another quality had no sex, they formed here another sort, which denoted those of neither of the other two qualities. For the same reason as they suited the adjectives to the declension of case, so also they would do that of gender, hence *equus bonus, equa bona, pratum bonum*.

As more objects than one of the same sort occurred, it was necessary to distinguish betwixt the singular person and those cases where there were more than [one] together; and as abstract numbers are also of difficult comprehension, they here likewise invented another variation to denote number. Hence the singular, dual, and plural number. ⟨The original languages have all the dual, as the Hebrew and Slavonic.⟩ To this declension or variety, also, they accommodated their adjectives, for the same reason that we before mentioned. Hence came *equus, equi,* ἀνήρ, ἀνέρε, ἀνέρες, and to these adjectives, *bonus, boni,* and ἀγαθός, ἀγαθώ, ἀγαθοί.

Hence we may see how complex their declensions must have become. The substantive nouns, declined through cases in three numbers, will have fifteen varieties, and the adjectives, having besides three genders, will have forty-five.

Besides these various parts they would have occasion for some words to describe or express certain actions. Everything we say is either affirming or denying something, and to do this some other master sort of word was necessary, and this was the reason of the invention of verbs, for without [them] no one thing could be expressed. Hence, probably, verbs of the impersonal form would be the first invented of any, as they would express a whole sentiment or assertion in this way. So *pluit, ningit* are complete assertions. The savages we supposed together might, for instance, use the word *venit* to express the coming of some terrible animal, as a lion, which they expressed completely in one word. Afterwards, other beasts coming, they would naturally use the same word to give the alarm. So this word would come to signify some terrible beast; then any frightful object; and lastly, any approach, in the abstract. For the same reasons [as] they invented number and person in nouns, they would in the verbs, as a greater or less number might be coming. According to the time, different variations would also be made. They might indeed have used the same word for different tenses, had they known the pronouns; but these were not invented in the early times we are talking of, as too abstract. The different words made for different things of the same origin is like the forming of the letters. The first writer would probably use a different character for each word, but this would soon be troublesome and occasion some other contrivance; so different flexions of words would be also invented.

In this complex state languages would probably have continued had it not been for the mixtures of different nations. The only thing that could have had any effect was this so great complexity, which would make them at a loss and might run them into improprieties of grammar. And so we see the Greeks and Romans were forced to instruct their children in the grammar of their own tongue. But the chief cause of the declension from this custom was the inter-mixture of different nations. Those who are most simple are all most complex.[1] When two nations thus met, when [a member of one] was at a loss to express himself in the other language, he would be led to supply this defect in some easy manner. The most obvious is that of the substantive and possessive verbs. The substantive verb *sum* with the passive participle, would supply all the Passive voice, and the auxiliary, or, rather, possessive, *habeo*, would by a stranger, with the help of the supine, be made to supply the whole of the Active. The prepositions would be put in place of the declensions of nouns. A Lombard, when he had forgotten *amor* for *I am loved*, would say *ego sum amatus; a citizen of Rome, civis de Roma*; for *I have loved, Ego habeo amatum*, instead of *amavi*.

These mixtures, the more they are multiplied, the more the language would lose of its complexness and be supplied in this manner. The simpler the language, the more complex. The Greek seems to be very original, as all the primitives are only about three hundred. The Latin, formed of it, and the Tuscan, is complex, but much less so. The French, of the Latin and the native of the country, still less; and the English less still, being formed from the French and the Saxon.

The languages in this have made advances a good deal similar to those in the construction of machines. They at first are vastly complex, but gradually the different parts are more connected and supplied by one another. But the advantage does not equally correspond. The simpler the machine the better, but the simpler the language the less it will have variety and harmony of sound, and the less it will be capable of various arrangement. And, lastly, it will be more prolix.

[1] In the MS this sentence has a cancel stroke.

II

# 4

Wednesday, 24 November 1762

As such great defects have been unavoidably introduced into the English language by the very manner of its formation, it will be proper to consider how far and by what means they have been remedied.

The first of those defects which comes to be considered is the prolixity necessarily attending a language which has so few flexions in its nouns and verbs. To remedy this, many contractions have been made in the words themselves. The *e* which formerly made the final syllable of the third person of many verbs has been universally thrown out where it possibly could, and in many cases where it had been better retained, as in *judged*; but the general rule is followed.[1] Most of our own native words consist of but one or two or at most three syllables. There are fewer of one than in any other language whatever. ⟨* The Italian and French are compounded of simple languages, but into the composition of the English there enters a language already compounded, viz. the French.⟩ When we borrow from other languages words of more syllables, they are shortened by the manner of pronunciation. This is very remarkable in the words *refractory, concupiscence*. In other words, too, when this cannot be done, we fairly strike off one-half, as in *plenipotentiary, incognito*, which in the mouths of some would sound *plenipo, incog*. The pronunciation of sentences is likewise shortened in the same manner by throwing the accent as near the beginning as possible, which makes it much sooner pronounced. This method is exactly contrary to that in use in the French language, where the accent, both in words and in periods, is thrown on to the last syllable or the concluding word. The former is what seems most likely to produce a melodious sound, and it is a known rule in music that the first note of a bar, or the first pitch of any note that is to be repeated with a uniform accent, should be sharpest, whereas the manner of the French pronunciation makes the sentence

---

[1] Smith seems to have shared Swift's opinion. Cf. *A proposal for Correcting, Improving and Ascertaining the English Tongue*, 1712. (*Works*, Bohn ed., Vol. XI.)
* This sentence is on the opposite page and in the second hand.

continually more and more precipitate, till at last it breaks off short. From this contrariety we may see the reason why a Frenchman will never be able to speak English with the proper accent, nor an Englishman French, if the habit be confirmed by time. To shew that the English manner of pronouncing a sentence, high at first and lower in the end, we need only observe that it is the manner in which all those speak who have a cant or whine, whether in reading, preaching, or crying 'oysters!' or 'broken bellows!': the first is always the high note, and the last part dies away and is hardly felt.

The melody of sound has likewise been attended to in many respects. The harsh and uncouth gutturals which so much prevailed have been almost entirely laid aside: *thought, wrought, taught,* are now pronounced as if there were no guttural in them. *Ch,* which was some time ago pronounced as the Greek *X,* is now pronounced as when it ends a word, as in *charming, change,* etc. or as *K* in *character, chimera.* The final syllable *-ed,* which has a sound nearly as harsh as *-eth,* is now laid aside as often as possible, and even sometimes when [it] had better been continued; but when common use, which has the supreme determination in these matters, is determined otherwise, 'tis in vain to stand out.

*Eth,* as we just now mentioned, is often now [changed] into *-s, loveth* into *loves, willeth* into *wills.* This change, however, is still faulty, and increases the hissing of the language, already very remarkable, as most of the pronouns and plural nouns end in the letter *s.* But though the sound may not be altogether harmonious, yet it is much better than the other, which, as well as *-ed,* approaches nearly to a whisper and dies away to nothing.

The frequent use of the letter *s* and the hissing thereby occasioned is commonly ascribed to the defect of a musical ear in the English nation. But this does not seem to be the case.[1] The introduction of it here is of real advantage; and besides, there is no reason to think there is any defect in the point of a musical ear. For there is as general and good taste for music in England as in any other nation except the Italians, and what is still of more weight, no nation attends more to a musical pronunciation, as is hereafter to be observed.

Some authors, indeed, have written constantly *-eth,* and *-ed,* as Swift and Bolingbroke, but if they were now to read their own words they would undoubtedly read *flows, brings, avow'd,* which are certainly

[1] Smith seems to have been touchy on this point; see below, Lecture 30, p. 192.

smarter words than *floweth, bringeth, avowed,* the pronunciation of our more deliberate and sober ancestors.

⟨In order also to curtail the phrases we omit prefixing the particles to every word, as in translating the title of the Abbé du Bos' book,[1] yet this sure[2] is the accurate method and that without which we are exposed to ambiguity. It is thus that we write on public monuments, etc. Here again the general rule betrays us into an error.⟩

Besides these alterations in the pronunciation of the consonants, there are several attempts to remedy the harshness of the language in the pronunciation of the vowels and diphthongs, which are indeed but very few. The first vowel, *a,* is softened into the same sound as in other nations is given to the Greek *η,* unless in a few words where it would be disagreeable, as in *walk, talk.* The second vowel, *e,* is sounded as other nations do the third, *i,* which in English has a different sound when it is long and when it is short. In the first case, it is sounded as a diphthong, as in *idol;* in the latter it has the same as they give *e,* as in *intelligible.* The fifth vowel, *u,* has also two sounds: in one case it is pronounced as the diphthong *ou,* as in *use,* pronounced as *eu* in *Eugene;* and in other cases it has the same sound as in other languages, as in *undone.* The diphthongs also have their full strength and are sounded stronger than in any other languages, as in *faith, mourn,* etc.

But what has a greater effect on the sound of the languages than all the rest is the harmonious and sonorous pronunciation of the English nation. There is a certain singing in their manner of speaking which foreigners can never attain. Hence it is that this language, which when spoken by the natives is allowed to be very melodious and agreeable, in the mouth of strangers is strangely harsh and grating. The English have been led into all these practices, without thinking of them, to remedy the natural harshness of their language, which they have effected.

I proceed next to make some observations on the arrangement of words, which will naturally lead to the consideration of what I call style.

A period is a set of words expressing a complete sense without the help of any other. The members of a period are those phrases which make up that sense, and may frequently have a sense of their own, complete enough without the other, and only referring to it by some word or two.

[1] Smith is probably alluding to the work by the Abbé du Bos, translated in 1748 by Nugent under the title *Critical Reflections on Poetry, Painting, and Music,* in which the word 'on' is not repeated before 'Painting' and 'Music'.
[2] *sure*: reading uncertain.

In one member there are generally three principal parts or terms, because every judgement of the human mind must comprehend two ideas, between which we declare that relation subsists or does not subsist. In two of these we affirm something or other, and the third connects them together and expresses the affirmation. One of these is that which is the chief part or subject of the member, and is therefore called the 'subjective' term; the middle one, which connects the extremes, is called the 'attributive'; and the other, of whom the assertion is made, is called the 'objective', as of inferior rank to the former ones. These three must generally be placed in the order we have mentioned, as otherwise the meaning of the sentence would become ambiguous. It is also to be observed that in sentences expressed by neuter verbs there is no adjective; it is when the verb is active that the term can be used. In imperative and interrogative expressions the order of the terms is also different. Besides these terms there [are] other two which frequently occur, though not necessary to constitute a perfect member of a period or phrase, and denote the [one] how far, and the other in what circumstances, the proposition expressed by the three fore-mentioned terms is to be understood. The former is called the 'terminative', and the latter the 'circumstantial'. Though the other three are a good deal limited in their order, yet these are hardly at all confined, but may be placed in almost any way that one inclines.

The only remaining terms are the 'conjunctive' and the 'adjunctive'. The 'conjunctive' is that which connects the different terms of a sentence or period together. The 'adjunctive', again, points out what particular opinion the speaker has of it, the person to whom it is addressed, and such like. The 'adjunctive' is that which expresses the habit of the speaker's mind in regard to what he speaks of, or the sentiment it excites, as 'tis strange, alas, etc. Sir, is an 'adjunctive' which denotes your addressing yourself to a particular person. All interjections are 'adjunctives'.

These being the constituent parts of any sentence, it comes now to be considered in what order these parts are to be placed in the composition of a sentence. Now it is plain that must be the best order which most naturally occurs to the mind and best expresses the sense of the speaker concerning what he speaks. But this is not the simple order in which they would be placed by one that was no way affected with what he said, but varies according as any of the different terms is the chief or essential one in the sentence, as that must first occur to the mind. The most plain

15

order we could suppose and in which idiots, etc. speak, would be this: 1st, the subjective; 2nd, the attributive; 3rd, the objective; 4th, the terminative; 5th, the circumstantial. The conjunctive and adjunctive would probably be at the beginning or end, and the adjunctive in different places according to its different designs.

But this order would very ill suit many expressions: nothing lively or spirited could be said in this arrangement. The general rule, therefore, is that whatever is most interesting in the sentence, on which the rest depends, should be placed first; and so on through the whole. That the strong members should precede those of less consequence is also confirmed by the observation already made of ranters; they raise the first and most important part of the sentence to the high note, as they are most in earnest.

⟨Thus* would a man always speak who felt no passions; but when we are affected in anything, some one or other of the ideas will thrust itself forward, and we will be most eager to utter what we feel strongest. Eloisa regrets her vain endeavours to check her passion and the breaking of her heart.

> In vain lost Eloisa weeps and prays;
> Her heart still dictates and her hand obeys.[1]

Make it:

> Lost Eloisa weeps in vain and prays;
> Still her heart dictates and her hand obeys,

the line, though still a pretty one, has lost much of its force. In the same manner: 'The soul proud Science never taught to love'.[2]

Translations which are literally done from one language to another, particularly from the ancient to the modern, are very defective in this respect. They do not, indeed, stick by the natural and grammatical order, but then they frequently [use] one worse suited to the subject than it would be. The reason is, that as the different parts might be more disjoined in them, so when they are put in another language where such liberty cannot be taken, they only breed confusion. They need a different arrangement before the same spirit can be given the sentence when in another language. The most animated and eloquent works, whether ancient or modern, if turned into the grammatical order, would appear to be wrote by dull fellows or an idiot. If therefore we find the

[1] Pope, *Eloisa to Abelard*, ll. 15-16.
[2] Pope, *Essay on Man*, I, l. 101: 'His soul proud science never taught to stray.'

first turn we give a sentence does not express our sentiment with suitable *aise*, we may reasonably imagine it is owing to some defect on the arrangement of the terms (that is to say if the words be proper English), and when we hit this, it is not only language but style, not only expresses the thought but also the spirit and mind of the author.

Hence it is that literary translations have been from the beginning of the world and to its end will be, insufferably languid and tedious. Any member of the phrase may thus on certain occasions intrude into the first place, sometimes even the conjunctive.

An example may be taken from a fine passage in Bolingbroke. 'There have been in our little world as well as in the great one, ages of gold, of silver, of brass',[1] etc. If our dissatisfaction be owing to the impropriety of our words, that we will instantly perceive if we understand language; but oftimes it arises from somewhat that we cannot explain, and in this case we may always be sure that it is from the words not arranging themselves in the order of the ideas.

Ammianus Marcellinus observed[2] the great dignity which Livy had given his style by his inversions. He thought, therefore, that by inverting still more and more frequently he might give a greater energy to his; but not knowing that which gave propriety to Livy's, he has become insufferably obscure; for example, the beginning of his third book.

This general axiom it is fit to have in mind when we compose; but it is not to be expected, nor is it advisable, that we should adjust every phrase by a minute examination of the order our ideas have or ought to have.⟩

[1] I have not found the passage.
[2] *observed*: in the sense 'noticed', not 'remarked upon'. Ammianus Marcellinus does not comment on Livy's style.

# 5

Friday, 26 November 1762

IT is a great defect in the arrangement of a sentence when it has what they call a tail coming after it, that is, when the sense appears to be concluded when it is not really so. This is always avoided by placing the terminative and circumstantial term before the attributive. This, by rendering the sense incomplete, prevents our thinking it is concluded before the whole is expressed. It likewise keeps the mind in suspense, which is of great advantage on many occasions.

If these rules be observed, the expression, though not perhaps so pompous and regular as that of Lord Shaftesbury amongst the moderns, or Isocrates and the other most ancient orators, will probably have more force and life, and be every way more natural and eloquent, than the laboured periods of those authors. The chief thing they aimed at in the arrangement of their words was the agreeable cadence of the periods. This was much more easily attained in the ancient than modern languages. The similarity of sound in the different members, one great help in this case, was always to be come at without any great labour, their verbs and nouns, generally, having the same or similar terminations in the same parts. By this means the cadences of their sentences were easily rendered smooth and uniform. But in modern languages the case is very different, as neither the verbs nor nouns have such similarity in their terminations. The chief help in our language to a good cadence is to make the different members end nearly with the same number of words, and those of the same sort. When other ways are attempted, or when even this is carried too far, it often hurts the propriety and perspicuity of the sentence, which are still more to be regarded.

The ancient authors of the best character generally avoid this by throwing the verb, and sometimes the nominative also, into the end of the sentence. Livy and Cicero commonly end every third sentence in this manner. And later authors, thinking to attain their grandeur and dignity by following them in this, frequently carry it too far, so as to end perhaps two out of four with the verb or nominative. Cicero was ridiculed for his . . . *esse videatur*.[1]

⟨There* is a passage in the *Oratio pro Marcello* in which there is an example of couplets and of alternate rhyme. Another passage in Shaftesbury's *Essay on Virtue* gives a specimen of his great care. The passage is a description of the judicious traveller.[2]⟩

In many cases this uniform and regular cadence is not at all proper. Joy and grief generally burst out into periods, regularly decreasing or increasing, both in strength and the quickness of their movements, according as the passion is becoming more violent or beginning to subside. ⟨The* bursts of laughter and of crying observe this regularity of increase or diminution.⟩ Pompous lofty expressions generally run into sentences of a tolerable length and of a slow movement. Cicero has many passages that shew the proper style of grief and joy in this respect: he often makes use of those stronger passions. But Demosthenes, a man of more hard and stubborn materials, never introduces those passions, and accordingly has none of those regular and uniform cadences. Lord Shaftesbury may serve as example of the pompous and grand style. ⟨Demosthenes* never expresses a weak passion, joy, grief, or compassion, never once[3]: he is that hard, unfeeling man. Nor does he ever express pomp, as Cicero often does. He is altogether familiar, though severe.

Indignation, everyone knows, is the most irregular of all passions in its movements. It is so in its expression also, and this it is which gives the variety to Demosthenes' periods.⟩ On the other hand indignation has a sort of regularity in its cadence; and anger is of all the most broken and irregular.

A good and harmonious sound is also promoted by avoiding harsh clashings of consonants or the hiatus arising from the meeting[4] [of] many vowels. The latter our language is in no great danger of; the more frequently vowels and diphthongs occur it is generally the sweeter. Waller has a vast sweetness in his compositions, from the smooth and melodious words he generally makes use of. Waller has a whole copy of

[1] *esse videatur*: cf. Tacitus, *Dialogus*, 23, 1 (speech of Asper); Quintilian x, 2, 18.
[2] *traveller*: I have been unable to find this passage. There is a vivid description of man's interest in travel in *Characteristics, Advice to an Author*, pt. 3, sect. 3, and a tale of travellers in *ibid., Miscellaneous Reflections*, Misc. 2, ch. 3.
[3] Smith's confidence in his complete knowledge of Demosthenes is worth noting. Cf. his description of Aristotle, above, p. 5, as one 'who never once deviates from [the plain style] in his whole works'.　　[4] *meeting*: reading doubtful.

verses to Delia[1] in which the only harsh words are *stretch* and *God's.*

> Delia let not us inquire
>   What has been our past desire,
> For if joys we now may prove
> Take advice of present love.

Swift in his severe, ironical manner, says

> Our barren island hardly bears
>   One sprig of bay in fifty years;
> Yet every fool his claim alleges
>   As if it grew on common hedges.[2]

Swift, again, is harsh and unpleasant in many of his compositions. This style suits well enough with the morose humour of that author, but would be very unpleasant in most sorts of compositions.

Long sentences are generally inconvenient, and no one will be apt to use them who has his thoughts in good order. This is not to say that we are to be so restricted as Demetrius Phalereus and other authors would have us, as never to have above three or four members at most in a period. There are many sentences in Bolingbroke and Shaftesbury which have twice that number, and are nevertheless very perspicuous.

In the same manner as when we are taken with any subject and full of it, we are eager and impatient to speak of it and bring it into every conversation, so whichsoever it is among the ideas which constitute a phrase that most deeply affects us, that we bring forth first. As we are naturally disposed to begin with the most interesting idea and end with those which are least so, in like manner those who are little attentive to their manner of speaking begin always in a high key and end in a low one. This is the manner of all those who have a monotony, who whine, whether in the pulpit, or the Bar, or in conversation.

When in obedience to the arrangement of ideas the objective comes first, it requires the subjective to be placed immediately after.

---

[1] *Verses to Delia.* Waller's poem, the *second* with the title, is *To Phyllis*, which has 'you and I', not 'us' (l. 1), and 'the joys', not 'if joys' (l. 3). (*Poems*, ed. Thorn-Drury, p. 84).

[2] The exact text is:

> Our chilling Climate hardly bears
> A Sprig of Bays in Fifty Years:
> While ev'ry Fool his Claim alledges,
> As if it grew in Common Hedges.
>     (*Poems*, ed. Williams, vol. ii, p. 640)

Whom have I hurt?   No poet yet or peer.[1]

Him, haply, slumbering on the Norway foam,[2] etc.

This, then, is the rule. Let that which affects us most be placed first; that which affects us in the next degree, next; and so on to the end.

I will only give one other rule with regard to the arrangement, which is subordinate indeed to this great one, and it is that your sentence or phrase never drags a tail. To limit and qualify what you are about to affirm before you give the affirmation has the appearance of accurate and extensive views, but to qualify it afterwards seems a kind of retraction, and bears the appearance of confusion or of disingenuity.

Many other rules for arrangement have been given, but they do not deserve attention.

[1] Pope, *Prologue to the Satires*, l. 95.     [2] *Paradise Lost*, I, l. 203.

# 6

Monday, 29 November 1762

*Of what is called the tropes and figures of speech.*

THESE are what are generally conceived to give the chief beauty and elegance to language; whatever is sublime and out of the common way is called a figure of speech.

After language had made some progress, it was natural to imagine that men would form some rules according to which they should regulate their language. These rules are what we call grammar. The Greeks and Romans accordingly have done so, but as their languages were very complex in their form, particularly in their conjugations and declensions, it was not easy to accommodate these rules to all possible cases. Neither were they made in the best manner they might have been. They were only accommodated to the most plain and vulgar expressions. But when they came to find that many expressions could not be reduced to these rules, they were not candid enough to confess the grossness of their error and allow that these were exceptions to the general [rule] they had laid down, but stuck close to their old scheme. That they might do this with the greater appearance of justice, they gave this sort of expressions the name of tropes or figures of speech. Thus imperative and interrogative expressions, which plainly contradict the general rule that in every sentence there must be a nominative, a verb, and an accusative, and in a certain order, were not considered as exceptions but as figures of speech, and accordingly we find them among the first of the *figurae sententiarum* of Quintilian and Cicero. They had only accommodated their rules to the narrative style, and whatever varied from this was considered as a figure of speech. In these, as we mentioned, they tell us all the beauties of language, all that is noble, grand, and sublime, all that is passionate, tender, and moving, is to be found. But the case is far otherwise. When the sentiment of the speaker is expressed in a neat, clear, plain, and clever manner, and the passion or affection he is poss[ess]ed of and intends, *by sympathy*, to communicate to his hearer, is plainly and cleverly hit off, then and then only the expression

22

has all the force and beauty that language can give it. It matters not the least whether the figures of speech are introduced or not. ⟨When* your language expresses perspicuously and neatly your meaning and what you would express, together with the sentiment or affection this matter inspires you with, and when the sentiment is nobler and more beautiful than such as are commonly met with, then your language has all the beauty it can have, and the figures of speech contribute or can contribute towards it only so far as they happen to be the just and natural forms of expressing that sentiment.⟩ They neither add to, nor take from, the beauty of the expression. When they are more proper than the common forms of speaking, then they are to be used; but not otherwise. They have no intrinsic worth of their own. That which they are often supposed to have is entirely derived from the expression they are placed in. When a man says to another, 'Go blow the fire', there is no one that will affirm there is any beauty or elegance in this expression. Yet it is as much a figure of speech, and as far from the common or grammatical form, as when Dido says *I peti* [sic] *Italiam ventis*,[1] which everyone allows to be a neat and strong expression. But the beauty of it flows from the sentiment and the method of expressing it being suitable to the passion, and not from the figure in which delivered.

The grammarians, however, finding that the best authors frequently deviated from their general rules and introduced those figures of speech, as they called them, and finding also that they were most frequently met with in the most striking and beautiful passages, [un]wisely[2] concluded that these figures gave the passage all its beauty; not considering that this beauty flowed from the sentiment and from the elegance of the expression, and that the use of figures was only a secondary mean, sometimes proper, to accomplish this end, to wit, when they more fitly expressed the sense of the author than the common style. This being often the case in strong and striking passages, was the reason of these being so found in them, and [of] this mistake of grammarians in founding the beauty of a passage in the figures found in it.

It is, however, from the consideration of these figures, and divisions and sub-divisions of them, that so many systems of rhetoric, both ancient and modern, have been formed. They are generally a very silly set of books and not at all instructive. However, as it would be reckoned strange in a system of rhetoric entirely to pass by these figures that have

[1] *Aeneid*, IV, 381: 'I, sequere Italiam ventis, pete regna per undas'. Quintilian uses the illustration.　　　　　　　　[2] [un]*wisely*: conjectural emendation.

23

so much exercised the wits of men, we shall offer a few observations on them, though not on the same plan as the ordinary writers proceed on.

Whenever, then, an expression is used in a different way from the common, it must proceed either from the words of the expression or from the manner they are used in. The first forms what the ancients called tropes, when a word τρέπεται turned from its original signification. The second produces what is more properly called figures of speech.

⟨Hudibras* says justly

> For all the rhetoricians rules
> Are but the naming of his tools.[1]

It is impossible to assign the distinct limits of the ancient figures. Thus, when the shout of the fallen angels is said to have 'torn Hell's concave',[2] this figure might be asserted with equal reason to be an Hyperbole, a Metonymy, or a Metaphor.⟩

Again, if it proceeds from anything in the words, it must be either from the words being new and not in common use, or being used in a sense different from the common one. No one will venture to form words altogether new and not related to those already in use. Such could never be understood, being mere creatures of his own brain. They must either be formed from words in common use, or by old ones brought again into use, or be borrowed from some other language. The language we use most to borrow from is the Latin, as we think that as all in the character of gentlemen commonly understand this language, our words will be easily understood. Words of this sort are commonly reckoned to add to the dignity of writing, as they shew the learning of the author, and besides, what is foreign has some privileges always attending it. But as we shewed before, these foreign intruders should never be received but when they are necessary to answer some purpose which the natives cannot supply. That they are many ways prejudicial to the language has been already shewn, and need not again be insisted on.

Old words are often introduced into grave and solemn narrations or descriptions; sometimes because they answer the purpose better, as Mr. Pope says 'the din of battle' instead of 'the noise of battle'; and sometimes merely because we are apt to think everything that is ancient

[1] Butler, *Hudibras*, pt. 1, canto 1, ll. 89-90:
> For all a rhetorician's rules
> Teach nothing but to name his tools.

[2] Milton, *Paradise Lost*, 1, l. 542.

24

is venerable, whether it be so or not. Our forefathers, we always think, were a much [more] sober and grave, solemn sort of people than we are, and by analogy every [thing] that relates to them conveys to us the idea of gravity and solemnity. Spenser has studied this through all his works; he is much more obsolete than any of his contemporary writers, than Shakespeare or Sidney.

Compound words are thought by some to give a great majesty to a language, as well as the others; but we see they are generally used rather by the middling than the upper class of authors. Lucretius, Catullus, and Tibullus have many of this sort which we will never meet with in Virgil or Horace. ⟨I* have seen a Greek ode by the fellow of a college, on Ad. Vernon,[1] more abounding in such compounds than either Æschylus or Homer.⟩ Milton has but very few. Thomson, again, never thinks he has expressed himself well but when he has put two or three. There does not seem to be any great merit in barely tacking two or three words together, unless it be that they are more concise, as 'the violet-enamelled vale' of Milton is shorter than 'the valley enamelled valley'.[2] But no one surely would admire Colley Cibber's *un-come-at-able*, or the Seceders' *Pull-off-the-crown-of-Christ* heresy[3].

When the alteration of the word is in its signification, it must either be in giving it one to which it has some resemblance or analogy, or when it gets one to which it has no resemblance but is some way connected. Thus when we say *the slings and arrows of adverse fortune*[4] there is some connection betwixt the crosses of bad fortune and the slings and arrows of an enemy; ⟨Rhetorical and grammatical paronomasia:⟩ but when we say that one 'drinks off a bowl' for the liquor that is in it, there is here no sort of resemblance betwixt the glass and the liquor, but a close connection. The first of these is what the rhetoricians call a *metaphor* or *translatio*, and the latter is what they call an *metonymy*. In each of these there are several distinctions which we shall pass over as of little consequence, and when we use these words it shall be in the sense above-mentioned.

In every metaphor it is evident there must be an allusion betwixt one object and another. Now as our objects are of two classes, intellec-

---

[1] Smith went to Oxford in June 1740, when Admiral Vernon's capture of Porto Bello (November 1739) was still exciting the country. But the same admiral's orders regarding the seamen's 'grog' (August 1740) might equally excite a college fellow.

[2] *Sic.* Probably a mistake for 'with violets'.

[3] The second hand has noted on the opposite page: 'off Christ's head crown plucking heresy'.          [4] *Hamlet*, Act III, l. 58, which reads 'outrageous fortune'.

E                    25

tual and corporeal, the one of which we perceive by our mind only, and the other by our bodily senses, it follows that metaphors may be of four different kinds: 1st, when the idea we borrowed is taken from one corporeal object and applied to another intellectual object; or 2ndly, from one intellectual object to another corporeal; or 3rd, betwixt two corporeal; or 4th, betwixt two intellectual objects. When we say the 'bloom of youth', it is a metaphor of the 1st kind. When we say 'one covets applause', this is an instance of the 2nd sort of metaphor. 'The lust of fame' is an instance of the 1st kind, betwixt a corporeal [and] an intellectual object. ⟨The* 'lust of fame' is a transposition of a word from denoting a corporeal passion to another mental, equally gross and indelicate.⟩ And when necessary in the Scripture language, *The fields rejoiced and were glad, The floods clapt their hands for joy*,[1] an example of the 2nd kind.

Now it is evident that none of these metaphors can have any beauty unless it be so adapted that it gives due strength of expression to the object to be described, and at the same time does this in a more striking and interesting manner. When this is not the case, they must either carry us to bombast on the one hand, or into burlesque on the other. When Lee makes his Alexander say, 'clear room there for a whirlwind, or I blow you up as dust'. ⟨'Avaunt* and give a whirlwind room, or I will blow you up like dust',[2]⟩ the objects compared are noways adequate: the strength of a whirlwind is a much more terrible object than the fury of even an Alexander, though perhaps as dangerous to some individuals. Homer has some metaphors which border near on the burlesque, as when he says Diomede resembled an 'ass driven by boys'.[3] Thomson seems to be very faulty in this respect ⟨of expressing ever too much, and more than he felt⟩: his description of the horse will shew this very well. ⟨Compare* Thomson's horse with Virgil's, from which it was translated.[4]⟩ Virgil, again, is always just and exact in his metaphors. Milton,

[1] Cf. 1 *Chron.* 32, 'let the fields rejoice, and all that is therein'; *Ps.* 98, 'Let the floods clap their hands; let the hills be joyful together'.
[2] Roxana, in Nathaniel Lee's *Rival Queens* (Act II, sc. ii), says:
   Away! away! and give a whirlwind room;
   Pride, indignation, fury, and contempt
   War in my breast, and torture me to madness.
Perhaps the speaker confused this passage with Alexander's words in Act v, sc. i.
   Away, ye slaves, stand off!—Quick let me fly
   On lightning's wings;—nor heav'n nor earth shall stop me.
[3] It is Ajax who is so described. *Iliad*, XI, l. 558. The thistles are Smith's addition.
[4] Thomson, *Seasons*, 'Spring', 807, 809; Virgil, *Georgics*, III, ll. 250-4. Cf. Aretino's *L'Orazia*, v, 25-36.

too, keeps them always within just bounds. When he compares the grating of Hell gates to the thunder,[1] the metaphor is just; but if he had compared the noise of the gates of a city to thunder, the metaphor would not have been so just, and still [less] if to the door of a private house, though perhaps the noise might have been as great as in the former case. Homer is not always so exact in this point: his comparison of Ajax to a gad-fly[2] that continually pestered the milking woman is hard on the borders of burlesque; as also that other when he compares Diomede to an [ass] whom the boys are driving before them, 'but ever and anon he plucks up some thistles as he passes'.[3]

What has been said of the justice or propriety of metaphors is equally applicable to other figures, as metonymies, similes, allegories and hyperboles. Metaphors are nearly allied to metonymies, as we observed before. Allegories are also closely connected with them, insomuch that metaphors are called contracted allegory, and an allegory is named by some a diffused metaphor. Had Spenser been [able] to use that comparison of Shakespeare's before-mentioned, of the arrows of an enemy to the uneasiness of bad fortune, he would have described fortune in a certain garb, throwing her darts around her, and would[4] those that were under her power.

One thing farther we may observe is that two metaphors should never be run and mixed together, as in that case they can never be both just. Shakespeare is often guilty of this fault, as in the line immediately following that before cited, where he goes on *or bravely arm ourselves and stem a sea of troubles.*[5] Here there is a plain absurdity, as there is no meaning in one's putting on armour to stem the sea. ⟨Shakespeare's 'sea of troubles' has been converted in a late edition into a 'siedge', but the former reading is so like Shakespeare's manner that I dare to say he wrote it so.[6]⟩ Thomson has several slips of this sort, though much fewer than Shakespeare. There [are] I believe three or four in the four first lines of his *Seasons*.[7] In the first line Spring is addressed as some

---

[1] Milton, *Paradise Lost*, ii, ll. 879-83.
[2] The only reference in Homer to the gad-fly is in *Odyssey*, xxii, l. 300, where the suitors, as they are slaughtered, are compared to cows herding together as a gad-fly attacks them.    [3] See note 3 on preceding page.    [4] *Sic*. Probably an error for 'wounding'.
[5] As so often, Smith (or his reporter!) misquotes; *Hamlet*, iii, ll. 1, 59-60: 'Or to take arms against a sea of troubles, And by opposing end them!'
[6] Pope (1725) thought the reading should be 'siege'.
[7] *Seasons*, 'Spring', ll. 1-4:
> Come, gentle Spring, ethereal mildness, come;
> And from the bosom of yon dropping cloud
> While music wakes around, veiled in a shower
> Of shadowing roses, on our plains descend.

genial quality in the air, but in the next it is turned into a person and bade *descend, to the sound of music,* which I believe is very hard to be understood; as well the next, *Veil'd in a shower of dropping roses.* What sort of a veil a shower of roses would make, or connection such a shower has with the spring, I cannot tell. These lines, which I believe few understand, are generally admired, and, I believe, because few take the pains to consider the author's real meaning or the significance of the several expressions, but are astonished at these pompous sounding expressions.

The hyperbole is the coldest of all the figures, and indeed has no beauty of itself. When it appears to have any, it is owing to some other figure with which it is conjoined. To say that a man was a mile high would not be admired as a lofty expression, but when Virgil compares the two heroes, Turnus and Æneas, coming to battle, to two huge mountains, the grandeur of the two objects is suitable to each other and the hyperbole appears[1] on the same grounds as we determined when a metaphor appears so.

⟨Quantus Athos aut quantus Eryx aut ipse coruscis
　　Cum tonat fremit ilicibus, quantus, gaudetque nivali
　Vertice assorgens pater Appenninus in auras[2]⟩

When he compares the ships before the battle of Actium to the Cyclades[3] loosened from their foundations and floating on the sea, the grandeur of the idea of islands loosened and floating on the sea makes the hyperbole appear just and agreeable. But if he had said the ships were half-a-mile broad, the beauty would be entirely lost, though the hyperbole would not be so great and the fact asserted nearer the truth.

Besides these, many other species of these figures are mentioned, as the *paronomasia,* when we don't name but describe a person, as 'the Jewish law-giver' for Moses, the [blank], when we call an orator a Cicero, a brave warrior an Alexander. When we speak improperly, as when we say 'a brass ink-glass, a silver box' etc. these are all made figures of speech, and in general when we speak in a manner different from the common, they call it a figure. But these we shall pass over and proceed to the second class of figures.

---

[1] *Sic.* Probably an error for 'appeals'.
[2] Virgil, *Aeneid,* XII, ll. 701-03. The second and third line should read: *Cum fremit ilicibus quantus gaudetque nivali Vertice se attollens pater Appenninus ad auras.*
[3] *Aeneid,* VIII, l. 692.

# 7

Wednesday, 1 December 1762

BESIDES those tropes and figures, as they are called, of which we treated in the last lecture, there are others that consist in the meaning the word is taken in or in the arrangement of the words. The first they call *figurae verborum*, the second, *figurae sententiarum*. When we use a fem[inine] for a mascu[line], or even give another gender to a neuter, this is a *figura verborum*. *Figurae sententiarum*, on the other hand, are such as imperative, interrogative, or exclamatory phrases. But these, as we observed above, give no beauty of their own: they only are agreeable and beautiful when they suit the sentiment, and express in the neatest manner the way in which the speaker is affected. When the common form of speech well enough describes the thing we want to make known, or sufficiently communicates our sentiments, yet perhaps it does not express clearly and with sufficient life the manner we ourselves regard it—if in this case the figurative way of speaking is more suited to our purpose, then it surely ought to be used preferably to the other. But we may observe that the most beautiful passages are generally the most simple. That passage of Demosthenes[1] in which he describes the confusion at Athens after the battle of Elateia, is reckoned by Longinus[2] the most sublime of all his writings; and yet there is not one figure or trope through the whole of it. Very often the figures seem to diminish rather than add to the beauty of an excellent passage. Two of the most beautiful passages in all Pope's work are those in which he describes the state of mind of an untaught Indian,[3] and the other in which he considers the various ranks and orders of beings in the Universe.[4]

⟨Lo* the poor Indian whose untutored mind
Sees God in clouds and hears him in the wind, etc.

[1] Demosthenes, *De Corona*, 169.
[2] Longinus, *On the Sublime*, x, 7.
[3] Pope, *Essay on Man*, I, ll. 99ff.
[4] *Ibid.* I, ll. 233-4. Pope's text reads:
  See, thro' this air, this ocean, and this earth,
  All matter quick, and bursting into birth.

The words 'watery waste' had been better exchanged for 'ocean' but that the rhyme required them.

> Behold above, around, and underneath
> All nature full and bursting into birth, etc.⟩

In the latter of these there is not one figurative expression, and the few there are in the other are no advantage to it.

On the other hand there is nowhere more use made of figures than in the lowest and most vulgar conversation. The Billingsgate language is full of it. Sancho Panza and people of his stamp, who speak in proverbs, always abound in figures. For we may observe that a proverb always contains one, at least, and often two metaphors.

Upon the whole, then, figures of speech give no beauty to style: it is when the expression is agreeable to the sense of the speaker and his affection that we admire it.

But the same sentiment may often be naturally and agreeably expressed and yet the manner be very different, according to the circumstances of the author. The same story may be considered either as plain matter of fact, without design to excite our compassion; or in a moving way; or, lastly, in a jocose manner, according to the point in which it is connected with the author. There are variety of characters which we may equally [sic] admire as equally[1] good and amiable, and yet these may be very different. It would then be very absurd to blame that of a good-natured man because he wanted the severity of a more rigid one. A man of superior sense and penetration is not to be condemned because he gives his assent to the opinion of the company with the same ease as one of a more soft temper and of less parts (whose character is for this reason very often acceptable) will do. Other characters, all very commendable, cannot be blamed because they want some perfections we are apt to miss, for these perhaps are not all consistent with them, and can hardly meet in the same person. The consideration of this variety of characters affords us often no small entertainment, and forms one of the chief pleasures of a social life, and few are so foolish as to blame it or consider it as any defect.

In the same manner the various styles, instead of being condemned for the want of beauties perhaps incompatible with those they possess, may be considered as good in their kind and suited to the circumstances

---

[1] The repetition of *equally* could be a typical copyist's slip: but it might as easily be caused by the lecturer's change of construction.

of the author. This observation confirms what we before observed, that the expression ought to be suited to the mind of the author, for this is chiefly governed by the circumstances he is placed in. ⟨The style of an author is generally of the same stamp as their character. Thus the . . . of . . . and the . . . of the flowery modesty of Addison, the pert and flippant insolence of Warburton, . . . of . . . appear evident in their words and point the very character of the men.[1]⟩

A didactic writer and historian seldom make use of the bolder figures which an orator frequently introduces with advantage. The end they have in view is different, and so the means by which they hope to accomplish that end must be so too.

It is here to be observed that an orator or didactic writer has two parts in his work. In the one he lays down his proposition, and in the other he brings his proof of that proposition. An historian, on the other hand, has only one part, to wit the proposition. He barely tells you the fact, and if he has anything as a proof of it, [it] is only a quotation from some other author in a note or parenthesis. From this it is that though the circumstances of an orator and a didactic writer are very different, there is a much greater resemblance betwixt their styles than even betwixt that of the latter and the historian's. The orator and historian are indeed in very different circumstances. The business of the one is barely to narrate the facts, which are often very distant from his time, and in which he is, or ought to be and endeavours to appear, noways interested. The orator, again, treats of subjects he or his friends are nearly concerned in; it is [his] business, therefore, to appear—if [he] is not really—deeply concerned in the matter, and [he] uses all his art to prove what he is engaged in. Their styles are no less different. The orator insists on every particular, expresses it in every point of view, and sets off every argument in every shape it can bear. What the historian would have said barely and in one sentence, by this means is brought into a long series of different views of the same argument. The orator frequently will exclaim on the strength of the argument, the justice of the cause, or anything else that tends to support the thing he has in view; and this, too, in his own person. The historian, again, as he is in no pain what side seems the justest, but acts as if he were an impartial narrator of the facts, so he uses none of these means to affect his readers. He never dwells on any circumstance, nor has he any use for insisting on arguments, as he does not take part with either side, and

[1] In the MS 'flippant insol.' is cancelled for what stands.

31

for the same reason he never uses any exclamations in his own person. When he does so we say he departs from the character of the historian and assumes that of the orator. Amongst the ancient historians I remember but three instances of such exclamations in the first person: one in Velleius Paterculus on the death, the other in Florus on the eloquence, of Cicero; the third is in Tacitus' life of Agricola, at the end, on the character of that Roman. ⟨Virgil* has but three exclamations in the *Æneid*, one on the love of Dido, another on the death of Pallas, a third on that of Nisus and Euryalus, *Felices animae si quid mea carmina possunt.*[1]⟩

The didactic writer, as his circumstances are nearer to those of the orator, so their styles bear a much greater resemblance to each other. The orator often lays aside the dictatorial style and barely offers his arguments in a plain modest manner, especially when his discourse is directed to those of greater judgement and higher rank than himself.

The didactic writer sometimes assumes an oratorial style, though it may be questioned whether this be altogether so proper. Cicero often does so, not only in those writings which are wrote in the manner of dialogues, but where he speaks in his own person he often runs out into oratorial exclamations, and dwells on the same argument, and repeats it in different manners. Most other writers of this sort often do so as well as he. Aristotle among the ancients and Dr Mandeville[2] among the moderns are perhaps the only two who have adhered closely to this peculiar style of a didactic writer. They trust solely to the strength of their arguments, the ingenuity and newness of their thoughts and discoveries, to gain the assent of their readers.

Such is the variety of styles that those which appear the most like have still a great difference. No two styles have a great[er] connection than a plain and a simple one, but they are far from being the same. A plain man[3] is one who pays no regard to the common civilities and forms of good breeding. He gives his opinion bluntly, and affirms without condescending to give any reason for his doing so; and if he mentions any sort of a reason, it is only to shew how evident and plain a matter it

---

[1] Velleius Paterculus, II, 66 or II, 129-31; Florus, II, 13, 94 (death of *Julius Cæsar*); Tacitus, *Agricola*, 45, 3; Virgil, *Aeneid*, IV, ll. 65-7 *or* 408-12; x, l. 507; IX, l. 446. The line quoted should read *Fortunati ambo.*

[2] *Dr Mandeville* has been cancelled, and corrected by the second hand to *Macchiavel.*

[3] Smith proceeds to give a set character sketch at some length, somewhat irrelevantly. Was he using 'stock' he had for other purposes?

was, and expose the stupidity of the others in not perceiving it as well as he. ⟨He is not at all ruffled by contradiction or any irritation whatever, but is at pains to shew that this proceeds from his confidence in his own superior sense and judgement. He never gives way either to joy or grief; such affections would be below the dignity and complacence of mind which he affects. Compassion finds little room in his breast. Admiration does not at all suit his wisdom: contempt is more agreeable to his self-sufficient, impervious temper.⟩ He is not at all sedulous to please: on the contrary, he affects a sort of austerity and hardness of behaviour, so that when the common civility of behaviour would be the most natural and easy manner, he industriously avoids them. He is so far from affecting any graces or civilities that he affects the contrary, and renders himself more severe than his nature would naturally lead him to be. ⟨He despises the fashion in every point, and neither conforms himself to it in dress, in language, nor manners, but sticks by his own downright way.⟩ Wit would ill-suit his gravity. He is more apt to think that others have ill motives even when they act well, than that they are only in a mistake and do not err knowingly when they act amiss. ⟨He* affirms without mitigation or apology.⟩ In ordinary conversation he thinks it enough to support what he says that it is his opinion, and is at no pains to inquire into those of others.

Such a character is what clergymen generally assume, and those come to age. It does well enough in those of superior abilities, who have had greater opportunities than common, or longer experience; but young men generally avoid it. Modesty and diffidence are more suited to their years than the assuming arrogance of this character, which even though accompanied with age [and] knowledge, renders the possessor rather the object of our respect and esteem than of our love.

The simple man, again, is not, indeed, studious to appear with all the outward marks of civility and breeding that he sees others of a more disingenuous temper generally put on; but then, when they naturally express his real sentiments, he readily uses them. He appears always willing to please, when this desire does not lead him to act disingenuously. At other times the modesty and affability of his behaviour, his being always willing to comply with customs that don't look affected, plainly shew the goodness of his heart, He is not over-ready to give his opinion, and when he does, 'tis with that unaffected modesty which displays itself in all his behaviour, and in nothing more than in his conversation, where his diffidence of his own judgement leads him to

33

offer all the reasons he had to be of that mind,[1] to shew that he does not assert anything merely because it is his opinion. Contempt never enters into his mind; he is more ready to think well than meanly both of the parts and of the conduct of others. His own goodness of heart makes him never suspect others of disingenuity. He is always open to conviction, and is not [at] all irritated by others contradicting him: but the reason of this is not any stubborness, but the diffidence he entertains of his own capacity. ⟨This leads him to speak very often in the first person, to shew the mean opinion he has of himself, and sometimes to childish prating.⟩ He is more given to admiration and pity, joy, grief and compassion than the contrary affections; they suit well with the softness of his temper. This temper is what we often find in young men, and in them is very agreeable. Old men are generally not so apt to be of this character. It renders one more an object of love and affection than [of] regard and esteem.

When the characters of a plain and a simple man are so different, we may naturally expect that the style they express themselves in will be far from being the same. Swift may serve as an instance of a plain style, and Sir W. Temple of a simple one. Swift never gives any reason for his opinions, but affirms them boldly without the least hesitation, and when one expects a reason he meets with nothing but such expressions as 'I have always been of opinion that', or 'because it seems to me'. This we find that he does in the beginning of his *Considerations on the Present State of Affairs*. He is so far from studying the ornaments of language that he affects to leave them out even when natural, and in this way he often throws out pronouns, etc., that are necessary to make the sentence full, but would at the same time lead him into the uniformity of cadence which he industriously avoids. This, however, makes his style very close. No word can be passed over without notice; every other one must be strongly accented to draw the attention of the hearer, for a word lost would spoil the whole. This makes us read his works with more life and emphasis than those [of] most authors. In Shaftesbury and Bolingbroke, or others who study this uniformity of cadence, there are many superfluous words which we huddle together as being of very small importance to the sense of the period. He never introduces (in his grave works) any sort of figure; and that for the same reason as he avoids harmony and smoothness of cadence. He never expresses any passion, but affirms with a dictatorial gravity.

[1] Replaces 'arguments he can think of' cancelled in MS.

Temple, on the other hand, is not anxious about ornaments; but when they are natural he does not reject them. His style has neither the hardness of Swift's, nor the laboured regularity of Shaftesbury. The most common and received opinions he never [blank] but the most [*sic*] manner possible, as that saying that wit and solid judgement are seldom found together, which he brings in[to] his character of the Dutch nation.[1] He does not avoid a figurative style when agreeable to his subject, as in the comparison betwixt the life of a merchant and a soldier, ⟨in which there are a great many antitheses. These Swift never used in his grave works. They savour too much of the paradox, that is, of wit, to suit his gravity.⟩ He uses more obsolete words here than I would expect in a writer of his age. This we never find in Swift. The knowledge of the world which [he] affects and which he chiefly employs to satirize and turn it to ridicule, will not allow him to use anything that is out of the present taste. But Temple is led to them by the notion that everything belonging to our forefathers has more simplicity than those of our times, as [if] they were a more simple and honest set of men. His love of a modest, simple style leads him, (but in a different manner from Swift) to use the first person very often, as well as to run into 'prating and quibble'. The description he gives of [blank] may serve as an instance of both the former. When he says, 'The *earth* of Holland is better than the air' and 'the love of interest stronger than the love of honour',[2] it is a mere quibble on the words 'earth' and 'profit' [*sic*], 'air' and 'honour'. Xenophon and most other writers of this sort, as well as he, abound in jokes we are surprised to find in such grave writers.

[1] *Observations upon the United Provinces of the Netherlands*, ed. Clark, Cambridge 1932, ch. 4, passim.  [2] *Ibid.* p. 115.

# 8

Friday, 3 December 1762

HAVING in the foregoing lecture made some observations on tropes and figures, and endeavoured to show that it was not in their use, as the ancient rhetoricians imagined, that the beauties of style consisted, I pointed out what it was that really gave beauty to style, that when the words neatly and properly expressed the thing to be described, and conveyed the sentiment the author entertained of it and desired to communicate to his hearers, then the expression had all the beauty language was capable of bestowing on it. I endeavoured to shew, also, that the form of the style was not to be confined to any particular point. The view of the author, the means he takes to accomplish that end, must vary the style, not only in describing different objects or delivering different opinions, but even when these are the same in both; as the sentiment will be different, so will the style also. Besides this, I endeavoured to show that when all other circumstances are alike, the character of the author must make the style different. One of grave cast of mind will describe an object in a very different way from one of more lively; a plain man will have a style very different from that of a simple man. There is, however, no one particular which we esteem, but many are equally agreeable. Extreme moroseness and gravity, such that no risible objects will in the least affect, would not be admired: neither would one of such levity that the smallest incident would make lose himself. But it is not in the middle point betwixt these two characters that an agreeable one is alone to be found: many others that partake more or less of the two extremes are equally the objects of our attention. In the same way it is with regard to a spirited and silly behaviour, and every two other opposite extremes in the characters of men.

These characters, though all good and agreeable, must nevertheless, as they are different, be expressed in very different styles, all of which may be very agreeable. And here likewise the rule may be applied, that one should stick to his natural character. A gay man should not endeavour to be grave, nor the grave man to be gay, but each should regulate that

36

character and manner that is natural to him, and hinder it from running into that vicious extreme to which he is most inclined.

This difference of style arising from the character of the author, I endeavoured to illustrate by comparing the style of two celebrated English writers, Swift and Sir Wm. Temple; the one as an example of the plain style, and the other of a simple one. Both are very good writers. Swift, as I observed, is remarkable for his propriety and precision; the other is not perhaps so very accurate, but he is perhaps as entertaining, and much more instructive. I shall now proceed to make some further observation on the style of Dr. Swift.

There is perhaps no writer whose works are more generally read than his, and yet it has been very late that very few, in this country particularly, understand his real worth. He is read with the same views and the same expectations as we read *Tom Brown*.[1] They are considered as writers just of the same class. Swift's graver works are never almost read; they are looked upon as silly and trifling. His other works are read merely for their humour.

We shall therefore endeavour to find out what are the causes of this general taste. And first: Swift's sentiments in religious matters are not at all suitable to those which have for some time past prevailed in this country. He is indeed no friend to tyranny, either religious or civil; he expresses his abhorrence to them on many occasions. But then he never has such warm exclamations for civil or religious liberty as are now generally in fashion. This would not suit his character: the plain man he affects to appear would never be subject to such strong admiration. The levity of mi[nd], as well as freedom of thought, now in fashion, demands warmer and more earnest expressions than he ever allows himself.

Another circumstance that will tend to confirm this opinion is, that the thoughts of most men of genius in the country have of late [blank] to abstract and speculative reasonings, which perhaps tend very little to the bettering of our practice. ⟨Even* the practical sciences of Politics and Morality or Ethics have of late been treated too much in a speculative manner.⟩ These studies Swift seems to have been rather entirely ignorant of, or, what I am rather inclined to believe, did not hold them to be of great value. His general character, as a plain man, would lead him to be of this way of thinking; he would be more inclined to prose-

---

[1] Tom Brown (1663-1704), an amusing light-weight satirist and translator. His *Letters from the Dead to the Living* and *Amusements Serious and Comical* (1700) are his chief works. (The name is underlined in the MS.)

37

cute what was more immediately beneficial. Accordingly we find that all his writings are adapted to the present time, either in ridiculing some prevailing vice or folly, or exposing some particular character. We cannot now enter altogether into the true spirit of these; and besides, as I said, such confined thoughts do not suit the present taste, which delights only in general and abstract speculations.

But his language may possibly have brought about the general disregard for his serious works, as much as any other part of his character. We in this country are most of us very sensible that the perfection of language is very different from that we commonly speak in. The idea we form of a good style is almost contrary to that which we generally hear. Hence it is that we conceive the further one's style is removed from the common manner, it is so much nearer to purity and the perfection we have in view. Shaftesbury, who keeps at a vast distance from the language we commonly meet with, is for this reason universally admired. Thomson, who perhaps was of the same opinion himself, is equalled with Milton, who, amongst his other beauties, has this also, that he does not affect forced expressions even when he is most sublime. Swift, on the other hand, who is the plainest as well as the most proper and precise of all the English writers, is despised as nothing out of the common road: each of us thinks he would have wrote as well. And our thoughts of the language give us the same idea of the substance of his writings. But it does not appear that this opinion is well grounded. There are four[1] things that are required to make a good writer: first, that he have a complete knowledge of his subjects; secondly, that he should arrange all the parts of his subject in their proper order; thirdly, that he paint [or] describe the ideas he has of them several in the most proper and expressive manner—this is the art of painting or imitation (at least we may call it so).

Now we will find that Swift has attained all these perfections. All his words shew a complete knowledge of his subject. He does not, indeed, introduce anything foreign to his subject, in order to display his knowledge of his subject; but then he never omits anything necessary. His rules for behaviour[2] and his *Directions for a Servant*[3] shew a knowledge of both these opposite characters that could not have been attained but by the closest attention continued for many years. ⟨It* would have

---

[1] Smith lists only three.

[2] Probably *A Treatise of Good Manners and Good Breeding*. 'Directions' cancelled in MS. and 'rules' substituted.  [3] i.e. *Directions to Servants*.

been impossible for anyone who had not given such attention to allege so many particulars.⟩ The same is apparent in all his political works, insomuch that one would imagine his thoughts had been altogether turned that way.

One who has such a complete knowledge of what he treats will naturally arrange it in the most proper order. This we see Swift always does. There is no part that we can think would have been better disposed of. That he paints but each thought in the best and most proper manner, and with the greatest strength of colouring, must be visible to anyone at first sight. ⟨That he does this when he speaks in his own person we observed already, and that he does so when he takes on the character of another is sufficiently evident from his *Gulliver*.⟩

Now, that a writer who has all these qualities in such perfection should not make the best style for expressing himself in, with propriety and precision, cannot be imagined. Notwithstanding of all this, perhaps for the reasons already shewn, his graver works are not much regarded. It is his talent for ridicule that is most commonly and, I believe, most justly admired. We shall therefore consider how far this talent is agreeable to the general character we have already given of him, and whether or not he has prosecuted it with the same exactness as the other subjects we mentioned. But before we enter upon this it will be necessary to make a few previous observations on this talent.

Whatever we see that is great or noble excites our admiration and amazement; and whatever is little or mean on the other hand excites our contempt. ⟨This Leibnitz, and, after him, Mr Locke, supposed to be excited by the viewing of some mean object; but that this is not the case will appear from what follows.⟩ A great object never excites our laughter, neither does a mean one, simply as being such. It is the blending and joining of those two ideas which alone gives that emotion. ⟨The foundation of ridicule is either when what is in most respects grand, or pretends to be so, has something mean or little in it, or when we find something that is really mean with some pretensions and marks of grandeur.⟩ Now this may happen either when an object which is in most respects a grand one, is represented to us and described as mean; or *e contra*, when a grand object is found in company as it were with others that are mean; or *e contra*, when our expectation is disappointed, and what we imagined was either grand or mean, turns out to be the reverse. These different combinations of ideas afford each a different form or manner of ridicule.

39

If we represent an object which we are apt to conceive as a grand one, or of no dignity, and turn its qualities into the contrary, the mixture of the ideas excites our laughter, though neither of them separately would do so. Hence comes the ridicule conveyed by burlesque or mock heroic compositions. The circumstances a thing is in, also, if there be any great contradiction betwixt the objects, for the same reason excites our laughter. A tall man is no object of laughter, neither is a little; but a very tall man amongst a number of dwarfs, like Gulliver amongst the Lilliputians, or a little man amongst a set of very tall men, as the same Gulliver in Brobdingnag, appears very ridiculous. There is no real foundation for laughter here, but the odd association of grand and mean or little ideas. ⟨In* this and similar cases it is the group of figures, and no individual one, which is the object of our ridicule.⟩ ⟨The ridicule in *The Rape of the Lock* proceeds from the ridiculousness of the characters themselves, but that of the *Dunciad* is owing altogether to the circumstances the persons are placed in. Any two men—Pope and Swift themselves—would look as ridiculous as Curll and Lintot, if they were described running the same races.⟩ We laugh against our will at the employment of Socrates, when we see him in the *Clouds* of Aristophanes measuring the length of the flea's leap by the length of the same flea's foot,[1] or suspended in a bucket making observations.[2] If this philosopher had been so employed, he would have appeared ridiculous, and the great contrariety of the idea makes the very supposition appear so.

⟨The wit of some of the French comedians as [blank] is founded on this principle. The lover in Fougu[3] is no ways ridiculous but by the circumstances.⟩ The Italian comedians at Paris, as they are called, as soon as any grave or solemn tragedy appears on the theatre, give the same play, that is, the same incidents, applied to some very opposite character. Generals and Emperors become burghers or turn mechanics. The ridicule here is owing to the contrast between the high idea connected with the incidents we have seen attendant on great characters, and the same incidents happening to persons of a rank so much lower. When what we expect to find great and noble turns out otherwise, we are in the same manner moved to laughter, and *e contra*. A sow wallowing in the mire is certainly a loathsome object, but no one would laugh at it, as it is agreeable to the nature of the beast. But if he saw the sow afterwards in

---

[1] Aristophanes, *Clouds*, ll. 143-52.                                    [2] *Ibid*. ll. 218ff.
[3] *Sic*. Le Fougueux is doubtless intended, see below, p. 42. I have been unable to identify this play.

a drawing-room, the case would be altered. On the other hand a lean, poor-looking raw-boned horse excites one's laughter, as ⟨that noble animal seems to lay claim to our admiration⟩ we expect something great and noble in the appearance of that animal. We would not laugh at a bad prospect, as there [is] no contradiction in supposing one, unless we had been made to expect a fine one; but we laugh at a bad picture, because we expect that art is exercised in some noble manner.

'Tis from such combinations chiefly that ridicule proceeds. We may laugh, too, at things we contemn, but in a different manner. A coxcomb walking on the street and looking around him to see those about him admiring him as he expects, is a subject of laughter to the graver sort: but then this laughter that proceeds from an object we contemn is evidently mixt with somewhat of anger. But if this same coxcomb should slip a foot and fall into the kennel, the same gentlemen would laugh, but from a different motive, at the ridiculous plight such a fine fellow was in—which was the very condition they at their hearts would have wished him.

Some philosophers, as [blank], observing that laughter proceeds sometimes from contempt, have made that the original of all ridiculous perceptions. But we may frequently laugh at objects that are not at all contemptible. A tall man amongst a number of little men, or *e contra*, makes us laugh, but we don't contemn either. Things that have no sort of connection, but where the ideas we have are strangely contradictory, excite our laughter. I remember once a mouse, running across the area of a chapel, spoilt the effect of an excellent discourse. Any such trivial accidents excite our laughter when they happen at any solemn or important work, as a funeral. 'Tis for this reason that we are diverted with those phrases that we are accustomed to connect in our imagination with noble objects, when we meet with them applied to mean and trifling ones. Hence comes the ridiculousness of parodies (or applying whole passages of an author, by a sort of translation, to subjects of a very different sort, and centos where single phrases are applied.) The Cento of Apuleius,[1] where the grave and chaste Virgil is made to speak in his own words on a very different subject and not very chaste language, nowhere makes us laugh but in the story of the marriage. ⟨All the ridicule of Scarron's *Virgil Travesti*, in the same manner, proceeds from the grave and solemn adventures of Æneas being told in the most ridiculous language and trivial, mean expressions.⟩ The modern Latin poets, Vida,

---

[1] An error for Ausonius, *Cento Nuptialis* (Loeb ed., vol. I, pp. 370-93).

Sanazzaro, etc. are all parodies on some of the ancient Latin poets. These, not being on trivial subjects, but such as are equally important, do not excite our laughter, but are rather tedious and wearisome. The English poets are more original: they do not usually borrow from others —such dealings would be counted no better than stealing—and for that reason are not so tiresome. *The Splendid Shilling*[1] diverts us by the ridiculous appearance Milton's language makes when used to extol the charms of a shilling. ⟨The incongruity of the language to the subject has also its effect here, as well as in works of the contrary sort, as *Virgil Travesti*.⟩ But so far is it from being a sign of any passage's being a mean one, that a parody has been made upon it, that 'tis rather a sign of the contrary, as the more sublime and pompous a passage is, the greater the contrast will be when the same phraseology is applied to trivial subjects. Thus we see the soliloquies of Hamlet, the last speech of Cato,[2] have undergone more parodies than any others I know, and indeed make very good ones. For the same reason parodies on the Scriptures, though very profane, are at the same time very ridiculous.

⟨Puns, which are the lowest species of wit, are never wholly agreeable but when there is some contrast betwixt the ideas they excite: a mere quibble is never agreeable.⟩

There are two species of comic writing derived from two species of ridiculous circumstances. The one is when characters ridiculous in themselves are described in ridiculous circumstances. The . . . in or . . . of . . . is an instance of the former, and the lover of . . . in *Le Fougueux* of . . .[3] is an instance of the latter. The whole of Congreve's wit consists in the ridiculousness of his similes, as his comparing two persons bespattering one another to two apples roasting; or the young lady newly come to town, gaping with amazement, he compares her wide-open mouth to the gate of her father's house. Lucian has chosen the one of these two sorts of comic subject, and Swift the other.[4]

It is proper to be observed that of all these species of ridicule, Burlesque, Doggerel, Mock Heroic, Parodies, Centos, Puns, Quibbles, and even that sort of comedy which ridicules characters not from their real defects but from the circumstances they are brought into, are all of the buffoonish sort and unworthy of a gentleman who has had a regular education; and whenever such an one exercises his wit in this manner,

[1] *The Splendid Shilling* (1705), by John Philips.
[2] Addison's *Cato*. Probably the reference is to the last speech of Lucius, Act v, sc. iv, l. 100.      [3] MS has many blanks.
[4] In the MS this sentence has a cancel stroke.

42

he lays aside that character to assume that of a buffoon: at least for the time he does so. The only species of ridicule which is true and genuine wit is that where real foibles and blemishes in the characters or behaviour of men are exposed to our view in a ridiculous light. This is altogether consistent with the character of a gentleman, as it tends to the reformation of manners and the benefit of mankind.

⟨The* objects of ridicule are two: either those which, affecting to be grand, or being expected to be so, are mean; or, being grand in some of their parts, are mean in others; or such as, pretending etc. to beauty, are deformed.⟩

# 9

Monday, 6 December 1762

As there are two sorts of objects that excite our admiration, viz., when an object is grand, or when it is beautiful; and two that excite our contempt, viz. those that are little or mean, or such as are deformed or disagreeable in themselves; so there must be two sorts of ridicule proceeding from the combinations of these different objects: firstly, when mean objects are exposed by considering them as grand; or secondly, when grand ones, or such as pretend or are expected to be so, are ridiculed by exposing the meanness and the littleness which is found in them. Swift has chosen the former, and Lucian the latter of these sorts.

The characters of these different men would naturally lead them to chose these contrary subjects. Swift's natural moroseness, joined to the constant disappointments and crosses he met with in life, would make contempt natural to his character; and those follies would most provoke him that partake of gaiety and levity. This was so prevalent a part of his character that we are told he studiously avoided what are called the common forms of civility and good breeding. When he saw those that had little else to recommend [them] not only have some tolerable character and pass through life with some sort of applause, but even be preferred before himself, the reverence he had for his own good sense and judgement, which he thought far above that of the common stamp, he would surely be prompted[1] to expose to the utmost of his power these and such like follies and silliness in men. Accordingly we find all his less serious works are wrote with a design to ridicule some one of the prevailing gay follies of his time. They are chiefly levelled against coxcombs, beaus, belles, and other characters, where gay follies [prevail] rather than the graver ones. These he never attacks in any of his works, except the *Tale of a Tub*, which was wrote when he was very young, and is a work of a very different sort from all the rest. It is much less correct than those which he wrote when more advanced in life.

We may observe he never uses that sort of ridicule which may be

[1] Smith seems to have intended to say 'would surely prompt him'.

44

thrown on any subject by the choice of words. His language is always correct and proper, and no ornaments are ever introduced, nor does he ever write but in a manner most suitable to the nature of the subject. As his morose temper directed him to make choice of the gayer follies of men to exercise his talent for ridicule, so the character of a plain man, which he affected, hindered him from ever making us laugh to excess at any subject, in however ridiculous a light he may set [it]. This he does when he speaks in his own person. But when he has a mind to throw a great degree of ridicule on any subject, he puts it into the mouth of some other person, as in *Gulliver's Travels* and the *Drapier's Letters*. Even in these works he never uses any expressions but what are suitable to his subject. The most common manner in which he throws ridicule on any subject, when he speaks in another character, is to make them express their admiration and esteem for those things he would expose. As ridicule proceeds from a combination of the ideas of admiration and contempt, it is very evident he could not take a more effectual method to ridicule any foible or silly object than by making someone express the highest admiration for it, as the contrast is here the strongest. In those works that appear the most silly and trifling, as his *Song of Similes*,[1] and that other of Ditton and Whiston,[2] he ridicules the folly that then prevailed, in a very strong light.

Lucian, if we may judge of the man from his works, has been of a very different turn. He was of a more gay and jovial temper, with a not inconsiderable portion of levity. ⟨He was a follower of the Epicurean, or rather of the Cyrenaic sect. His principles are all adapted to that scheme of life where the chief thing in view is to pass it easily and happily, and with as much pleasure as we possibly can. And as life is short and transitory, he lays it down as a maxim that we ought not to omit any present happiness in expectation of a greater to come, but lay hold of the present opportunity. Friendship and the exercise of the social affections are in his opinion the chief fund for enjoyment, and consequently chiefly to be cultivated.⟩ The characters which Swift[3] exposes were those which best suited his taste. Grave men who had anything of levity or folly in their character were those that he most despised, as those who went about their follies with an air of importance appeared most despicable in the eyes of the morose Swift. Agreeably to these different casts of

[1] i.e. *A New Song of New Similes*, 'My passion is as mustard strong', etc. (*Works*, ed. Roscoe, vol. I, p. 790).

[2] i.e. *Ode for Music*. On the Longitude. 'The longitude miss'd on', etc. (*ibid.* vol. I, p. 788).      [3] *Sic*, but probably an error for Lucian.

mind, they chose different characters to expose by their wit. Swift, as we said, exposed none but empty coxcombs, fine gentlemen, beaus, belles, and any that encouraged themselves in employments of no moment or importance of life. Lucian ⟨exposes* only grave characters and the graver pursuits of men, as the mean and ambitious man;⟩ on the other hand has pitched on, for the subject of his ridicule, persons of the most solemn and respectable character, as gods, goddesses, heroes, senators, generals, historians, poets, and philosophers, as those wherein the graver sort of follies are most commonly found. Of such personages all his dialogues are composed, and those writings in which he talks in his own person turn chiefly on such follies. His discourse *De Luctu*[1] will serve as an example both of the subject and his manner of treating it. We may observe he never uses any witticisms derived from language, nor any ornaments of that sort, but what his subject naturally leads him to. He never makes any digressions from his subject, his fruitful imagination always affording him matter enough on every subject, without being obliged to call in another to his assistance, perhaps very little connected with it. His design of surprising and diverting his reader sometimes leads him into seeming digressions, that his return to his subject after keeping one in suspense may be the more entertaining. One way he often does this is by putting the comparison before the subject to which it is compared. Thus he puts the fatal effects of the fever at Abdera before his complaint on the number of historical writers then in Greece.[2] And the same may be seen in the comparison betwixt Diogenes tumbling his tub, and his own labours.[3] ⟨He often brings in the illustration before that which it illustrates, because commonly it is the most diverting, e.g. in the beginning of his *Directions for the Writing of History*. A graver author would have followed the natural order.⟩

By the different ends that Swift and Lucian have had in view, they have formed a complete system of ridicule. There is hardly any folly of the gayer sort that Swift passes over, and scarce any of the graver that is omitted by Lucian. Either of them taken alone might be apt to prejudice one in favour of the follies contrary to those he ridicules, but both together form a system of morality from whence more sound and just rules of life for all the various characters of men may be drawn than from most systems of morality.

[1] *Of Funerals* (Loeb ed., vol. IV, p. 112).
[2] *How to Write History* (Loeb ed., vol. VI, pp. 2-5).
[3] *Ibid.* pp. 5-7.

Nor are Lucian's works altogether confined to subjects of a ludicrous nature: he has many discourses of a serious cast, recommending the different virtues. These are all very excellent; his manner in them is no less agreeable than in his other works; he always keeps to his subject, and never is necessitated to betake himself to general praises of virtue in order to recommend any particular one (as has been the fashion for some time), that the discourse might have the appearance of a complete system and be drawn out to the length of a pocket volume. In a word, there is no author from whom more real instruction and goodness can be found than Lucian.

⟨There* are scattered through his works moral essays very much in the manner of Mr Addison, wherein he illustrates the virtue he would recommend, with all the graces of serious composition, and yet never departs from the consideration of its particular nature, nor launches out into those vague and general declamations suited to any virtue whatever, and shewing thus chiefly that the author is not particularly acquainted with his subject. In this respect he may be an excellent model to those whose particular business it is to teach morality, in opposition to a very different manner which prevails at present.⟩

47

# 10

THERE is perhaps no English writer who has more of this gaiety than Mr Addison; though neither has he so much as Lucian. This is the chief character of all his prose works. He frequently, in the manner of Lucian, begins his discourses with a story, which he places before the subject itself, as in his address[1] to the Tory ladies in *The Freeholder*; but he never carries these so far as Lucian does, nor so minutely. This perhaps may be owing to a sort of modesty, of which he is said to have been possessed in a very great degree, in the common affairs of [life], ⟨and* which breathes indeed through all his works;⟩ and [of] which the other author does not appear to have had any considerable share, from several stories he tells of himself, as that of his biting the thumb of the impostor Alexander.[2] ⟨The* ludicrous incident of biting Alexander's thumb is related in his life of that impostor, than which few things are more entertaining.⟩ ⟨His [*sc.* Addison's] modesty hinders him from those bold and extravagant strokes of humour which Lucian uses —he would not, for instance, put a ludicrous speech into the mouth of a dead man or a god—or from throwing out such biting sarcasms in his own person, as Swift often does.⟩ The floweriness of Mr Addison naturally leads him to make frequent use of figures in his discourses: the chief of these are metaphors, similes, and allegories. But in the use of these he always displays the modesty of his character. It may seem strange how the use of allegories especially should seem consistent with that modesty we have attributed to him, ⟨as they are the boldest and strongest kind of figures;⟩ but the manner in which he introduces them is always such as makes it appear that there was nothing forced or uneasy in the forming of them. He often introduces them in the form of a dream, and at the same time shews us the train of thought that led him into such conceptions, and by this means makes us imagine that the circumstances he was in naturally suggested them, without his being at

[1] It is doubtful whether Smith has one particular number of *The Freeholder* in mind.    [2] Lucian, *Alexander the False Prophet* (Loeb ed., vol. IV, p. 245).

48

any pains about it; ⟨as that where he compares the different characters of men to different musical instruments.[1]⟩ In the same manner his similes are always represented as naturally presenting themselves.

This modesty we have ascribed to him causes him likewise to deliver his sentiments in the least assuming manner, and this would incline him rather to narrate what he had seen and heard, than to deliver his opinions in his own person; and at the same time he will not seem to be at great pains to give nice and curious circumstances; it is more consistent with the natural modesty of his temper to give us only a few of the most striking and interesting. He neither presumes, as Shaftesbury and Bolingbroke, nor dictates, as Swift. ⟨Shaftesbury* and Bolingbroke display their superior dignity, and Swift his superiority of sense.⟩ For the same reason he neither writes with the precision and nice propriety of the latter, nor have his sentences that uniform cadence in their several members as the two former writers always affected. His sentences are neither long nor short, but of a length suited to the character he has of a modest man, who naturally delivers himself in sentences of a moderate length and with a uniform tone. Accordingly we find those of Mr Addison are of this sort. They generally consist of three, four, or five phrases, and are so uniform in their manner that we read them with a sort of monotony. The modest man will not use long sentences, as they are either proper for declamation, which he never uses, or bespeak a confusion of ideas that is not to be attributed to Mr Addison. He would not, either, deliver himself in short sentences, as that would appear like a snip-snap, or the language of presumption and a dictating temper. ⟨As he does not pretend that everything he says is of the utmost importance and an infallible rule, so he is much more lax in his writings than Dr Swift. Every word of *his* writings is of importance: when, on the other hand, Mr Addison frequently turns up the same things in the different phrases of a sentence, only placing it in a different light,⟩ ⟨and* is rather inaccurate in the use of words and repetition of synonyms, which the concluding of the essay on the *Pleasures of the Imagination*[2] will be an example of, if examined with that in view.⟩

He frequently makes quotations from the poets, which gives his writings an air of gaiety and good humour. This gaiety, joined to the modesty that appears in his works, has gained him the character of a most polite and elegant writer. His descriptions are not near so animated

[1] Addison, *The Tatler*, No. 153.
[2] *The Spectator*, Nos. 411-21, deal with the Pleasures of the Imagination.

as those of Lucian, and this may proceed both from his natural modesty and from his imagination not being altogether so lively. This will appear to be the case in any of his descriptions, if compared with [that] of Jupiter carrying off Europa,[1] in Lucian, which is remarkably animated, and gives as complete a notion of the several transactions as words can convey.

[1] Lucian, *Dialogues of the Sea-Gods*, No. 15 (Loeb ed., vol. VII, pp. 232ff).

# 11

Wednesday, 15 December 1762

IN some of our former lectures we have given a character of some of the best English prose writers, and made comparisons betwixt their different manners. The result of all which, as well as the rules we have laid down, is that the perfection of style consists in express[ing] in the most concise, proper, and precise manner the thought of the author, and that in the manner which best conveys the sentiment, passion, or affection with which it affects—or he pretends it does affect—him, and which he designs to communicate to his reader. This, you'll say, is no more than common sense: and indeed it is no more. But if you will attend to it, all the rules of criticism and morality, when traced to their foundation, turn out to be some principles of common sense which every one assents to: all the business of those arts is to apply these rules to the different subjects, and shew what the conclusion is when they are so applied. 'Tis for this purpose we have made these observations on the authors above-mentioned. We have shown how far they have acted agreeably to that rule which is equally applicable to conversation and behaviour, as [to] writing. For what is it that makes a man agreeable company? Is it not, when his sentiments appear to be agreeably expressed, when the passion or affection is properly conveyed, and when their thoughts are so agreeable and natural that we find ourselves inclined to give our assent to them? A wise man, too, in conversation and behaviour, will not affect a character that is unnatural to him; if he is grave, he will not affect to be gay; nor, if he be gay, will he affect to be grave. He will only regulate his natural temper, restrain [it] within just bounds, and lop all exuberances, and bring it to that pitch which will be agreeable to those about him. He will not affect such conduct as is unnatural to his temper, though perhaps in the abstract they may be more to be wished.

In like manner what is it that is agreeable in style? It is when all the thoughts are justly and properly expressed in such a manner as shews the passion they affected the author with, and so that all seemed natural and easy. He never seems to act out of character, but speaks in a manner

51

not only suitable to the subject, but to the character he naturally inclines to.

The three authors we have already considered seem all to have acted agreeably to this rule. Every one speaks in his own style, and such an one as is agreeable to his general character. Hence we see there is a certain uniformity in their manner: there are no passages that remarkably distinguish themselves; their admirers don't seem particularly fond of any one more than the rest; there are none which they get by heart and repeat with admiration, as they would a piece of poetry. These authors did not attempt what they thought was the greatest perfection of style, but that perfection which they thought most suitable to their genius and temper.

But there is another English author, who, though much inferior to these three, yet for the same reason as Thomson and others of that sort, had till very lately in this country a character much superior to that of the others. The reason, as we mentioned before, was the ignorance of true propriety of language. I believe that I need hardly mention that I mean Lord Shaftesbury. This author seems not at all to have acted agreeably to the rule we have given above, but to have formed to himself an idea of beauty of style abstracted from his own character, by which he proposed to regulate his style.

If we attend to the character and circumstances of this nobleman we will easily perceive what it was which led him to this conduct. He was connected with a father and educated under a tutor who had no very strong affection to any particular sect or tenets in religion, who cried up freedom of thought and liberty of conscience in all matters religious or philosophical, without being attached to any particular men or opinions. If these friends of his were inclined to any one sect, it was rather to the Puritans than the Established Church, as their tenets best suited with that liberty of conscience they strenuously maintained. Shaftesbury himself, by what we can learn from his letters, seems to have been of a very puny and weakly constitution, always either under some disorder or in dread of falling into one. Such a habit of [body] is very much connected, nay, almost continually attended by, a cast of mind in a good measure similar. Abstract reasoning and deep searches are too fatiguing for persons of this delicate frame. Their feebleness of body, as well as mind, hinders them from engaging in the pursuits which generally engross the common sort of men. Love and ambition are too violent in their operations to find ground to work upon in such frames, where the passions are not very strong. The weakness of their appetites and passions hinder them from being carried away in the ordinary manner: they find no great difficulty in conforming their conduct to the rules they have proposed to themselves. The fine arts, matters of taste and imagination, are what they are most inclined to cultivate. They require little labour, and at the same time afford an entertainment very suitable to their temper and abilities. Accordingly we find that Lord Shaftesbury, though no great reasoner nor deeply skilled in the abstract sciences, had very nice and just taste in the fine arts, and all matters of that sort. ⟨We are told he had some figure as a speaker in both Houses of Parliament, though not very extraordinary, but we do not find that he was ever distinguished in debate or deliberation in political matters.⟩ Natural philosophy he does not seem to have been at all acquainted with; but on the other hand he shows a great ignorance of the advances it had then made, and a contempt for its followers. The reason plainly is that it did not afford the amusement his disposition required, and the mathematical part particularly required more attention and abstract thought than men of his weakly habit are generally capable of. The pleasures of the imagination, as they are more easily acquired and of a very delicate nature, are more agreeable to them. ⟨The contempt he expresses for such studies is such as could proceed from no cause but very great ignorance.⟩

Men of this sort, when they take a religious turn, are generally great enthusiasts, and much disposed to mystical contemplations on the being and nature of God and his perfections, and suchlike topics. But the delicacy of his temper, together with the plan of his education, gave him a different turn. The scheme of revealed religion which he was best acquainted with, as we said, was that of the Puritans. The grossness of their conduct, the little decency or appearance of devotion that they used in their manner of worship, shocked his delicate and refined temper, and in time prejudiced him against every scheme of revealed religion. The selfish and confined systems of Hobbes and [blank] could not agree with the delicacy of his sentiments. The School philosophy was still less agreeable. The futility, sophistry, barbarism and meanness of their schemes was very visible, and very disagreeable to his turn of mind. This made him desirous of forming some system to himself more agreeable to his own inclinations and temper. The intimate acquaintance which he had with the ancients, and the great knowledge he had early acquired in the ancient languages, inclined him to apply to them in this

53

research. The system which of all others best suited his disposition was that of the Platonists. Their refined notions both in Theology and Philosophy were perfectly agreeable to him, and accordingly his philosophy and theology is the same in effect with theirs, but modernized a little and made somewhat more suitable to the taste then prevailing. In these he intermixes somewhat of the philosophy of Hobbes and his preceptor Locke. This latter, as he was of a very different cast from his pupil, so his philosophy did not suit with [sic], being too metaphysical and not capable of affording him entertainment to his mind. But though he endeavours to run down these philosophers, yet he sometimes takes their assistance in forming his own plan.

⟨Such* is Lord Shaftesbury's undertaking to overthrow the old system of religion and philosophy, as Hobbes before him had done, but still more, which Hobbes never had attempted to do, to erect a new one. Let us see how he has executed it, in what style and manner.⟩

Such is the subject of Lord Shaftesbury's writings. Let us next consider how far his style is suitable to the same character that led him to this scheme of philosophy. His weakly state of body, as it prevented the violence of his passions, did not incline him greatly to be of any particular temper to any great height. His style, therefore, would not be naturally more of one sort than another. As, therefore, he was not led to have any particular style, by the prevalence of any particular inclination, it was natural for him to form some model or idea of perfection which he should always have in view. ⟨His letters, where we should expect to meet with some distinguishing marks of the character of the man more than in his other writings, are not near so animated as those of Swift and Pope, of Cicero and the noble Romans who corresponded with him. They are indeed full of what we call here sentiments (that is, moral observations), but have no marks of the circumstances the writer was in at the time he wrote, nor any reflections necessarily suited to the time and circumstances.⟩

As he was of no great depth in reasoning, he would be glad to set off by the ornament of language what was deficient in matter. This, with the refinement of his temper, directed [him] to make choice of a pompous, grand, and ornate style. His acquaintance with the ancients inclined him to imitate them, and if he had anyone particularly in view it was Plato. As he copied him in his theology, and in a great measure in his philosophy, so he seems to have copied his style and manner also, tempering it in the same manner, so as to make it more suitable to the times he lived in. Theocles in his *Rhapsody*[1] is exactly copied from Socrates. But as Socrates' humour is often too coarse and his sarcasms too biting for this age, he has softened him in this respect and made his Theocles altogether polite, and his wit such as suits the character of a gentleman.

⟨He has indeed succeeded better in this attempt to form a style than we could have expected, and much better than anyone could do in an attempt to form a plan of behaviour. The writer may review and correct anything that is not suitable to the character he designs to maintain: but in common life many accidents would occur which would be apt to cause him to lose his assumed character, and if they are not immediately catched there is no remedy.⟩

⟨The* character which a writer assumes he is not obliged on any occasion to maintain without premeditation, but many incidents happen in common life to which, if the manners are not conformed in a moment, the affectation will be betrayed.⟩

Polite dignity is the character he aimed at, and as this seems to be best supported by a grand and pompous diction, that was the style he made choice of. This he carried so far that when the subject was far from being grand, his style is as pompous as in the most sublime subjects. The chief ornament of language he studied was that of a uniform cadence, and this he often does in contradiction to precision and propriety, which are surely of greater consequence. ⟨He has this so much in view that he often makes the one member of his sentence an echo to the other, and often brings in a whole string of synonyms to make the members end uniformly.⟩

⟨Socrates always, in his longer discourses, points out distinctly his transitions from one object to another. But as this looked too formal, he chose to do this by the more polite and easy manner of beginning a new paragraph, and he is at pains to tell us that he had reasons for his order, even though we can perceive no connection.⟩

⟨This* is the manner of marking transitions which has come so much in vogue in modern times; whatever advantages it may have in elegance, in perspicuity it falls short.

Socrates in Plato is always made to say 'Having considered this thing, we are next to consider such another thing'.⟩

In the choice of his subjects he was almost the same as Lucian. The design of both was to overthrow the present fabric of theology and

---

[1] *The Moralists: A Philosophical Rhapsody* (1709), in *Characteristics*, vol. II (1757).

55

philosophy. But they differed in this: Lucian had no design of erecting another in its place, whereas Shaftesbury not only designed to [destroy] the structure, but to build a new edifice of his own in its room. He judged, and indeed he judged rightly, that the destruction would be easier accomplished, and more to the taste of the times, by ridicule than by confutation. But even in those works where he designs to banter and laugh at his adversary, he does it with the same pompous diction he uses in other works. By this means he hardly ever makes us laugh: only in two places in the whole *Characteristics*: one in the introduction to [blank][1], and the other in his description of a match at football a little after.[2] His similes and metaphors are often very ingenious, but are spun out to such a [blank] as is tiresome both to himself and his readers ⟨as that of the Indian.[3]⟩ In his treatise, where he ridicules Mr Hobbes,[4] there is not one passage which would make us laugh. Mr Hobbes' book would make us laugh, but *his* ridicule of it would never affect us.

⟨As all copiators [*sic*] exceed the original, as paintings may be known to be a copy from being larger than that from which they were copied, so those who affect either in behaviour or in style carry their imitation too far. One who affects to be merry always laughs the loudest and longest of any in the company. In the same manner as Shaftesbury affects to be pompous, he often exceeds and applies a grand diction to a subject of a very different kind. A stranger who did not understand the language would imagine the most trivial subjects to [be] something very sublime, from the manner and sound of his periods.⟩

This nobleman sometimes allows himself even to run into burlesque: his pompous style and humorous thoughts joined together make it almost unavoidable. But this species of ridicule is always buffoonish, and he surely falls greatly off from the polite dignity he studies to maintain, when he allows himself a species of wit that is greatly beneath the character of a gentleman. Nay, this strenuous advocate for the [blank] and justness of thought even condescends now and then to make use of a pun, and those of the silliest kind, as where [blank].

⟨When* Shaftesbury is disposed to be in a rhapsody, it is always unbounded, over-violent, and unsupported by the appearance of reason; as, for instance, in his address to the Sun in his *Rhapsody*, in which address not one circumstance is mentioned which ought to excite

---

[1] Probably *Miscellaneous Reflections*, Misc. 1, ch. 1 (*Characteristics*, vol. III).
[2] *Ibid*. Misc. 1, ch. 2.   [3] *Ibid*. Misc. 5, ch. 3.
[4] *Essay on the Freedom of Wit and Humour*, pt.2, sect. 1 (*Characteristics*, vol. I).

56

rational admiration. Compare this with the most rapturous passage in all Virgil, his encomium on rural life in the *Georgics*.[1]

> O fortunatos nimium, sua si bona norint,
> Agricolas, etc. etc.

Here every circumstance, every word, has an energy and force in displaying the liberty of the country, and deprecating the tinsel and tumult of a town life. Virgil, when he is disposed to be in a transport, does not run mad.⟩

[1] *Georgics*, II, l. 458ff.

# 12

## Of Composition

BEFORE we enter on the different parts and species of composition, it will be proper to acquaint you with the method in which we are to proceed. Every discourse proposes either barely to relate some fact or to prove some proposition. The first is the kind of discourse called a narrative one; the latter is the foundation of two sorts of discourses, the didactic and the rhetorical. The former proposes to put before us the arguments on both sides of the question in their true light, giving each its proper degree of influence, and has it in view to persuade no further than the arguments themselves appear convincing. The rhetorical, again, endeavours by all means to persuade us, and for this purpose it magnifies all the arguments on the one side, and diminishes or conceals those that might be brought on the side contrary to that which it is designed that we should favour. Persuasion, which is the primary design in the rhetorical, is but the secondary design in the didactic. It endeavours to persuade us only so far as the strength of the argument is convincing: instruction is the main end. For the other, persuasion is the main design, and instruction is considered only so far as it is subservient to persuasion, and no further.

⟨One who was to give an account of any controverted point, as of the disputes about the right of two princes to a throne, would state the claims of each in the clearest light, and show their several foundations in the custom and constitution of the country, without being, or at least appearing to be, any way inclined to the one more than the other. But if one was to plead the cause of one of the contending parties before some supreme court or another prince, as Edward was made the judge betwixt Bruce and Balliol, he would not probably think it his business, nor would it be his duty, to lay the cause open before him. He would give all the strength he could to those arguments that supported his side, and soften and pass over with little attention those which made against him.⟩

There are two different sorts of facts: one external, consisting of the transactions that pass without us, and the other internal, to wit, the thoughts and sentiments or designs of men which pass in their minds. The design of history, compounded of both these, is to state the remarkable transactions that pass in different nations, and the designs, motions, and views of the most remarkable men in those times, so far as they are necessary to explain the great changes and revolutions of states which it is intended to relate.

In our observations on this I shall observe the following division. First, I shall consider what facts are proper to be narrated; secondly, in what manner; thirdly, how they are to be arranged; fourthly, in what style these may be most conveniently expressed; fifthly and lastly, what writers have succeeded most happily in these branches. ⟨As* there are two kinds of objects which may become the subject of description, I shall consider first the description of simple objects, first of simple visible objects, then of simple invisible objects. Then we shall consider the description of compound visible objects, as of an action; next, of compound invisible objects, as of a character; and last of all, of the rhetorical style and description of actions and characters, in treating of which I shall observe five things. We shall then proceed to didactic and rhetorical compositions.⟩

The distinction made by the ancients came pretty nearly to the same. They divided Eloquence into three parts, according to the three species which were most in use amongst them. The first they called the Demonstrative; the second, Deliberative; and the third, Judicial. ⟨It is rather reverence for antiquity than any great regard for the beauty or usefulness of the thing itself which makes me mention the ancient divisions of rhetoric.⟩

The Demonstrative is so called not because it was that sort which is used in mathematical demonstrations, but because it was chiefly designed to demonstrate or point out the eloquence of the orator. This was one of the most early sorts of eloquence. Discourses of this kind, merely for ostentation, were delivered in the assemblies of the whole people, and were thence called πανηγυρικά. The subjects of such discourses were generally the praises or the discommendation of some particular persons, communities or actions, exhorting the people to or deterring them from some particular conduct. As it was more safe to commend than to discommend men or actions, these discourses generally turned that way, and hence what we call elogiums came to be denominated by the name of panegyrics.

59

The Deliberative was such as they used in their councils and assemblies on matters of consequence to the State; and the Judicial was that used in proceedings before a court of justice.

To begin with the Demonstrative, as it is the most simple, and[1] proceed in it in the same order as I proposed to follow when I come to treat of historical discourses, 1st of the facts, 2nd the manner of treating them, 3rd the arrangement, 4th the style, and 5th the writers.

⟨We shall begin with the historical, and the most simple part of it is the narration of one simple fact. These are either external or internal. After having explained their difference, we proceed to shew how they are to be expressed, in what order they are to be arranged, and in what expressions the idea of them will be best conveyed. Then we shall treat of the expressing a sentiment, and last of all of describing a character. History comprehends all these and we shall therefore treat of it next.⟩

First, then, we are to treat of the facts that are to be described or related. These, as we observed, are either external or internal. We shall begin with the first, as most simple and easily conceived. Mr Addison observes[2] that facts may be agreeable either from their being grand, new, or beautiful. As those facts[3] that are agreeable will be apt to make the greatest impression, we shall consider them first, and then we can easily apply the rules laid down for them to objects of other kinds. The idea of a fact[4] that is grand may be conveyed in two ways, either by describing it and enumerating various particulars that concern it, or by relating the effect that it has on those who behold it. ⟨The* first of these, viz. describing the thing itself by its parts, I call—for it is necessary to give names to things—direct description; the other, indirect.⟩ Milton makes use of the first in his description of Paradise,[5] and of the second in the account Adam gives the angel of the effect Eve's presence had on him.[6] He makes use of the first again where he described the view which Satan had of the burning lake.[7] Shakespeare again uses the second manner in the description of Dover Cliff in *King Lear*.[8]

The manner of describing an object often makes it agreeable when there is nothing in the object that is so. There would surely [be]

---

[1] In the MS this sentence is cancelled as far as the word 'and'.

[2] *The Spectator*, No. 412: 'I shall first consider those pleasures of the imagination which arise from the actual view and survey of outward objects; and these, I think, all proceed from the sight of what is great, uncommon, or beautiful.'

[3] MS: 'objects' cancelled, and 'facts' written above.

[4] MS: 'object' cancelled, and 'fact' written above.

[5] *Paradise Lost*, IV, ll. 205ff.   [6] *Ibid*. VIII, ll. 595ff.

[7] *Ibid*. I, ll. 59ff.   [8] *King Lear*, Act IV, sc. vi, ll. 11-24.

nothing agreeable in a picture of a dunghill, neither is the object agreeable, nor can there be anything extraordinary in painting it. For the same reason it would be altogether unsufferable in prose. It might be tolerable if it was done in good language and flowing verses, as it would shew the art of the writer. It might please still more if this was done in burlesque; but neither here does the pleasure arise from the object itself, but from the consideration of the ingenuity of the artist in turning grand and sublime expressions to describe such an object in an accurate manner. Even when there is no burlesque, the applying grand expressions, or such as seem not easily applicable to the subject, pleases us from the same cause. Thus Mr Gray's description of the appearance of Harlequin[1] on the stage will always be agreeable. The art required in adapting the style and manner and versification of Spenser to an object so different gives us a great opinion of the capacity and skill of the writer. Had it been in prose there would have been nothing agreeable in it, as all the art of the author, in which alone the beauty of it consists, would have been lost.

New objects are never agreeable in description merely from being new. There must be something else in them than mere novelty before they can please us much. New objects may have somewhat agreeable when we really behold them and have them present before us, because then they may strike us with wonder. The whole object is at once conceived. But in descriptions, the idea is presented by degrees; the objects open up slowly, so that the surprise cannot be great at the novelty of the object. Mr Addison observes[2] that there is no author who abounds [more] in descriptions of this sort than Ovid. In his *Metamorphoses*, every change that happens is described in all its stages. We hear of men with the heads and paws of bears,[3] women who are beginning to take root in the ground and their hair and hands sprouting into leaves.[4] Mr

[1] I have not found this reference.
[2] The reference here and in what follows is probably to *The Spectator*, No. 417: 'Ovid . . . describes a miracle in every story, and always gives us the sight of some new creature at the end of it. His art consists chiefly in well-timing his description, before the first shape is quite worn off, and the new one perfectly finished; so that he everywhere entertains us with something we never saw before, and shows monster after monster, to the end of the metamorphosis.' But there are numerous comments of a like kind in Addison's *Notes on Ovid's Metamorphoses*, for example, on Fable V, where Ovid is 'the greatest admirer of this mixed wit of all the ancients, as Cowley is among the moderns'.
[3] Probably *Metamorphoses*, II, l. 477, where Callisto is changed to a bear by Juno's jealous anger.
[4] Examples are: Daphne changed into a tree (*Metamorphoses*, I, ll. 548-52); Myrrha into a tree (*ibid*. x, ll. 489ff); Heliades into poplars (*ibid*. II, l. 346).

Addison seems to be pleased with these descriptions; but to me they don't at all seem pleasing, both for the reason I already mentioned, and because they are so very much out of the common course of nature as to shock us by their incredibility. For my part, when I see Tithonus in a picture with the wings and legs of a grasshopper, I feel no pleasure at seeing such an unnatural and inconceivable object. Novelty, indeed, joined to any other quality that makes an object agreeable, heightens the pleasure we feel in the description of it.

# 13

Monday, 20 December 1762

THAT way of expressing any quality of an object which does it by describing the several parts that constitute the quality we want to express, may be called the direct method. When, again, we do it by describing the effects this quality produces on those who behold it, [this] may be called the indirect method. The latter in most cases is by far the best. We see accordingly Shakespeare's descriptions are greatly more animated than those of Spenser. Shakespeare, as he wrote in dialogues, had it always in his power to make the persons of the dialogue relate the effects any object had upon them. Spenser describes everything directly, and has in adhering to this plan described several objects directly which no other author attempted in that manner. ⟨Spenser* was constrained to take this method because he dealt in allegorical personages, without existence or form but what he conferred on them.⟩ Pindar, Homer, and Milton never attempt to describe music directly; they always do it by describing the effects it produced on some other creatures. Pindar[1] relates the effects it had not only on the earthly beings, but even goes to the Heavens and to Tartarus for objects that might strengthen this description. ⟨Mr Hervey has imitated the passage here mentioned[2] in an extremely beautiful manner, but though the circumstances are as well, or perhaps better, pointed out than in Pindar, yet one chief beauty is lost, by his omitting the effects of the music on Jupiter himself, the thunderbolt falling from his hand, and the eagle settling herself at that particular moment on his hand. In the *Merchant of Venice* music is described by the effects it produces.⟩ ⟨The* man that hath not music in himself.⟩ But this, which none of these great men ever attempted, Spenser has not only attempted, but has succeeded in, in the account of the Knight of Temperance destroying the Bower of Bliss.[3]

The describing or expressing internal, invisible objects is a matter

---

[1] *Pythian Odes*, I, ll. 1ff.
[2] I have not found this reference.
[3] Spenser, *Færie Queene*, Book II, Canto 12.

of far greater difficulty. One would imagine that it would be easy to express an internal one in either of the fore-mentioned ways. But we find it requires no inconsiderable degree of skill to accomplish this into a considerable perfection. But whatever difficulty there is in expressing the external objects that are the objects of our senses, there must be far greater in describing the internal ones, which pass within the mind itself and are the object of none of our senses. We have here no parts into which we can separate them, nor any by describing which we can convey the notion we desire. ⟨The* exact way of describing an object is by its parts: how then describe those which have no parts.[1]⟩

The causes of these internal facts or objects, in like manner, are either internal or external. The internal are such dispositions of mind as fit one for that certain passion or affection of mind, and the external are such objects as produce these effects on a mind so disposed. ⟨There* can be but two ways of describing them, by the effects they produce either on the body or the mind: both these are indirect.⟩ A mind not ruffled by any violent passions, but calm and tolerably serene, filled with some degree of joy, though not so great as to withdraw the attention, is that state of mind in which one is most disposed to admiration. 'Tis in this state the poets have been when they have burst out into those rapturous expressions on the pleasures of a country life. The calm[2] tranquil scene it affords would then be most agreeable. If any beautiful object is presented to one in these circumstances, he is fixt in the place he was in, his arms fall down loose by his sides, or, if the emotion is very violent, are laid across his breast, he leans forward and stretches out his neck, with his eyes fixt on the object, and his mouth a little opened. The affection he feels is mixt with some degree of desire and hope towards the object, and this inclines [him] to draw nearer towards it, imagining that by coming nearer towards it he will enjoy it in greater perfection. ⟨A College,* seen at a certain distance, is an agreeable object, and we are apt to suppose the inhabitants of a College (perhaps contrary to experience) innocent and happy.[3]⟩ This affection is most apt to take place in those of an easy-pleased temper, but not in one where vanity or self-conceit is predominant; such persons are too much engaged with themselves to be greatly affected with other objects.

Any new object affects one with surprise, particularly if it be great and important. This affection does not, as the other, fix the person to

[1] *parts*: reading uncertain.                    [2] *calm*: reading uncertain.
[3] Perhaps Smith had in mind Gray's *Ode on a Distant Prospect of Eton College*.

his place, but makes him start back, his hands stretched out, and his eyes staring. ⟨The turn of mind most fitted to this is when. . . .⟩ If the object is grand and he is fixt to his place, but does not, as in the first case, desire to approach the object, he rather inclines to draw back. This is what we properly call admiration. It does not partake of hope or desire, but rather of a reverential awe and respect that gives one a fear of displeasing. ⟨Surprise is most violent in the first beholding the object, but admiration gradually increases, comes to its greatest height, and again decreases.⟩ The turn of mind that inspires one most to this is. . . .

Other passions affect the body still more violently and distort it in different ways. We do not mean that all these should be described, but only such as are most striking and distinguishing. The different passions all proceed in like manner from different states of mind and outward circumstances. But it would be both endless and useless to go through all these different affections and passions in this manner. It would be endless because, though the simple passions are of no great number, yet these are so compounded in different manners as to make a number of mixt ones almost infinite. It would be useless, for though we had gone through all the different affections, yet the difference of character and age and circumstances of the person would so vary the effects, that our rules would not be at all applicable. Grief[1] is the passion that affects Mezentius, Evander, and the mother of Euryalus, but its effects on them are very different. Mezentius at the same time . . . ⟨In* Mezentius the effect it produces on a ferocious tyrant, abandoned by his subjects, pursued by the vengeance of heaven, is a continuous fury and despair. The grief of Evander was perfect weakness, such as naturally became an old man who had lived in innocence and simplicity.⟩ Evander is affected with a plain simple grief. The mother of Euryalus displays a sort of vivacity in her grief, common to that sex after they have passed a certain age; their passions seem then (contrary to what happens to men) to have acquired greater strength and acuteness than they had before. ⟨The* diversity of the same affection in different characters is finely instanced in the sentiment of our first parents on quitting Paradise; Eve[2] regrets leaving the flowers and walks, and chief the nuptial bower; Adam,[3] in a very sublime passage, the scenes where he had conversed with God.⟩

---

[1] Mezentius, *Aeneid*, x, ll. 833-908; Evander, *ibid.* xi, ll. 148-81; Euryalus, *ibid.* ix, ll. 473-502.

[2] *Paradise Lost*, xi, ll. 268-85.    [3] *Ibid.* xi, ll. 315-29.

The addition of certain objects tending to the same point is often of great benefit. The *L'Allegro* of Milton and his *Il Penseroso* are set out to great advantage by the various additional personages joined in the scene. These additional objects may be of three kinds:—1st, such as are immediately affected by the principal objects, and tend to give strength to the design in view; 2nd, such as are not produced by the principal object, but are connected with it, and are of the same kind, and tend to produce the same emotion; and 3rd, such as neither are affected by the object nor are connected with it, but are some ways suitable to the main design and tend to produce the same emotion. When Vi[rgil] describes the tumbling of a torrent down a rock,[1] he strengthens the picture by describing a traveller astonished and surprised at hearing it below him. The rocks themselves, broken, steep, and hanging over the ground is [*sic*: are] an object very agreeable in a country scene. Titian often added a goat clinging on the rocks to his pleasant landscapes; this added greatly to the agreeableness of the rocks. But when he drew the shepherd lying on the ground and diverting himself with beholding its motions, he made a great addition to the mirth and the pleasure of the piece. The humming of a swarm of bees and the cooing of a turtle give us ideas agreeable and soothing, but this is greatly heightened when Virgil describes Meliboeus[2] lulled asleep by their soothing sound. These are examples of the first kind, where the additional objects are affected by the principal one. (We may observe here that a landscape is where the chief object is the inanimate or irrational part, and a historical where the human figures are designed chiefly to attract our attention.)

The second method is that which Milton makes use of in his *L'Allegro*. The milkmaid singing along, and the mower sharping his scythe,[3] do not immediately respect the landscape described, but are connected with it and tend to excite the same emotion. ⟨Salvator* Rosa[4]⟩ has drawn many landscapes in which the rocks, cascades, woods and mountains make objects. Here he often places a philosopher meditating under the shade of the mountain, a magician at the mouth of a cavern, and a hermit amidst the desert and torrents. Here neither the philosopher is contemplating the mountain, the magician the cavern, nor the hermit the desert. But these objects are connected together and excite the same

---

[1] Smith probably had in mind *Aeneid*, II, ll. 304-8, though the 'traveller' there is a shepherd. A traveller watches a hail-storm in *Aeneid*, x, ll. 803-10.

[2] Virgil, *Eclogues*, I, ll. 54-6. It is Meliboeus who speaks; he refers to Tityrus.

[3] *L'Allegro*, ll. 65-6.

[4] A blank in the MS has been filled with this name in the second hand.

emotion. ⟨A* philosopher reading on a book. . . .⟩ The philosopher adds to the awful, majestic appearance of the mountain, the magician to the gloomy horror of the cavern. The hermit tends to excite in a strong degree the emotions we are apt to conceive at the sight of a desert. Solitude gives us an idea of something very awful. We imagine that some superior beings are generally present in such places, and when we do not see them we conceive them to present the invisible. The fairies, nymphs, fauns, satyrs, dryads and such divinities were all inhabitants of the forest. ⟨If* they are ever brought into the city, it is in the silence of the night, which is a species of solitude.⟩ In such places all communication with superior beings is conceived to be had; prophetical inspirations and revelations have all been given in solitude. It was not in the palaces of Troy but in the solitary mountains of Ida that the goddesses are said to have presented themselves to Paris. By this means hermits and other religious persons are fit additions to such solitary places where we would have an awful and gloomy emotion excited.

⟨Poussin,* in his *Night-Piece,* has added the story of Pyramus and Thisbe, as of the same sort with the rest; but here there is no connection, and the unsuitableness renders the effect not very agreeable. The same he has done in others, where he has brought in the history of Phocion. This sort, where there is no connection, seems proper in historical paintings, because. . . .⟩

We shall now give some general rules for the description of objects. 1st, the whole of the objects described should tend to excite the same emotion, otherwise the end will not be answered. Where the chief design is to excite mirth and cheerfulness, nothing should be brought in that is gloomy or horrible; and, on the other hand, where one would raise awful, grand sentiments, the whole must tend that way. Milton's *L'Allegro* and *Il Penseroso* answer exactly to this rule. Thomson seems frequently to have broken through it. The plan he laid down of giving an account of the seasons often led him to describe objects of different and contrary natures; by which means his descriptions, though sometimes good enough, lose their effect in raising any strong emotion. They ought all to have been arranged in such an order as not to have contrasted one another, but tended to the same end.[1]

A third direction may be, that we should not only make our circumstances all of a piece, but it is often proper to choose out some nice and curious ones. A painter, in drawing a fruit, makes the figure very striking

---

[1] In the MS this sentence is cancelled.

if he not only gives it the form and colour, but also represents the fine down with which it is covered. The dew on flowers, in the same manner, gives the figure a striking resemblance. In the same manner in description we ought to choose out some minute circumstances which concur in the general emotion we would excite, and at the same time but little attended to. Such circumstances are always attended with a very considerable effect.

Another thing that is necessary is that the description should be short and not tedious by its length. But here there is a difficulty, to attain this conciseness and at the same time bring in those circumstances which give a description vivacity and force. This may often be accomplished by picking out some of the most curious and striking circumstances which may suggest the others to the reader. This Virgil has done excellently in the description[1] of an Argive commander, where he says:

Sternitur in humum
Et dulces moriens meminiscitur Argos.

A poet of less merit would have made him express all the tender sentiments this naturally suggests to the reader. This Thomson has done in the description of the man dying in the snow.[2]

Conciseness in the expression may also be attained consistently with the strength of the imagery, if every member of a sentence represents one at least, and, if possible, two or three different circumstances. This makes the description still more lively. Thus in Milton's *Il Penseroso* and *L'Allegro* almost every word tends to convey some idea suited to the subject, and the same may be seen in Virgil's account[3] of the horse dying in the Norican [murrain].

⟨Another* direction is that the circumstance should not be a curious one, and, if such as is not subject to common observation, then it will be sure to strike. Thus we are greatly pleased with those paintings of flowers or fruit which represent the down or the dew, which is not what is commonly observed, although to it the fruit and flowers owe their beauty.⟩

---

[1] *Aeneid*, x, ll. 781-2; the text should read: *Sternitur infelix alieno vulnere, caelumque Aspicit, et dulces moriens reminiscitur Argos.*
[2] *Seasons*, 'Winter', ll. 276-317.
[3] A generalised description of a horse's death by plague is in *Georgics*, iii, ll. 498-502; a more dramatic account of an *ox's* death, in iii, ll. 515ff.

# 14

HAVING some given general rules for the description of objects, I shall now proceed to give some particular rules for the description of different sorts of objects. These are indeed the former applied to particular cases, and are no more than common sense dictates to any man, though he had never heard there was such a rule.

Objects are either corporeal or incorporeal. Corporeal objects are, again, either natural or artificial. Natural objects may be considered as of two sorts: either, 1st, such as exist completely at the same time, or 2nd, such as subsist in a succession of incidents.

First: For describing such natural objects as exist altogether at the same moment, as prospects, it is not necessary that we should arrange the objects, but describe them in any order that seems easiest. Milton does this in his description of Paradise[1] and in his *L'Allegro* and *Il Penseroso*. When authors attempt to arrange the objects in such descriptions, the reader endeavours to arrange them in the same manner in the idea he forms of the thing described, and is always at a loss to follow it out, as no words can convey an accurate idea of the arrangement of objects unless they be assisted by a plan. ⟨Such* descriptions require all the attention and exertion of mind which is required by a mathematical demonstration.⟩ Pliny[2] has given us a description of his villa in this manner, with great minuteness, But notwithstanding his great exactness, his commentators are not at all agreed with regard to the situation of the several objects described; each has formed a different plan according to the way in which he arranged them in his mind. And I believe if any unprejudiced person were to read the description he would form an arrangement of the several objects in his mind different from what either of them has given us. ⟨The later Sophists often make use of such descriptions as these, as Achilles Tatius,[3] etc.⟩ ⟨They* deal

---

[1] Already used as an illustration. *Paradise Lost*, IV, ll. 205ff.

[2] Pliny, *Letters*, Bk. V, Epist. 6.

[3] The MS has 'Hercules Statius'! The second hand has cancelled 'Hercules' and substituted 'Achilles'.

very much in description and tell you that on the right hand was a wood, on the left a rock, and so on.⟩

Mr Balzac,[1] in imitation of Pliny, gives us an account of his villa and the arrangement of the several objects in it. I believe that if it be Mr Balzac's fate to be an ancient and have commentators, they won't agree one whit better than Pliny's have done. The Earl of Buckingham[2] has given a very accurate description of his house and gardens in a letter to Mr Pope. Yet though it be very exact and done in an extremely lively manner, anyone who sees Buckingham's house will find it very different from the idea he had formed from the description.

When, therefore, we describe a natural object which can be comprehended in one view, we need not be at great pains with regard to the arrangement, as the reader will arrange them to himself in the manner which suits his taste best, and will not be perplexed by the arrangement we have given, which will never be sufficient without the assistance of a plan to give a just notion of the thing described.

Second: If the circumstances regarding the object to be described are not existent in the same moment, we should deliver them in the same succession as that they existed in, as Virgil does in his description of the murrain.[3] This is evident, otherwise the order would impose on the reader.

Third: Artificial objects are either entirely the contrivance of man, or they are made in imitation of the works of nature. For describing the former (I mean in poetical descriptions) it is much better to follow the indirect than the direct description. We form a much better idea of these works from the effects they have on the beholder than by any description of their several parts. Mr Addison has described St Peter's at Rome[4] in this manner, and we form a more distinct notion of the size and proportions of that building from his account than if he had gone to describe each part and given us the most exact dimensions, ⟨without* a plan.⟩

Fourth: On the other hand, if the objects are imitations of nature,

[1] The MS has 'Mr Blenac' cancelled and corrected in the second hand. See J. L. Guez de Balzac, *Oeuvres*, II, p. 426 (ed. Moulard 1854). Smith may have used a translation by Sir R. Baker, London 1654, vol. I, Letter 15. The letter is addressed to M. de la Motte Aigron and dated 4 September 1622.

[2] Buckingham's *Works* (1726), vol. 2, pp. 212-21. Letter to the Duke of Shrewsbury communicated to Pope, who imitated and mocked it in a highly imaginative account of the house in which he was then staying (*Works*, ed. Elwin-Courthope, x, pp. 148-52).

[3] *Georgics*, III, ll. 478-566.

[4] *Remarks on Italy*, in *Works*, ed. Hurd, I, pp. 417-8 (Bohn ed.).

they cannot be described too minutely, for it is in the exact symmetry and [?]-bleness[1] of the several parts that the excellence of such productions consists. Lucian's description[2] of Apelles' painting of the marriage of Alexander and Roxana is admirable in this way: he gives us a complete notion of the whole piece. But if he had wrote on purpose to describe that picture, and had not mentioned [it] only to illustrate another subject, he would (as he himself hints) have entered much more minutely into the several parts, and not only given us an account of the general scheme of the piece, but of the chief lines and colouring of every figure in it.

Fifth: Internal objects, as passions and affections, can be well described only by their effects. These again [are] either internal or external. The best rule that can be given on this head seems to be that if the passion is very violent and agitates the person to any high degree, the best method is to describe it by the external effects it produces, and these ought to be enumerated pretty fully and in the most striking and expressive manner. ⟨The* sentiments which a violent passion excites in the mind are too tumultuous and rapid for your description to keep pace with.⟩ On the other hand when the passion is less violent, we must have recourse to the internal effects: the external ones are not strong enough, nor sufficiently remarkable, to point out the state of the person's mind and characterise the passion he feels. The enumeration of circumstances in this case should neither be very full nor very particular. One or two well-chosen are more expressive than a greater number less striking. Virgil has described the passion of Dido[3] on the departure of Æneas in a very [words omitted] from that of Æneas on the same occasion. Her bitter anguish[4] is admirably pointed out by a great variety of circumstances, all external and very nicely chosen. The grief of Æneas,[5] again, as he does not seem to have been so deeply affected, is expressed by a few well-chosen circumstances, and these all internal. The cause of the passion may sometimes be brought in to advantage, but is seldom sufficient to characterise it, without the addition of some of its effects.

Homer and Virgil both describe the joy of Latona on seeing her daughter preferred to other Oreads, by a single expression, and this readily suggests the state of mind she was in. We may have observed

[1] Word indecipherable.
[2] In *Herodotus*, or *Aëtion*. Loeb, vol. VI.
[3] *Aeneid*, IV, ll. 362-87.
[4] MS has 'her violent grief and bitter anguish', with cancel stroke through the first three words.    [5] *Aeneid*, IV, ll. 333-61.

that Virgil's description[1] is somewhat more exact than Homer's. That author barely says she γέγηθε φρένα,[2] an expression he used to denote any kind of joy, and often applies in a very different sense, as when he says γέγηθε δὲ ποιμήν.[3] Virgil, again, points out in a very delicate manner the kind of joy she felt. Those nice and delicate emotions were either not greatly felt or not much attended to, in the age of the Greek poet.

Sixth: In describing natural objects we should not introduce two circumstances the one of which is included in the other. ⟨Such* circumstances as necessarily suggest one another may be called synonyms.⟩ The modern Sophists, as Achilles Tatius[4] and Apuleius, etc. are often guilty of this. They will tell us that a man who leant forwards had one foot placed before another; if he leant his head to one side, they tell us that he leant his body to the other. The latter of these circumstances is included in the other, and would be easily conceived from it. They were probably led to this manner of description by seeing that those authors whose descriptions were most admired followed it. But they did not consider that those authors described imitations of nature, and not natural objects. This last species of writing was greatly [admired][5] in the time of Trajan and the Antonines; and as we observed before, the excellence [is] in detailing every particular, as it is in the exactness and symmetry of them that the excellence of the workmanship consists.

The Abbé du Bos, in his description of the statue of the slave who discovered the conspiracy amongst the Romans,[6] describes every particular attitude. But if he had been to describe the posture of the slave himself, he would have told us that he stood listening to what he heard them talking of, but at the same time so as to seem minding his work, though in reality he had given it up for that time.

Seventh: We ought not only to avoid those circumstances that include one another, which we may call synonymous circumstances, but also those [that] are contrary to the nature of the object we would describe. Thus when a modern poet describes the appearance of a mountain to those who saw it at a distance from sea, he tells us that they saw it appear black, which could not be the real appearance of a mountain at a dis-

---

[1] *Aeneid*, I, l. 502: *Latonae tacitum pertemptant gaudia pectus.*

[2] *Odyssey*, VI, l. 106. Homer reads γέγηθε δέ τε φρένα Λητώ (and Leto rejoiced in her heart). The MS has γέγηθεν φρῆνα.

[3] *Iliad*, VIII, l. 559. γέγηθε δέ τε φρένα ποιμήν. The MS has γέγηθεν δὲ ποιμήν.

[4] The MS has 'Hercules Statius', as before.

[5] Conjectural addition.

[6] *Critical Reflections on Poetry, Painting, and Music*, trans. T. Nugent (1748), Vol. I, pp. 311-12. Cf. Livy, II, 4 and Juvenal, *Satires*, 8, l. 266.

tance, as it is tinged of a bluish white by the colour of the atmosphere. Those who think themselves bound to describe, when they are very ill qualified and know little of the object they would describe, are most apt to fall into this error.

Seventh [*sic*]: It would appear needless to guard you against using epithets that are contradictory or not applicable to the object, if we did not find that some of the greatest English writers have fallen into it, in many places. Mr Pope frequently applies adjectives to substantives with which they cannot at all agree, as when he speaks of the *brown horror of the groves*.[1]

> ⟨Deepens* the murmur of the falling flood,
> And sheds a browner horror o'er the wood.⟩

'Brown' joined to 'horror' conveys no idea at all. Thomson is often guilty of this fault, and Shakespeare almost continually.

---

[1] *Eloisa to Abelard*, ll. 169-70. Pope's words are:
> Deepens the murmur of the falling floods,
> And breathes a browner horror o'er the woods.

# 15

HAVING made some observations on the description of objects in general, and given some directions for the describing simple objects whether internal or external, I shall proceed in the next place to give some observations on the proper manner of describing more complex objects. These are either the characters of men, or the more grand and important actions and conduct of men. I shall begin with the first, as it is chiefly the character and disposition of a man that gives rise to his particular conduct and behaviour, and the manner of describing the former will be better understood when the causes of it are first considered.

A character, then, may be described either directly or indirectly. When we describe a character directly, we relate the various parts of which it consists, what mixture of each particular passion or turn of mind there is in the person. To do this in any tolerable degree of perfection requires great skill, deep penetration, an accurate observation, and almost perfect knowledge of men. Accordingly we find that very few of the ancients have attempted to describe characters in this manner altogether. Sallust has described[1] the character of Catiline in this manner. Tacitus, too, though he seldom sets himself on purpose to give an account of a man's character, yet generally gives some strong lines of it at first, which are illustrated afterwards by the many reflections he afterwards makes on each person's conduct, and the pains he is at to discover and explain the motives of his conduct.

This way is seldom sufficient, unless remarkably well executed, to give us a just notion of the character; the general distinctions do not serve alone to distinguish the character we describe, from others perhaps a good deal different. It is not so much the degree of virtue or vice, probity or dishonesty, courage or timidity, that form the distinguishing part of a character, as the tincture which these several parts have received in the forming his character.

[1] *Bellum Catilinae*, 5.

74

⟨A Turenne[1] and Saxe[2] were both perhaps equal in courage, but the activity of the one and the caution of the other made their characters very different. In our own country, Cromwell and Montrose, who lived in the same period, were I believe of equal military skill, but the open boldness of the one and the suspicious designing temper of the other sufficiently distinguished them.⟩

⟨Men* do not differ so much in the degrees of virtue and wisdom as in the peculiar tinges which these may receive from the other ingredients of their character.⟩

The Abbé de Retz[3] is one of the chief writers amongst the moderns who has followed this method. His characters, a few excepted, are all drawn in this manner. His method is to set before us the different passions and inclinations, aversions and desires, of the person whose character he would give us, and the different proportions which each of them bears to the others.

⟨The* method followed by Cardinal de Retz was that of describing a character as it existed in the person, and he had perhaps in this excelled all others, had it not been for some affectation and too much subtlety: for example, who can have any idea of his strange character of Anne of Austria?[4]—That, too, of Mademoiselle Chevreuse[5] is disfigured by its conclusion.⟩

This manner of writing, as it requires very nice observation, and as it cannot give us a just idea of the character described unless it be by pointing out very nice and minute peculiarities, has frequently led those who followed it into too great refinements in the description of their characters. The Abbé seems frequently to have fallen into errors of this sort; and Tacitus, too, seems often to have had recourse to causes too minute and too trivial, in order to account for the conduct of the persons he has occasion particularly to insist on. Many of the characters drawn by the Abbé are altogether unintelligible, some from [blank] and others from an ill-timed affectation. His character of the Queen of France is

---

[1] Vicomte de Turenne (1611-75), Marshal of France.

[2] Comte Hermann Maurice de Saxe (1696-1750), Marshal of France.

[3] Cardinal de Retz (1614-79), French ecclesiastical politician; author of a book of *Mémoires*, from which Dumas later drew much material.

[4] See de Retz, *Mémoires* (Amsterdam 1731), vol. I, bk. II, p. 214.

[5] *Ibid.* p. 221. Smith may have confused the *longer* sketch of *Madame* de Chevreux which ends 'she knew of no duty but that of pleasing her lover' with the *very short* one of her daughter which follows it and ends: 'But she soon treated her lovers as she did her gowns, which she put in bed by her whilst they pleased her, and two hours after burnt them out of mere aversion' (English trans. 1723).

an instance of the first, and the character of Madame de Nivers[1] of the second. 'Who can make anything of this character?', cried I, on reading the first. The second, on the other hand, is entirely spoiled, and is almost deprived of any meaning, by the misapplied witticism with which it is concluded.

The indirect description of a character is when we do not enumerate its several component parts, but relate the effects it produces on the outward behaviour and conduct of the person. Now the first [thing which] strikes one on seeing a person whom they had not before known, is not the prevalency of any part of his temper, but the air of the man, as we call it; this it is which first gives one an opinion of a man, whether it be ill or whether it be good. But this air is a matter of so simple a nature that it can hardly admit of description, and accordingly no one has attempted it. We must therefore have recourse to the more particular effects of the character, and this may be done either by relating the general tenor of conduct which the person follows, which we may call the general method, or by descending into particulars and pointing out how he would act in such and such instances: this we may call the particular method.

The general method is that in which Monsieur La Bruyère has wrote the greater part of his Characters. This manner differs from the direct manner, as it does not relate the general principles that govern the conduct of men, but tells us in what manner those principles, when brought into action, influence the general conduct of the man. ⟨La Bruyère's* character of a discontented man[2] may be taken as an example of his favourite manner. Had Theophrastus been to describe it he would probably have done it thus.⟩ The difference betwixt these two methods will be more clearly seen if we should compare the character of Catiline by Sallust, with that of the same person drawn by Cicero.[3] The first is in the direct way, and the latter in the general indirect one. We will see likewise, by this comparison, that the latter is considerably more interesting and gives us a fuller view of the character.

Theophrastus is one of the chief who have given us characters drawn in the particular manner. He always begins his 'characters' with a definition of the character he is to describe, and then gives us a description of it by telling us in what manner the person of that character would

---

[1] Not in the *Mémoires* of de Retz. It may be an allusion to Mme de Montbazon.
[2] Possibly that of *Demophile*. See Rowe's translation of La Bruyère's Works (1776), vol. I, pp. 234ff. Cf. Aldington, *A Book of Characters*, London n.d., p. 516.
[3] Cicero, *In Catilinam*.

act in such and such circumstances. This manner, though not always most proper, is generally the most interesting and agreeable. In so much that though La Bruyère has drawn his characters in many different manners—sometimes he laughs at the person he characterizes, sometimes expostulates with them, and sometimes gives him serious advice—yet notwithstanding of this variety of method, there is perhaps none of them all so agreeable as that of Theophrastus.

⟨We may observe that it would be no difficult matter to turn one of Theophrastus' characters into the manner of Bruyère; the circumstances are so well chosen as readily to suggest the general character. But, on the other hand, it would be very difficult to express one of La Bruyère's in the manner of Theophrastus, it being a very nice matter to pick out single instances that sufficiently mark out the general character we would describe.⟩

Accordingly we find that Theophrastus is generally more read than La Bruyère. Nay, this method is so far superior with respect to the pleasure it gives, that the only character La Bruyère has drawn in that manner, though perhaps a worse one than any of the others, is more admired than any of them. Though it ⟨viz., that of Menalcas[1] or absent-minded man⟩ ⟨mutato* nomine de te fabula narratur, said Mr Herbert of Mr Smith⟩[2] has less variety and less spirit than perhaps any of the rest, yet [blank] has thought it deserved to have a comedy founded on the plan of it. None of the others have been honoured in this manner, though there are few that do not deserve it as well ⟨or* better.⟩ ⟨The* comedy was wrote by Mr [blank] a comic writer of secondary[3], an imitator of Molière's and no bad one⟩ ⟨There* is a certain order and arrangement in the pictures exhibited by Bruyère which the least alteration of any member of it would destroy. But Theophrastus's are tumbled together without much arrangement, and that circumstance which concludes the whole might have stood first.⟩

If we were to state a comparison of the excellences of these three methods of describing a character, we might perhaps give the preference in point of agreeableness to that of Theophrastus. But in writing a history it would probably be the best method to describe the characters in the same order as the different views of the characters naturally present themselves to us. That is, first to give an account of the prevailing temper and passions of the man as soon as he is brought into the scheme

[1] See Rowe's translation of La Bruyère's Works, vol. I, pp. 256-64.
[2] See Introduction, pp. XIX-XX.   [3] *secondary*: reading doubtful.

of the history, and afterwards to give such observations on his conduct as will open up the general principles on which he acts; ⟨to* give an account of his disposition and the general manner in which it had led him to act, reserving the particulars to be interwoven in the subsequent narration.⟩ The particular manner would but ill suit the dignity of a history. A number of particular actions, perhaps very trifling ones, thrown all together, gives a work the appearance of a comedy or a satire, and it is in such works only that it can be applied with propriety. The characters of Theophrastus, though very agreeable, yet have so great similarity, both in their plan and execution, that they soon fatigue us. Bruyère's, again, have a great deal of variety and elegance. They of all works of this sort are most proper for those who would study the rhetorical art, and are extremely well worth reading.

⟨His* book abounds with a species of reflections equally distant from trite and unentertaining ones as from the paradoxical ones at present so much in vogue among authors. La Bruyère's are sufficiently obvious at first view, yet such as would not readily have occurred to one.⟩

The same methods that are proper to describe a particular character are also applicable to that of a nation or body of men. La Bruyère[1] has also given us characters of several nations, and particular professions and ways of life, as the courtier, etc., drawn in the same manner as those of persons. In describing the characters of the nations, the Government may be considered in the same view as the air of a single person: the situation, climate, customs, as those peculiarities which give a distinguishing tincture to the character, and form the same general outlines into very different appearances.

These authors whom I have mentioned are the chief who have excelled in the describing of characters. Lord Clarendon, likewise, in his *History*, is at great pains to give us the characters of the several persons as they appear in it. This he does by narrating the different circumstances of their past life, their education, and the advances or declining state of their fortunes; and from thence endeavours to collect their characters in a manner nearly allied to the direct method. Though he has not the penetration requisite for excelling in this way, yet his being personally acquainted with the most of those whom he describes makes it almost impossible that he should miss some circumstances that will give us at least a tolerable idea of the person's character. There is always something in a character which will make an impression on those

---

[1] The name is cancelled in the MS and 'wrong' written under.

who are of one's intimate acquaintance, and which they will readily express so as to make it known to others.

⟨An* instance of this may be seen in his [sc. Clarendon's] character of the Earl of Arundel and Pembroke.[1]

The great fault we are apt to fall into in the description of character is the making them so general that they exhibit no idea at all. Who, for example, can form any idea of Lord Falkland[1] from the character which Clarendon gives him? To avoid this there ought to be always some particular and distinguishing circumstance annexed, such as that description of Agricola by Tacitus. 'You would have known him by his look to be a good man, you would have rejoiced to have found him a great one.'[2] In fact, when you would do honour to and perpetuate the memory of a friend, you must take care not to ascribe to him those contrary virtues which the comprehension of the human mind is too narrow to take in at once.⟩

Burnet, in the characters he gives us, is so biting and sarcastical that he is not at all pleasing; he gives us a worse idea of his friends than Clarendon does of his very enemies. The latter, whatever we may think of him as a historian, certainly deserves our love as a man.

⟨Sir* William Temple in his essay on the Netherlands, has described the character of a nation very completely in all the several three ways. The conclusion is an example both of the direct and indirect character of a nation, where he says this is a place where profit is in more respect than honour,[3] etc. As in the characters of persons the great error we are exposed to is the making them too general, so is it that of nations. The English, French, and Spaniards may be equally brave, yet that virtue is certainly very different in each.⟩

---

[1] A convenient selection of these 'characters' is D. Nichol Smith's *Characters of the Seventeenth Century* (1920). Arundel's character is on pp. 29-32; Falkland's, pp. 71-95.

[2] *Agricola*, 44: *bonum virum facile crederes, magnum libenter.*

[3] Temple, *Observations upon the United Provinces of the Netherlands*, ed. Clark, Cambridge 1932, p. 115. 'Holland is a country where the earth is better than the air, and profit more in request than honour; where there is more sense than wit' etc.

# 16

Monday, 27 December 1762

HAVING in the three or four foregoing lectures considered the manner of describing single objects, as well internal as external, and given some particular rules for the describing the different species of them, and having also given you an account of the different manners of describing a character and the principal authors who have excelled in that art, I come now to make some observations on the proper method of describing the more complex and important actions of men. It is only the more important objects that are ever described; others less interesting are so far from being thought worthy of description that they are not reckoned to deserve much of our attention. As it is mankind we are chiefly connected with, it must be their actions which chiefly interest our attention. Other rational agents we are little acquainted with, and the transactions which pass amongst other animals are never of so great importance to us as to attract our notice. 'Tis therefore the actions of men, and, of them, such as are of the greatest importance, and are most apt to take our attention and make a deep impression on the heart, that form the ground of this species of description. The actions and perceptions which chiefly affect us and make the deepest impression on our minds, are those that are of the misfortunate kind, and give us in the perception a considerable degree of uneasiness. These are always found to be more interesting than others of the same degree of strength, if they are of a pleasant and agreeable nature.

⟨Whence this superior influence of uneasy sensations proceeds,⟩ whether from their being less common and so more distinguished from the ordinary pitch of human happiness, by being greatly below it, than our most agreeable perceptions are by rising above it, or whether it is thus ordered by the constitution of our nature, to the end that the uneasiness of such sensations as accompany what tends to our prejudice might rouse us to be active in warding it off, cannot be easily determined. For though pleasant sensations from what is of advantage might perhaps be dispensed with, and no great prejudice thereby accrue to our happiness, yet it seems absolutely necessary that some considerable degree of uneasiness should attend what is hurtful, for without this we should soon, in all probability, be altogether destroyed. But whatever be the cause of this phenomenon, it is an undoubted fact that those actions affect us in the most sensible manner, and make the deepest impression, which give us a considerable degree of pain and uneasiness. This is the case not only with regard to our own private actions, but with those of others. Not only in our own case misfortunate affairs chiefly affect us; but it is with the misfortunes of others that we most commonly, as well as most deeply, sympathise. A historian who related a battle and the effects attending, if he was in no way interested, would naturally dwell more on the misery and lamentations of the vanquished than on the triumph and exultations of the victors.

It is to be observed that no action, however affecting in itself, can be represented in such a manner as to be very interesting to those who had not been present at it, by a bare narration, where it is described directly, without taking notice of any of the effects it had on those who were either actors or spectators of the whole affair. Had Livy, when relating the engagement of the Horatii and the Curiatii,[1] told us that the Albans and Romans chose three brothers from each side to determine by the issue of their combat the fate of each nation; that they accordingly engaged; that the Curiatii killed two of the Romans, being at the same time wounded themselves; that the remaining Roman, betaking himself, as they imagined, to flight, brought them to follow him and by that means got the victory, which he could not have expected from an engagement with them all at once—this would have been a direct description, but very languid and uninteresting in comparison of the other sort, where the effects of the transaction, as well on the actors as on the spectators, are pointed out. The difference will appear very remarkable if we compare the above description to that which he has given us of the same transaction. The account he gives of the description[2] of Alba,[3] is another instance of great excellence in that method of description.

Thucydides might have given us in a very few words the whole account of the siege of Syracuse by the Athenians, which has filled the best part of the seventh book of his History, but no such account could have had [a] chance of equalling the animated and affecting description

---

[1] Livy, Bk. I, chs. 24-5.
[2] *Sic*. Probably an error for 'destruction'.
[3] *Ibid.* ch. 29.

81

he has given of that memorable event. ⟨There are many pages in Livy and other authors that deserve to be read on account of their excellence in this art; but these, I think, are sufficient to confirm the general rule, that when we mean to affect the reader deeply we must have recourse to the indirect method of description, relating the effects the transaction produced both on the actors and spectators.⟩

We observed that the emotions of grief are those which most affect us, both in reality and in description; but when these come to a very great height they are not to [be] expressed by the most accurate description, even, of them. No words are sufficient to convey an adequate idea of their effects. The best method in such cases is not to attempt any indirect description of the grief and concern, but barely relate the circumstances the persons were in, the state of their mind before the misfortune, and the causes of their passion. It is told of an eminent painter[1] that, drawing the Sacrifice of Iphigenia, he expressed a considerable degree of grief in Calchas the augur, still greater in [blank],[2] and all that his art could reach in the countenance and behaviour of Menelaus; but when he came to Agamemnon, the father of the victim, he could [not] by all his skill express a degree of grief suitable to what then filled his breast. He thought it more prudent therefore to throw a veil over his face. In the same manner when Thucydides described the distress and confusion of the Athenians retiring from Syracuse,[3] he did not attempt to describe it by the effects it produced on them. He chose, rather, to relate the circumstances of their misfortunes and the causes of their distress, and left the reader to frame an idea of the deep concern and affliction they must have been in. Dionysius [of] Halicarnassus observes[4] that Thucydides delights much more in relating the misfortunes and distresses of his countrymen than their prosperity, and so far his observation is just. But the reason he gives for it does not appear at all probable. He says that Thucydides, being banished by his countrymen, was so irritated by this bad usage that he was at pains to collect everything that tended to their dishonour, and was at pains to conceal all accounts of glorious and successful conduct, that he might by this lessen their reputation. For this reason he prefers Herodotus to him, who dwells more on the prosperity and good fortune of his countrymen, reckoning this to be a sign of a more humane and generous temper. But

---

[1] Timanthes. The story is told by several authors, e.g. Cicero, *Orator*, 74; Quintilian, *Institutiones*, II, 13, 12.

[2] Ulysses is probably intended.  [3] Thucydides, VII, 8off.

[4] Dionysius of Halicarnassus, *The Three Literary Letters*, ed. Roberts, p. 109.

if we consider the tempers of the men, as well as the nature of the thing itself, we may perhaps be of a different opinion. These tempers, if we may judge from their works, were very different. Herodotus appears to have been of a more gay disposition, was of no great experience amongst men; which temper, joined to the [blank] of old age, would make him inclined to insist much on the good fortune and happy incidents of the history. Thucydides, again, being of an age not much given to sallies of passion of any sort, and having seen men and things, would, as it were, be hardened against trivial and light bursts of joy, but would not, from the innate goodness of his heart, be insensible of the misfortunes of his fellows. He perhaps considered, also, that these melancholy affections were most likely to produce good effects on the minds of his readers, to soften and humanize them: whereas the other would rather tend to make the heart insensible to tender emotions. All this may incline [us] to be of a different opinion from the critic above mentioned.

We are here also to consider, that which was before hinted, that it is these uneasy emotions that chiefly affect us and give us a certain pleasing anxiety. A continued sense of prosperity would not give us near so much pleasure in the recital as an epic poem or a tragedy, which make but one continued series of unhappy events. Even comedy itself would not give us much pleasure, if we were not kept in suspense and some degree of anxiety by the cross incidents which occur, and either end in, or appear to threaten, a misfortunate issue. For this reason also it is not surprising that a man of an excellent heart might incline to dwell most on the dismal side of the story.

# 17

HAVING now given those observations I think necessary to the describing single objects, both external and internal, and the more important complex ones, as the characters of men and the more important and interesting actions, I might now proceed to shew how these are to be applied to the oratorical composition, what objects and what manner of describing them, and what circumstances were most proper to interest us, and, fixing our attention on one side, persuade us to be of that opinion.

But as the particular directions already laid down naturally lead us to consider how they are to be applied in the most distinct manner, and where they are all conjoined, I shall first consider how they are to be applied to the historical style. Besides, the narration makes a considerable part in every oration. It requires no small art to narrate properly those facts which are necessary for the groundwork of the oration. So that I would be necessitated to lay down rules for narration in general, that is, for the histo[rical] style, before I could thoroughly explain the rhetorical composition.

The end of every discourse is either to narrate some fact or prove some proposition. When the design is to set the case in the clearest light, to give every argument its due force, and by this means persuade us no farther than our unbiassed judgement is convinced, this is not to make use of the rhetorical style. But when we propose to persuade at all events, and for this purpose adduce those arguments that make for the side we have espoused, and magnify these to the utmost of our power, and on the other hand make light of and extenuate all those which may be brought on the other side, then we make use of the rhetorical style. But when we narrate transactions as they happened, without being inclined to any part, we then write in the narrative style.

The didactic and the oratorical compositions consist of two parts: the proposition which we lay down, and the proof which is brought to confirm this, whether this proof be a strict one, applied to our reason and sound judgement, or one adapted to affect our passions and by that means persuade us at any rate. But in the narrative style there is only one part, that is, the narration of the facts. There is no proposition laid down or proof to confirm it. When a historian brings anything to confirm the truth of a fact, it is only a quotation in the margin, or a parenthesis, and as this makes no part of the work, it cannot be said to be a part of the didactic. But when a historian sets himself to compare the evidence that is brought for the proof of any fact, and weigh the arguments on both sides, this is assuming the character of a didactic writer.

The facts which are most commonly narrated, and will be most adapted to the taste of the generality of men, will be those that are interesting and important. Now these must be the actions of men. The most interesting and important of these are such as have contributed to great revolutions and changes in States and Governments. The changes or accidents that have happened to inanimate or irrational beings cannot greatly interest us. We look upon them to be guided in a great measure by chance and undesigning instinct. Design and contrivance is what chiefly interests us, and the more of this we conceive to be in any transaction, the more we are concerned in it. A history of earthquakes or other natural phenomena, though it might contain great variety of incidents and be very agreeable to a naturalist who had entered deeply into those matters, and by that means conceived them to be of considerable importance, as we do everything that we have gone so far into as to have some notion of its extent, yet it would appear very dull and uninteresting to the generality of mankind. The accidents that befall irrational objects affect us merely by their external appearance, their novelty, grandeur, etc. but those which affect the human species interest us greatly by the sympathetical affections they raise in us. We enter into their misfortunes, grieve when they grieve, rejoice when they rejoice, and in a word feel for them in some respects as if we ourselves were in the same condition.

The design of historical writing is not merely to entertain; (this perhaps is the intention of an epic poem); besides that, it has in view the instruction of the reader. It sets before us the more interesting and important events of human life, points out the causes by which these events were brought about, and by this means points out to us by what manner and method we may produce similar good effects or avoid similar bad ones.

⟨Should one lay down certain principles which he afterwards con-

85

firmed by examples, this work would have the same end as a history, but the means would be different: it would be, not a narrative, but a didactic writing.⟩

In this it differs from a romance, the sole view of which is to entertain. This being the end, it is of no consequence whether the incidents narrated be true or false. A well-contrived story may be as interesting and entertaining as any real one. The causes which brought about the several incidents that are narrated may all be very ingeniously contrived and well adapted to their several ends, but still [as] the facts are not such as have really existed,[1] the end proposed by history will not be answered. The facts must be real, otherwise they will not assist us in our future conduct, by pointing out the means to avoid or produce any event. Feigned events and the causes contrived for them, as they did not exist, cannot inform us of what happened in former times, nor of consequence assist us in a plan of future conduct.

Some hints of this sort, pointing out the view with which the author undertook his work, whether he was induced to it by the importance of the facts, or whether it was to remedy the inaccuracy or partiality of former writers, and also showing us what we may expect to find in the work, would form a much better subject for the preface or beginning of the work (where Tacitus has applied them) than commonplace morality, as that with which Sallust introduces his works.[2] These, however pretty, have no connection with the matter in hand, and might have been anywhere else as well as where they are. This much with regard to the preface.

The next thing that comes to be considered in the course of the history is the causes which brought about the effects that are to be narrated. And here it may be questioned whether we are to relate the remoter causes, or only the more immediate ones which preceded the events.[3] If the events are very interesting, they will so far attract our attention that we cannot be satisfied unless we know something of the causes which brought them about. If these causes again be very important, we, for the same reason, require to have some account of the causes which produced them. But these need not be so accurately explained as

---

[1] *existed*: reading uncertain.

[2] Bolingbroke had made this point towards the end of his *Plan for a General History of Europe*.

[3] Here and elsewhere in this lecture Smith seems to adopt suggestions from the comparison by Dionysius of Halicarnassus of Herodotus and Thucydides. Cf. *The Three Literary Letters*, ut supra.

the more immediate ones, and so on, gradually diminishing the importance of the causes till at last we satisfy the reader.

In general the more remote any cause is, the less circumstantially it may be described. Thus Sallust, in his *Jugurthan War*, where the immediate cause of that event was the character of that prince and the state of the Numidian affairs at the death of Micipsa, dwells but little on the events that preceded that reign. These he points out more minutely, but less so than those that happened in Jugurtha's life; and in it, too, those that happened in his infancy, or when he was in the Roman camp, are much less accurately explained than those which immediately preceded and were intimately connected with the chief events. Had he dwelt more on the events that happened before Micipsa's reign, he would have been necessitated to have explained those that preceded them, and so on *ad infinitum*. By not attending to this method the introduction to the [blank] history fills a whole folio volume. Gordon, who translated Tacitus, tells us that when he set about writing the life of Oliver Cromwell, he found the events in that period so connected with those before the Reformation, and those again with the former reigns, that he was obliged to go as far back as the Conquest; and by going on in the same way he would have found himself reduced to the necessity of tracing the whole back even to the fall of Adam. It is always, however, necessary to give some reason for the events which more immediately preceded the chief cause, but this may often be done in such a manner as to prevent any farther curiosity: thus Sallust, when he tells us that the cause of the Catiline conspiracy was the temper and character of that man, and the circumstances of his life, joined with the corrupt manners of the people. Here we naturally demand how it came to pass that a people once strictly virtuous and sober should have degenerated so much: he tells us that it was owing to the luxury introduced by their Asiatic conquests. This altogether satisfies us, as those conquests and their circumstances, however interesting, appear no way connected with the matters in hand.

⟨The* more lively and striking the impression is which any phenomenon makes on the mind, the greater curiosity does it excite to know its causes, though perhaps the phenomenon may not be intrinsically half so grand or important as another less striking. Thus it is that we have a greater curiosity to pry into the causes of thunder and lightning and of the celestial motions, than of gravity, because they naturally make a greater impression on us. Hence it is that we have naturally a greater curiosity to examine the causes and relations of those things which pass without us, than of those which pass within us, the latter naturally making very little impression. The associations of our ideas and the progress and origin of our passions are what very few think of inquiring into. But when one has turned his thoughts that way and made some inquiries, he begins to think those matters to be of importance, and is therefore interested in them.

A historian therefore is to expose the causes of everything only in proportion to the impression it makes. Now the cause of the event makes a less impression than the event itself, and so excites less curiosity with regard to its cause; that cause therefore is to be touched upon more slightly, and by being so it excites but very little curiosity about its cause, which therefore may be still more superficially mentioned. It is thus that Sallust ascribes the conspiracy of Catiline to the characters and circumstances of certain persons in the state; these he traces to the general profligacy and luxury then prevailing in Rome; which at length he deduces from the conquest of Asia; where he leaves us fully satisfied that we know all that is necessary of the matter, and not disposed to enter into the origin of these conquests, however convinced that the enquiry would be curious at a proper time.⟩

The causes that may be assigned for any event are of two sorts, either the external causes which directly produced it, or the internal ones, that is, those causes that, though they no way affected the event, yet had an influence on the minds of the chief actors so as to alter their conduct from what it would otherwise have been. . . . We may observe on this head that those who have been engaged in the transactions they relate, or others of the same sort, generally dwell on those of the first sort. Thus Caesar, and Polybius, and Thucydides, who had all been engaged in most of the battles they describe, account for the fate of the battle by the situation of the two armies, the nature of the ground, the weather, etc. Those, on the other hand, who have little acquaintance with the particular incidents of this sort that determine events, but have made inquiries into the nature of the human mind and the several passions, endeavour, by means of the circumstances that would influence them, to account for the fate of battles and other events, which they could not have done by those causes that immediately determine them. Thus Tacitus, who seems to have been but little versant in military or indeed public affairs of any sort, always accounts for the event of a battle by the circumstances that would influence the minds of the combatants.

This difference in the manner of accounting for events is very plainly seen in the description of a battle in the night, one by Thucydides[1] and the other by Tacitus.[2] The former mentions all the causes[3] the nature of the circumstances would have on the armies; whereas the other has entirely omitted these, and mentioned solely those that would affect the minds of the combatants with lesser courage, etc. The first is the account of the attack of Syracuse by the Athenians, and the latter of the battle betwixt Vespasian and Vitellius' general.

The describing of characters is no essential part of a historical narration. The temper of the person of the actors at the different times will be sufficient. Xenophon, in his account of the retreat of the 10,000 Greeks, describes very accurately the characters of the three commanders who were betrayed by Artaxerxes.[4] In his Greek history likewise, though he does [not] enter on purpose on the describing of characters, but by the different circumstances and particular incidents he relates, the characters are sufficiently plain. ⟨Xenophon* is almost the only ancient historian who professedly draws characters.⟩ Herodotus and Thucydides hardly describe any characters. Herodotus, indeed, has some exclamations on the characters of the different persons, but such general ones as are not to be called characters, and might be equally applicable to a hundred others, ⟨as in the exclamations on the virtues of Pericles[5]—A man of [a] grave or a merry [disposition], of a good nature, or morose temper, may advance to battle or scale the walls with equal intrepidity.⟩

'Tis not the degrees of virtue or vice, of courage or good nature, that distinguish a character, as the particular turns they have received from the temper and turn of the mind of the several individuals. Thucydides gives us no account of characters at all. This we cannot attribute to want of ability, as he was personally acquainted with most of the characters he would have occasion to describe, and has shown his skill in this art in the admirable characters he has given of whole communities, as of the Athenians after the [blank][6]⟩ and of [blank] which is still more difficult than the describing of characters of single persons. We must, then attribute this conduct to an opinion that this was not at all necessary.

[1] Thucydides, VII, 43-5.
[2] Tacitus, *Historiae*, III, 22-4, Vespasian's general was Antonius Primus. Tacitus says that the Vitellians had no leader—*indigus rectoris* (III, 22).
[3] *causes*:? an error for 'effects'.
[4] *Anabasis*, II, 6. Clearchus, Proxenus the Boeotian, Menon the Thessalian.
[5] The *only* reference to Pericles in Herodotus is in VI, 131, where we are told that his mother, a few days before he was born, dreamt that she gave birth to a lion.
[6] Possibly Smith refers to the disaster of Syracuse; Thucydides, VIII, 1.

There is no author who has more distinctly explained the causes of events than Thucydides. He is in this respect far superior to Polybius, who is at such great pains in minutely explaining all the extreme causes of any event that his labour appears visibly in his works, and is not only tiresome, but at the same time is less pleasant, by the constraint the author seems to have been in. Thucydides, on the other hand, often expresses all that he [sc. Polybius] labours so much, in a word of two, sometimes placed in the middle of the narration, but in such a manner as not in the least to confound it.

Next to Thucydides comes Xenophon and Tacitus. This last has often been censured as being too deep a politician. The author of this remark was, I think, ⟨Trajan* Boccalini,[1]⟩ an Italian, who has been imitated[2] by all the petty critics since his time. This remark was very natural at that time, when such subtlety prevailed and Machiavellian politics were in fashion, but does not seem at all suitable to the ingenuous temper of Tacitus, nor is it confirmed by his writings. In the beginning of his history of the reign of Tiberius[3] he gives us some political remarks on the genius and temper of that prince, but this is sufficiently justified by the character of cunning and design given him by other authors. In other parts of his work the pains he is at to explain the causes of events from the internal causes seems to point out a contrary temper.

Livy seldom endeavours to account for events in either way, by the internal or external causes; and those who are acquainted with military affairs affirm that he is not altogether clear in his accounts of battles or sieges. He supports the dignity of his narration by the interesting manner in which he relates the several events, which he does so admirably that we enter into all the concerns of the parties, and are almost as much affected with them as if we ourselves had been concerned in them.

Events, as we before observed, may be described either in a direct or indirect manner. We observed also that in most cases the indirect method is much preferable, even when the objects were inanimate. Much more, then, will it be to be chosen, when we describe the actions of men, where the effects are so much stronger, as the actions themselves are more interesting. 'Tis the proper use of this method that makes most of the ancient historians, as Thucydides, so interesting, and the neglecting it that has rendered the modern historians for the most part so dull

[1] MS: 'Balthasar Castiglione' cancelled.
[2] *imitated*: reading uncertain.
[3] *Annales*, I, 4.

and lifeless. The ancients carry us, as it were, into the very circumstances of the actors; we feel for them as if it were for ourselves. ⟨They* show us the feelings and agitations of mind in the actors previous to and during the event. They point to us, also, the effects and consequences of the event, not only in the . . .[1] change it made on the situation of the actors, but the manner of behaviour with which they supported them.⟩

One method which most modern historians and all the romance writers take to render their narration interesting is to keep the events in suspense. Whenever the story is beginning to point to the grand event, they turn to something else, and by this means get us to read through a number of dull nonsensical stories, our curiosity prompting us to get at the important event, ⟨as Ariosto in his *Orlando Furioso*.⟩ This method the ancients never made use of; they trusted not to the reader's curiosity alone, but relied on the importance of the facts and the interesting manner in which they related them. Livy, when he relates the affecting catastrophe of the Fabii[2] and the Battle of Cannae,[3] does not endeavour to conceal the event, but on the other hand gives us a plain intimation of what will be the event of those expeditions before they are related. ⟨In* cassum missae preces.[4]⟩ Yet this does not in the least diminish our concern on the relation, which, by the lively manner in which he has executed it, engages us as much as if it had been entirely unknown. This method has, besides, this advantage, that we can then with patience attend to the less important intervening accidents, which, if the great event had been entirely concealed, our curiosity would make us hurry over. We would count the pages we had to read to get to the event, as we generally do in a novel. ⟨Nay,* in some cases the warning has a very manifest and considerable advantage. Thus after being given to know that the generous attempt of the Fabii was to fail, we read every future circumstance and the progress of their expedition with a melancholy which is extremely pleasing. Livy seems almost to design to give warning of the event of his battles, as of Thrasymene[5] and Cannae.⟩

As newness is the only merit in a novel and curiosity the only motive which induces us to read them, the writers are necessitated to make use of this method to keep it up. Even the ancient poets, who had not reality on their side, never have recourse to this method. The importance of the narration, they trust, will keep us interested. Virgil in the beginning of the *Aeneid*, and Homer in both his heroic poems, inform us in the begin-

---

[1] The text here is illegible.  [2] Livy, II, 48-50.
[3] Livy, XXII, 43-9.  [4] Livy, II, 49, 8.  [5] Livy, XXII, 4-6.

ning of the chief events that are told in the whole poem. Even in tragedy, where it is reckoned an essential part to keep the plot in suspense, this is not so necessary as in romance. A tragedy can bear to be read again and again. Though the incidents be not new to us, they are new to the actors, and by this means interest us, as well as by their own importance.

⟨The* gradual and just development of the catastrophe constitutes a great beauty in any tragedy, yet it is not a necessary one, otherwise we could never with any pleasure hear or see acted a play for the second time: yet that pleasure often grows by repetition.⟩

Euripides[1] often in his Prologues, by means of a god or a ghost, makes us acquainted with the events and puts us on our guard, that we may be free to attend to the sentiment and action of each scene, some of which he has laboured greatly.

[1] It is perhaps worth noting how seldom Smith mentions the Greek and Roman dramatists, or quotes from them: yet these were his favourite reading in his later years, and he expressed to Professor Dalzel his pleasure at returning to the studies which had given him the greatest delight when he was young.

# 18

⟨THE* order in which I proposed to treat of historical composition was, first, to treat of the end; next, of the means of accomplishing that end, of the materials of history; next, of the arrangement of these materials; next, of the expression; and lastly, of those who have most excelled in this subject.⟩

The next thing in order that comes to be considered with regard to historical composition is the arrangement in which the several parts of the narration are to be placed. In general, the narration is to be carried on in the same order as that in which the events themselves happened. The mind naturally conceives that the facts happened in the order they are related, and when they are by this means suited to our natural conception, the notion we form of them is by that means rendered more distinct. This rule is quite evident, and accordingly few historians have trespassed against it.

But when several of the events that are to be related happened in different places at the same time, the difficulty in this case is to determine in what order they are to be related. The best method is to observe the connection of place; which is to relate those that happened in the same place for some considerable succession of time, without interrupting the thread of the narration by introducing those that happened in a different place. 'Tis in this manner that Herodotus, after having followed the course of events in one country to some remarkable era,[1] passes on to those that happened during a period nearly of the same length in another country, resuming afterwards the former by itself where he had left it off.

But though the connections of time and place are very strong, yet they are not to be so invariably observed as to supersede the observance of all others. There is another connection still more striking than any of the former: I mean that of cause and effect. There is no connection with which we are so much interested as this of cause and effect. We are not

[1] *era*: reading uncertain.

93

satisfied when we have a fact told us which we are at a loss to conceive what it was that brought it about. Now there is often such a connection betwixt the facts that have happened at different times in different countries, that the one cannot be explained distinct from the other. They would appear altogether unintelligible unless those which produced them were also understood. The difficulty of accommodating the explaining the causes that have produced the different events with the distinctness which is necessary to give one a clear notion of any one series of events, has led different authors into error in both the distinctness of events and the connection of causes with events. Diodorus[1] of Halicarnassus accuses[2] Thucydides of having adhered so much to the connection of time that the different events he relates to have happened in different places at the same time are so jumbled together that it is impossible to form a distinct notion of what passed in any one place. This observation of the Halicarnassian is not, perhaps, altogether just with regard to Thucydides. The history he writes is that of a war, and the events of one campaign in each place he narrates by themselves. This period is not so short but one may form a distinct enough notion of the events that happened in each place. The criticism may, however, serve to show what disadvantages would attend the writing of history with too close an attention to the connection of time. Had Thucydides chosen much shorter periods, as a month, which the compilers of the *History of Europe*, a work published some years ago, did, no one could form any conception of the events any more than from a chronological table.

Mr Rapin,[3] on the other hand, having adhered too much to the connection of place, has often rendered the causes of the events altogether obscure. In his account of the Saxon Heptarchy, he relates the whole affairs of each of these separate states by themselves, in one continued account from their first establishment till their subversion by the West Saxons. The transactions that pass in any of these are so connected with what passed at the same time or a little before in another part of

[1] *Sic.* An error for Dionysius.

[2] *The Three Literary Letters*, ed. Roberts, pp. 111-13. 'Thucydides keeps close to the chronological order, Herodotus to the natural grouping of events. Thucydides is found to be obscure and hard to follow. As naturally many events occur in different places in the course of the same summer or winter, he leaves half-finished his account of one set of affairs and takes other events in hand. Naturally we are puzzled, and follow the narrative impatiently, as our attention is distracted.' Cf. also his *On Thucydides*, ch. 9.

[3] Rapin, *L'Histoire d'Angleterre*, 8 vols, Hague 1724. English version, 2 vols, 1725-31, with notes by Tindal.

England, that one cannot perceive by what means they were brought about, unless he is before informed of what passed in the neighbouring states. So that one cannot form any notion of the history of any one of these till he has read through the whole several times, and that with no small attention. The same may be observed of his account of the disputes betwixt the people and King Charles the First, which for distinctness' sake, as he says, he relates in the same manner, and the obscurity and incoherence that follows it is still greater as the affairs are still more clearly connected. ⟨For* distinctness' sake, says he, I shall relate separately the affairs of the Bishops, of the Militia, and of the Earl of Strafford. These are accordingly so interwoven that to understand what is done in one of them we must know what is doing in the others.⟩

The best method, therefore, is to adhere to the succession of time, as long as it does not introduce an inconvenience from the want of connection, and that when there are a number of simultaneous events to be related, we should relate by themselves those that happened in each place, recapitulating under each those concerning the others, so far as it is necessary to keep up the connection betwixt the cause and the event, and place the former always in order before the latter.

I shall only observe two things farther with regard to the arrangement of the narration. The first is, that there is another way of keeping up the connection besides the two above-mentioned, that is, the poetical method, which connects the different facts by some slight circumstances which often had nothing in[1] the bringing about the series of the events, or by some relation that appears betwixt them. This is the method which Livy generally has made use of, and to such good purpose that he has never been condemned for want of connection. ⟨Thucydides,[2] on the other hand, never observes any sort of connection in the circumstances he brings in. Those mentioned in his description of the battle in the night[3] would do equally well in whatever order they were placed. Tacitus, describing the distress an army was in,[4] says: They were without tents and in want of bandages, etc.⟩

The second is that we should never leave any chasm or gap in the thread of the narration, even though there are no remarkable events to fill up that space. The very notion of a gap makes us uneasy for what

[1] i.e. 'nothing to do with' etc.
[2] MS 'Tacitus' cancelled, and 'Thucydides' superscribed.
[3] The attack on Epipolae referred to above, Thucydides, VII, 43-4.
[4] Tacitus, *Annales*, I, 65. Caecina's army retreating from Germany: *non tentoria manipulis, non fomenta sauciis.*

should have happened in that time. Tacitus is often guilty of this fault. He tells us that the army of Germanicus, being attacked in their camp, gained a great victory over the enemy. This is in the middle of Germany: and in the next sentence we find them across the Rhine, supported by the assiduity and care of Agrippina, when they were in the utmost hazard.[1]

I shall now proceed to make some observations on the manner in which the narration is to be expressed and the difference betwixt the didactic, oratorical, and historical style. An historian, as well as an orator, may excite our love or esteem for the persons he treats of: but then the methods they take are very different. The rhetorician will not barely set forth the character of a person as it really existed, but will magnify every particular that may tend to excite the strongest emotions in us. He will also seem to be deeply affected with that affection which he would have us feel towards any object. He will exclaim, for example, on the amiable character, the sweet temper and behaviour of the man towards whom he would have us feel those affections. The historian, on the contrary, can only excite our affection by the narration of the facts and setting them in as interesting a view as he possibly can. But all exclamations in his own person would not suit with the impartiality he is to maintain and the design he is to have in view, of narrating facts as they are, without magnifying them or diminishing them. An historian in the same way may excite grief or compassion, but only by narrating facts which excite those feelings; whereas the orator heightens every incident, and pretends at least, to be deeply affected by them himself, often exclaiming on the wretched condition of those he talks of, etc.[2]

Few historians accordingly have run in[to] this error. Tacitus, indeed, has an occasional exclamation in the latter part of his character of Agricola. The Elder Pliny, too, has several times been guilty of this foolish affectation, as it certainly is in him, who in other respects is a very grave author; and the more so on the subject he writes on, which is natural history, a subject which, though it may be very amusing, does not appear to be very animating. Besides these there is no historian who has used them, unless it be Valerius Maximus and Florus (if he deserves the name of a historian, who is full of them from the beginning to the end).

[1] Tacitus, *Annales*, I, 68-9.
[2] The student or the copyist has here added in small script 'I could almost say damn it.'

As the historian is not to make use of the oratorical style, so neither has he any occasion for the didactic. It is not his business to bring proofs for propositions, but to narrate facts. The only thing he can be under any necessity of proving is the events he relates. The best way in this case is not to set [out] a laboured and formal demonstration, but, barely mentioning the authorities on both sides, to show for what reason he had chosen to be of the one opinion rather than of the other. Long demonstrations, as they are no part of the historian's province, are seldom made use of by the ancients. The modern authors have often brought them in. Historical truths are now in much greater request than they ever were in the ancient time. One thing that has contributed to the increase of this curiosity is that there are now several sects in religious and political disputes which are greatly dependent on the truth of certain facts. This it is that has induced almost all historians for some time to be at great pains in the proof of those facts on which the claims of the parties they favoured depended. These proofs, however, besides that they are inconsistent with the historical style, are likewise of bad consequence, as they interrupt the thread of the narration, and that most commonly in the parts that are most interesting. They withdraw our attention from the main facts, and before we can get through them they have so far weaken[ed] our concern for the issue of the affair that was broke off, that we are never again so much interested in them.

⟨The* dissertations which are everywhere interwoven into modern histories contribute, among other things, and that not a little, to render them less interesting than those wrote by the ancients.[1] To avoid a dissertation about the truth of a fact, a historian might first relate the event according to the most likely opinion, and when he had done so, give the other by saying that such or such a circumstance had occasioned such or such a mistake, or that such a misrepresentation had been propagated by such a person for such ends. This would be making a fact of it. The truth and evidence of historical facts is now in much more request and more critically examined than amongst the ancients, because of all the numerous sects among us, whether civil or religious. There is hardly one the reasonableness of whose tenet does not depend on some historical fact.⟩

Besides, no fact that is called in question interests us so much or makes so lasting impression, as those of whose truth we are altogether

[1] Robertson, who placed his dissertations at the end of his text, may well have profited from Smith's advice.

97

satisfied. Now all proofs of this sort show that the matter is somewhat dubious: so that, on the whole, it would be more proper to narrate these facts, without mentioning the doubt, than to bring in any long proofs.

The same objections that have been mentioned against long demonstrations hold equally against reflections and observations that exceed the length of two or three sentences. If one was to point out to us some interesting spectacle, it would surely be very disagreeable, in the most engaging part, to interrupt us and tear our attention from it, by desiring us to attend to the fine contrivance of the parts of the object, or the admirable exactness with which the whole was carried on. We would be uneasy by being thus withdrawn from what we were so much concerned in. The historian who brings in long reflections acts precisely in the same manner: he withdraws us from the most interesting part of the narration, and in such interruptions we always imagine that we lose some part of the transaction. Though the narration is broken off, we cannot conceive that the action is interrupted. The short reflections and observations made use of by the Cardinal de Retz and by Tacitus are not liable to the same objections. Of these two, Tacitus had evidently the superiority: his observations do not stand out from the narration, but often appear to make a part of it; whereas those of the Cardinal, though not too long, are entirely separate from the narration.

⟨'I* saw', says the Cardinal, 'the whole extent of my danger, and I saw nothing but what was terrible. There is in great danger a certain charm',[1] etc.⟩

Speeches interspersed in the narration do not appear so faulty, though they be of considerable length, as long observations or rhetorical declamations. Their style, indeed, is altogether different from that of the historian, as they are oratorical compositions. But then, they are not in the author's own person, and therefore do not contradict the impartiality he is to maintain. Neither do they interrupt the thread of the narration, as they are not considered as the author's, but merely a part of the facts related. They give also an opportunity of introducing those observations and reflections which, we observed, are not so properly made in the person of the writer. Livy often makes this use of them. Thus he introduces his reflections on the hazard, the importance, and generosity of the undertaking of the Fabii, not in his own person, but by making the

[1] de Retz, *Mémoires* (Amsterdam 1731), vol. I, bk. II, p. 152: '*Les plus grands dangers ont leur charmes, pour peu que l'on apercoive de gloire dans la perspective de mauvais succès, les mediocres dangers n'ont que des horreurs quand la perte de la réputation est attachée à la mauvaise fortune.*

design the subject of debate in the Senate,[1] which also adds to the sentiments he would inspire us with.

The only objection, then, that can be made against the using speeches in this manner is, that though they be represented as facts, they are not genuine ones. But then neither does [the historian] desire you to consider them as such, but only as being brought in to illustrate the narration. . . .[2]

[1] Livy, II, 48.
[2] The student or copyist here adds 'Not a word more can I remember.'

# 19

HAVING in the preceding lectures given you an account of the principal things necessary to be observed in the writing of history, I proceed to the *History of Historians*.

The poets were the first historians of any. They recorded those accounts that were most apt to surprise and strike the imagination, such as the mythological history and adventures of their deities. We find accordingly all the most ancient writings were ballads or hymns in honour of their gods, recording the most amazing parts of their conduct. As their subject was the marvellous, so they naturally expressed themselves in the language of wonder, that is, in poetry, for in that style amazement and surprise naturally break forth. Of the actions of men, again, military exploits would be the first[1] subject of the poets, as they are most fraught with adventures that are fit to amaze and gratify the desire men have, especially in the early period, for what is marvellous. Homer accordingly has recorded the most remarkable war that his countrymen had been engaged in before those days. All the other poets he mentions, for he mentions no writers but what were poets, had also followed the same plan: they related the most surprising adventures and warlike exploits of the great men in or before their time. In all countries we find poetry has been the first species of writing, as the marvellous is that which first draws the attention of unimproved men. The oldest original writings in Latin, Italian, French, English, and Scots, are all poets. There are, indeed, other writings perhaps as old as any of these poems, that are wrote in prose; but these are only monkish legends or others of that sort, which, as they are wrote in a foreign language, and in a different way from that naturally [*sic*] to the country, are evidently copied from the works of authors of another country. ⟨and* are not to be numbered in the productions of that country.⟩

The next species of historians were poets in every respect except the form of the language. Their language was prose, but their subjects alto-

[1] MS reads: 'military exploits as they would be the first'.

gether poetical. Furies, harpies, animals half-man and half-bird, or snake, centaurs, and others half-fish and half-man, that were bred in Tartarus and swam about in the sea; the intercourse of gods with women, and goddesses with men, and the heroes that sprang from them, and their exploits, were the subject of their works, according to Dionys[ius] of Halic[arnassus]. When one reads his account it will immediately put him in mind of the Geoffrey of Monmouth and the other earlier writers, their elves and fairies, dragons, griffins, and other monsters, with the accounts of which the greatest part of their books were [sic] filled. These are creatures of an imagination engendered by the terror and superstitious fear which is always found in the ruder state of mankind. Those writers that followed this method amongst the ancients confined their accounts to the memorable stories of some one country or province, and in the same manner the monkish legends are confined to one town or perhaps one monastery.

The first author who formed the design of extending the plan of history was Herodotus. He chose for this reason a period of two hundred and forty years before his time, and comprehends the history, not only of other foreign states, but also of all the barbarous nations. Those he has connected together in such an easy and natural manner as to leave no gap nor chasm in his narration. The style is graceful and easy; his narration crowded with memorable facts, and those the most extraordinary that happened in each country. He does not, however, confine himself to those that produced any memorable change or alteration in each country, but chooses out whatever is most agreeable. He has not near so many of those fabulous and marvellous accounts as we are told the authors who preceded him had; but then he has still a good number scattered in his work. His design, indeed, seems to have been rather to amuse than to instruct. This is confirmed by the long period he has chosen, and the wide tract of country which he has made the subjects of his history. By this means his facts could be more easily rendered amusing, and he has accordingly picked from the history of each country those which are most entertaining, whether they are of importance or not. We can learn from him rather the customs of the different nations and the series of events, than any account of the internal government, or the causes that brought about the events he relates: but in this way, too, we may learn a great deal.

History continued in the same state as Herodotus left it till Thucydides undertook a history of the Peloponnesian War. His design was different from that of former historians, and was that which is a proper design of historical writing. He tells us that he undertook that work that by recording in the truest manner the various incidents of that war, and the causes that produced [it], posterity may learn how to produce the like events or shun others, and know what is to be expected from such and such circumstances. In this design he has succeeded better perhaps than any preceding or succeeding writer. His style is strong and nervous, his narration crowded with the most important events. The subject of his work is the history of a war, which he relates in the distinctest manner, giving the history of each campaign by itself, so as that we have a complete notion of the progress of the war in each place. He never introduces any circumstances that do not some way contribute to the producing some remarkable change in the affairs of the two contending states. This is a fault most other historians are often guilty of. Tacitus and many others introduce all those circumstances which give them an opportunity of displaying their eloquence. Thus Tacitus, in one place,[1] stops short to describe a temple Titus happened to visit, and in another[2] the particular circumstances of the disorder in Verres'[3] army. The only place where Thucydides is guilty of it is in describing the concern of the soldiers at the recall of a favourite general, and for this, too, he makes an apology, acknowledging that such matters are not the subject of a history.[4] The events are all chosen so as to be of consequence to the narrations, and in his account of them he abundantly satisfies his design, accounting for every event by the external causes that produced [it], pointing out what circumstances of time, place, etc, in the side of either party determined the success of the enterprise they were engaged in. His narration is by this means very crowded; and though perhaps it is not so amusing as that of Herodotus, yet, as he himself says,[5] one who desires to know the truth, and the causes of the different success of the war, will be pleased with it. He gives a good deal more of the political and civil history of the two states engaged in the war than Herodotus, but neither does he seem to have had it much in his view. ⟨He renders his narration at the same time interesting by the internal effects the events produced, as in that before mentioned of the battle in the night, and also by the great number of speeches he introduces into his works,

[1] *Historiae*, II, 2-4.

[2] *Annales*, I, 61. Tacitus describes the weapons, bones, etc. at the scene of Varus's disaster, and which were still to be seen when Germanicus visited it six years later.

[3] *Sic*. An error for 'Varus's'.

[4] I have not found the reference.          [5] Thucydides. I, 22, 4.

and by which he opens up the different circumstances of the affairs at each time.⟩

⟨Thucydides* is the first who pays any attention at all to civil history: all who preceded him attached themselves merely to the military.⟩

The next author we come to is Xenophon. His style is easy and agreeable, not as strong as that of Thucydides, but perhaps more pleasant. Nor is [his] narration so crowded, as he often condescends to intermix circumstances that do not lend much to the chief events in the history, His *Retreat of the Ten Thousand Grecians* is commonly compared to Cæsar's *Commentaries*, as they are the accounts of the conduct of two generals wrote by themselves without the least ostentation. In this point, indeed, they bear a great resemblance, but in other matters they differ very widely. The plainness of Xenophon is very different from that of Cæsar, and displays an ingenuity and openness of heart that does not appear in the writings of the other. Cæsar's style is constantly crowded; he hurries from one fact of importance to another, without touching on anything that is not of importance betwixt them. It is not easy to convey a notion of Xenophon's beauties. There are no passages which taken by themselves could show his manner, and his peculiar excellences. ⟨He uses but a few circumstances in comparison of Thucydides in his descriptions. The precedent is always so much connected with every passage that we cannot enter into the beauties of any passage unless we are acquainted with the precedent.⟩ He must be read through to perceive his beauties and enter into his manner. In his *Expedition of Cyrus* he is at pains in all the circumstances of the narration, which would otherwise often have been of little consequence, tended [*sic*] to conciliate the affections of the soldiers to their commander, and by this means he engages us so much in his favour, that we are not less affected by the description he gives of the fate of the battle, though it be very plain and void of ornament, than we would have been by one of the most interesting of those drawn by Thucydides, with all the circumstances he brings in of the effect the events had on the actors, both in the action and afterwards. By thus drawing us gradually on, he becomes one of the most engaging, though not one of the most passionate and interesting, of authors. He does not raise those violent emotions that Thucydides does, but he pleases and engages fully as much. ⟨To speak in the painter's style, though neither the lines nor the colouring or expression be very strong, yet the ordonnance of the piece is such that it is on the whole very engaging and attractive.⟩ It is evident from this that no one passage can make us acquainted with his beauties.

On the other hand there are many passages in Cæsar which will give us a complete notion of his manner and his beauties. As all the events he describes are important, he is often induced to describe them in a striking and interesting manner.

Xenophon, too, has given us several descriptions of characters in his works, not indeed of set purpose, but by the circumstances he mentions, of the persons that occur in the course of his history. This he does particularly in his treatise of the Grecian affairs,[1] in which he takes up the history where Thucydides left it off, and by this means he gives us more insight into [the] political affairs of Greece than the fore-mentioned historians do.

The first writer, however, who enters into the civil history of the nations he treats of, is Polybius. This author, though inferior to Herodotus in grace, and to Thucydides in strength, and Xenophon in sweetness, and though his manner be not very interesting, yet by the distinctness and accuracy with which he has related a series of events, which would by their importance have been interesting though handled by a less able author, as well as by the view he has given us of the civil constitution of the Romans, is considered not only instructing but agreeable. Dio.[2]

Of all the Latin historians, Livy is without doubt the best; and if to be agreeable were the chief view of an author, he would merit the chief rank amongst the whole number. He does not, indeed, enter deeply into the causes of things in the same manner as the Greek historians do; but on the other he renders his descriptions extremely interesting by the great number of affecting circumstances he has thrown together, and that not without any connection, as is the method of Thucydides, but in an order natural to the times in which they happened and the circumstances themselves. The circumstances mentioned in the night battle are narrated in such a manner as if they had all happened at the same time; but those Livy relates in the confusion at Rome after the battle of [blank][3] are all related in the order they must have succeeded.

⟨But that which is the peculiar excellence of Livy's style is the grandeur and majesty which he maintains through the whole of his

[1] i.e. *Hellenica*.

[2] The letters 'Dio' are followed by a blank of half a page. Smith may have commented on Diodorus Siculus or Dion Cassius.

[3] Cannae. Livy, XXII, 54.

works, and in which he excels all other historians, though perhaps he is inferior in many other respects. 'Tis probably to keep up this gravity that he pays so much attention to the ceremonies of religion, and the omens and portents, which he never omits. For it is not to be supposed that he had any belief in them himself, in an age when the vulgar religion was altogether disregarded, except as a political institution, by the wiser sort. And of this he gives a hint in. . . .⟩

Livy is generally accused of being very inaccurate in his accounts of military affairs, but I imagine he is not so faulty in this respect as the common fame reports. He gives us, too, a very good account of the Roman constitution, not indeed so particular as that of the Halicarnass-ian,[1] but there is enough through the work to make us tolerably acquainted with it. It is to be considered, too, that Livy wrote for Romans, to whom it would have been impertinent to give a minute account of their own customs, whereas Dion[ysius] of Halicarn[assus] wrote for Greeks unacquainted with these matters.

Livy is compared[2] by Quintilian[3] with Herodotus, and Sallust with Thucydides. But Livy without question far excels Herodotus, and Sallust on the other hand falls no less short of Thucydides. He resembles him, indeed, in the conciseness of his manner and the suddenness of his transitions: but then he has neither his strength nor his accuracy. Nor is narration so crowded in the Catiline conspiracy (induced perhaps by the subject, which furnished him with no very wide field): he has thrown [in] several digressions of considerable length, very little connected with the subject. In both[4] the works that are now remaining he is very defec-tive in his descriptions: his circumstances are often so far from being adapted to the matter in hand that they are what we may call common-place, and such as would do equally well in any account of the same nature, though the state of the affairs were considerably different. His description of the battle with Jugurtha[5] would in almost all the circum-stances suit equally any other battle; it signifies indeed nothing more than that there was a great confusion. Thucydides, in his description of the night battle, though he represents nothing more than the confusion, yet it is such a confusion as in no other place, nor in no other condition,

---

[1] Of the twenty-two books of the History of Rome to 264 B.C., written by Dionysius of Halicarnassus, only the first nine, the greater parts of ten and eleven, and fragments of the others, have survived.

[2] MS has 'Generally' cancelled, as though the scribe's eye had caught the begin-ning of the previous paragraph.     [3] Quintilian, X, 1, 101.

[4] i.e. Sallust's *Catilina* and *Jugurtha*.     [5] Possibly *Jugurtha*, 97-9.

K

could possibly have happened. That described by Sallust is such as happens in every battle. In the same way the circumstances by which he represents[1] the luxury of the Romans and their depraved morals are such as attend the luxury in every country. But those by which Thucydides points out[2] the effects of s[edition[3]] in Greece are such as no other sort of sedition, no other state of a country, could have occasioned. Besides this, his conciseness, which it is plain he copied from Thucy[dides], is rather apparent than real. For though his sentences are always very short, yet the one signifies nothing more than was implied by the former, and in the following one. In the description of the battle above-mentioned, the first sentence[4] implies all the following ones. He supports, however, his narration by the aptness of his expression, in which perhaps he surpasses all the other historians, and by the variety of his speeches, which, as well as those of Thucydides, shall be considered when we come to Delib[erative] Eloquence. But from his descriptions one would imagine that he had inquired rather into the events, than into the different circumstances, with any accuracy. And as by this means he was necessitated to contrive incidents, he would naturally fall upon commonplace ones, such as would occur in every affair of the same sort.

[1] *Catilina*, chs. 1-13.    [2] *Thucydides*, III, 82-3.
[3] *sedition*: doubtful supplement. Could 'stasis' be intended?
[4] Possibly Smith is thinking of part of *Jugurtha*, 97, 5: *pugna latrocinio magis quam proelio similis fieri, sine signis, sine ordinibus equites peditesque permixti cedere alii, alii obtruncari, multi contra advorsos acerrume pugnantes ab tergo circumveniri.*

# 20

Wednesday, 12 January 1763

THE first historians as well as the first poets chose the marvellous for their subject, as that which was most likely to please a rude and ignorant people. Wonder is the passion which in such a people will be most easily excited. Their ignorance renders them credulous and easily imposed on, and this credulity makes them delighted with fables that would not be relished by a people of more knowledge. When, therefore, knowledge was improved, and men were so far enlightened as to give little credit to those fabulous relations which had been the entertainment of their forefathers, the writers would find themselves obliged to take some other subject. For what has nothing to recommend it but its wonderfulness can no longer please than it is believed: in the same way as we now see that the stories of witches and fairies are swallowed greedily by the ignorant vulgar, which are despised by the more knowing. As the marvellous could no longer please, authors had recourse to that which they imagine[d] would please and interest most: that is, to represent such actions and passions as, being affecting in themselves, or displaying the delicate feelings of the human heart, were likely to be most interesting. Thus it was that tragedy succeeded the fabulous accounts of heroes and centaurs and different monsters, the subject of the first romances, and thus also novels, which unfold the tender emotions or more violent passions in the characters they bring before us, succeeded the wild and extravagant romances which were the first performances of our ancestors in Europe.

The historians, again, made it their aim not only to amuse, but by narrating the more important facts, and those which were most concerned in the bringing about great revolutions, and unfolding their causes, to instruct their readers in what manner such events might be brought about or avoided. In this state it was that Tacitus found historical writing. He departed altogether from the plan of the former historians, and formed one of a very different sort for his own writings. He had observed that those passages of the historians were most interesting

107

which unfolded the effects the events related produced on the minds of the actors or spectators of those. He imagined, therefore, that if one could write a history consisting entirely of such events as were capable of interesting the minds of the readers by accounts of the effects they produced or were of themselves capable of producing their effect on the reader.[1] If we consider the state of the Romans at the time Tacitus wrote, and the dispositions of the people which it must necessarily occasion, we will find this plan of Tacitus to be a very natural one. The Roman nation [was], in the reign of Trajan, arrived to its greatest pitch of glory. The people enjoyed greater internal tranquillity and security than they had done in any of the former reigns, or indeed, in the last 150 [sc. years] of the Republic. Luxury and refinement of manners, the natural consequences of the former, were then as far advanced as they could be in any state.[2] Sentiment must be what will chiefly interest such a people. They who live in a great city where they have the free liberty of disposing of their wealth in all the luxuries and refinements of life, who are not called to any public employment but what they inclined and obtained from the favour and indulgence of the prince—such a people, I say, having nothing to engage them in the hurry of life, would naturally turn their attention to the motions of the human mind, and those events that were accounted for by the different internal affections that influenced the persons concerned would be what most suited their taste. The French monarchy is in much the same condition as the Romans under Trajan, and we find accordingly that those writers who have studied to be most agreeable have made great use of sentiment, ⟨This* is that in which the works of Marivaux and the younger Crebillon do excel.⟩ Marivaux and [blank[3]] resemble Tacitus as much as we can well imagine in works of so contrary a nature. They are always at great pains to account for every event by the temper and internal disposition of the several actors, in disquisitions that approach near to metaphysical ones.

We will find Tacitus has executed his works in a manner most suitable to this design. We shall consider chiefly his *Annals*, as it is in them that the character of Tacitus chiefly appears. We are told that his *History* was that which appeared first; perhaps he might have chosen to try first

[1] In the MS the words 'of themselves . . . reader' are cancelled.
[2] Trajan ruled A.D. 98-117; cf. Gibbon, *Decline and Fall*: 'If a man were called to fix the period in the history of the world during which the condition of the human race was most happy and prosperous, he would, without hesitation, name that which elapsed from the death of Domitian [A.D. 96] to the accession of Commodus' (ch. 3, *ad fin.*).
[3] Perhaps Crébillon was intended.

how a work would be relished in which his favourite plan was somewhat tempered with the usual manner of writing, before he would risk one where he kept in view entirely the notion he had conceived of the beauty of writing.

The period of time that makes the subjects of both these works contains no remarkable revolutions: the only two of any consequence that happened in that time, viz. the assassination of ⟨Caligula*⟩ and the expulsion of ⟨Nero*⟩, have not come down to our time, nor were these of a duration sufficient to fill a book or two. None, almost, of the events he relates, tended to produce any great change in the state of public affairs. He conjectured, however, and I believe justly, that the incidents of private life, though not so important, would affect us more deeply and interest us more than those of a public nature. The murder of Agrippina[1] and death of Germanicus' sons,[2] will perhaps affect us more than the description of the battle in the night by Thucydides. In private calamities one's passions are fixed on one, as it were concentrated, and so become greatly stronger than when separated and distracted by the affecting circumstances that befell the several persons involved in a common calamity. He describes all events rather by the internal effects, and accounts for them in the same manner, and where he has an opportunity of displaying his talents in these respects and affecting our passions, he is not greatly concerned whether the events be important or not. Thus he gives us a full description of the storms that attacked [blank][3] fleet,[4] the sedition of the German legions,[5] and the burial of Varus' soldiers by Germanicus,[6] although in the first there was but a ship or two lost, the second was no more but a mob, and the third was still less important than either of the former. Yet the method he describes these is so interesting, he leads us so far into the sentiments and minds of the actors, that they are some of the most striking and interesting passages to be met with in any history. In describing the more important actions he does not give us an account of their external causes, but only of the internal ones; and though this perhaps will not tend so much to instruct us in the knowledge of the causes of events, yet it will be more interesting and lead us into a science no less useful, to wit, the knowledge of the motives by which men act—a science, too, that could not be learned from. . . .[7]

[1] *Annales*, XIV, 1-13.
[2] Death of Drusus, *Annales*, VI, 23-4. Nero's death was described in the lost portion of the *Annales*, Bk. V.         [3] 'Germanicus's'.
[4] *Annales*, II, 23-4.         [5] *Ibid.* I, 31-49.
[6] *Ibid.* I, 61-2.       [7] After this word, a lacuna of two or three lines.

The events[1] he relates, as they are of a private nature, as the intrigues of ministers, the deaths or advancement of particular men, so they are not connected together by any strong tie, such as is necessary in the links of a history of the common sort, where the connections of one event with another must be clearly pointed out. But here they are thrown together without any connection, unless perhaps that they happened at the same time.

The reflections he makes on the different events are [rather] such as we might call observations on the conduct of the men than any general maxims deduced from particular instances, such as those of [blank].

In his *History* he gives us indeed some more insight into the causes of events, and keeps up a continued series of events: but even here he so far neglects connection as to pass over entirely those connecting circumstances that tend to no other purpose. Of this we saw an instance already in the retreat of the army of Caecina, after they had defeated the Germans.[2] The circumstances which intervened betwixt that defeat and the crossing of the Rhine were probably such as would have afforded no room for those descriptions or affecting narrations in which he thought the chief beauty of writing consisted.

⟨Such is the true character of Tacitus, which has been misrepresented by all his commentators, from Boccalini[3] down to Gordon.⟩

Machiavelli and Guicciardini are the two most famous modern Italian historians. The former seems to have had it chiefly in his view to prove certain maxims which he had laid down, as the impoliticness of keeping up a standing army, . . .[4] and others of the same sort, generally contradictory to the received politics of the times. The different courts of Italy at that time piqued themselves greatly on a refined and subtle politics. Nothing could then be a greater reproach to a man of genius than that he was of an open and undesigning character. But these politics he seems to have altogether despised, and has therefore given little attention to them, or represented them as of no great moment. He is to be commended above most modern writers on one account, as he does not seem to favour any one party more than another, and therefore is generally very candid in his relation ⟨which is the scheme of Lord Clarendon and Bishop Burnet.⟩

⟨Machiavelli* is of all modern historians the only one who has con-

---

[1] In the margin of the MS is a design of dots, 'doodled', and the words 'this is a picture of uncertainty'.     [2] *Ibid.* I, 63-8.

[3] MS has 'Machiavell' cancelled.     [4] A lacuna here of one line.

tented himself with that which is the chief purpose of history, to relate events and connect them with their causes, without becoming a party on either side.⟩

Guicciardini, on the other hand, seems as much to have esteemed the politics then in fashion as Machiavelli despised them, and is therefore at great pains to explain the schemes that brought about the several events of importance. In his account of his own country, Florence, he often dwells on particulars of very little moment, which makes Boccalini in his *Advices from Parnassus* cause Apollo [to] condemn [a learned Laconic] to read his account of the disputes betwixt Florence and Pisa, which he receives as a very hard task.[1]

⟨His* whole history is a critical dissertation on the schemes, and little—and often crooked—artifice of the times.⟩

Clarendon and Burnet are the two English authors who signalized themselves chiefly in writing history. As the thing he [*sc.* Clarendon] had in view was to represent the bad disposition of the one party, and justify the conduct of the other, so it is not those events which were of the greatest importance, and tended most to produce a memorable change, on which he insists, but such as tend most to unfold the dispositions of the different parties. In this manner it is that he dismisses in two or three sentences all the actions of Montrose in Scotland,[2] though of the greatest importance, and on the other hand relates at length[3] the whole proceeding of one of the Keepers of the Great Seal, Lord Lyttleton's flight to the King, though it produced nothing but a new Seal and a new Keeper, and to protest which[4] he was at the pains to tell us at full length. For the same reason it is that he is [at] such pains in describing characters, not to explain the transaction, but to display the characters of the parties by showing that of individuals; and for this reason there is hardly a footman brings a message but what he gives an account of his

---

[1] *Ragguagli di Parnaso*, first printed in 1612. Smith would appear to use the title of the English translation of 1705. Advice VI, p. 14, reads (in part): 'There was an unfortunate Laconic it seems, who spun out into three words a thought, which in the judgment of the Laconic Senate might have been fairly comprised in two. For which capital crime . . . the sentence was that he should read over Guicciardini's War of Pisa. But the very first leaf put the poor wretch into such a deadly sweat that away he ran immediately and threw himself at the feet of his judges, imploring them for the love of mercy to send him to the galleys for the rest of his days, shut him in a stinking dungeon, or flay him alive—anything, in short, but Guicciardini, and he could support it;' etc.

[2] Cf. Clarendon, *History* (Macray's ed.). Bks. VIII and IX.

[3] Clarendon, Bk. V, 203-14

[4] *which*: reading uncertain.

character. By crowding in so many trifling circumstances he has stretched the history of ten years, at most, to the size of three folio volumes.

Burnet again delivers his narration not as a complete history of the time, but only as an account of those facts that had come to his knowledge. His business plainly appears to have been to set the one party in as black a light as he could, and justify the other; so that he is to be considered rather as a party writer than as a candid historian. His manner is lively and spirited; his style very plain; but his language and expression is low, and such as we would expect from an old nurse, rather than from a gentleman. It has been the fate of all modern histories to be wrote in a party spirit, for reasons already mentioned.

Rapin[1] seems to be the most candid of all those who have wrote on the affairs of England.[2] Yet he has entered too much into the private affairs of the monarchs and the parties amongst the several great men concerned, so that his history, as many others, is rather an account of the lives of the princes than of the affairs of the body of the people.

[1] Rapin, *L'Histoire d'Angleterre*, see above, p. 94, *n.* 3.
[2] The MS has a marginal note: '10 years ago. A better now'. The first volume of Hume's *History* appeared in 1754; the last in 1761.

# 21

N.B. This lecture was delivered entirely without book.[1]

I HAVE now finished what I have to say with regard to the first species of writing, viz. the narrative, where the business is to relate facts, and come in the next place to treat of that where the design is to prove some proposition or series of propositions. The rules we have already given with regard to narrative composition will, with a few alterations, be easily accommodated to this species also.

We may observe, also, that the same rules will also be equally applicable to poetical compositions. For what it is that constitutes the essential difference betwixt a historical poem and a history? It is no more than this, that the one is in prose, and the other in verse. For what is it that induces one to write in verse rather than in prose? What is his design? It is certainly far more difficult, but at the same time it is much superior in beauty and strength. It is evident, therefore, that the author's design in writing is to amuse us. The way in which he writes is of all others best calculated to answer this end. ⟨There are many authors besides the poets who have made it their chief design to please, but they are the only writers who by the very manner in which they write fairly tell us that this is their design.⟩ The best prose composition, the best oratorical discourse, does not affect us half so much. An orator will often tell us the same thing in many shapes. If we should examine the best orations, we will find that the second, third, and fourth sentences often contain nothing more than is contained in the first, only turned into other words: whereas none but the lower class [of poems] have such repetitions. It is even necessary for an orator to do this, if he expects that the argument should have its full force. Some repetition is often absolutely necessary to make us affected in the manner the orator desires. But on the other

---

[1] The presence of this note, in the first hand, would seem to suggest that this lecture, at least, had been copied from another MS. Such a note would normally come at the end of a lecture, or would be written in the margin or in a cramped way under the heading, as an afterthought. In the MS space would seem to have been allowed for it.

hand repetition is so far from being necessary, that anyone who is the least acquainted with poetry, either by writing or reading, knows there is nothing more disagreeable than to have the next line in the next couplet express in other words the same thing that has been already expressed in the one before us. Mr Pope tells us that the reason which induced him to write his *Essay on Man* in verse rather than in prose was that he saw he could do it in a much shorter and concise manner.[1] I much doubt, indeed, whether this was his real motive, but it shows he was very sensible of the great superiority of poetry over prose in this respect. I mentioned this particular of the great conciseness of poetry, not that it is one of the chief of its beauties, but as it may prove the great advantage of poetical measures, and the great effect harmony and regular movement has on us, when it commands our attention so much that we are never necessitated to repeat the same thing over a second time. ⟨It is needless to prove the superiority of poetry over prose: everyone's experience and the common consent of mankind sufficiently confirm this.⟩ One expression in this manner has more effect on us than when the orator turns it in three or four different shapes.

The manner, however, as it is so vastly more difficult than prose writing, shows sufficiently that amusement and entertainment was the chief design of the poet. It is from our being satisfied that this is the design of poetry that what we call poetical licence has taken its origin.

There are some men who distinguish themselves chiefly in conversation by a certain knack of telling a story. They plainly show by their manner and the way in which they tell it that it is not their design to be believed. They do not care in the least whether they are or not; all they seem to have in view is to divert us by some ridiculous story. As we perceive that this is their design, we are not very anxious whether the story be just as they tell it or not. We give them the liberty to add to or take from the story what they think proper, to cut and carve as they please. For there is no story so completely of one sort that every circumstance tends to produce the same effect. There is no story, no adventure, so entirely ridiculous, that there is not some part of it of a grave nature; there is none so melancholy but what there is some part of it is prosper-

---

[1] Pope, *Essay on Man*, Preface: 'I chose verse, and even rhyme, for two reasons. The one will appear obvious; that principles, maxims, or precepts so written, both strike the reader more strongly at first, and are more easily retained afterwards: the other may seem odd, but it is true; I found I could express them more shortly this way than in prose itself; and nothing is more certain than that much of the force as well as grace of arguments or instructions depends on their conciseness.'

114

ous, nor any so prosperous that is not somewhat tinctured with adversity. Now as we are sensible of this, we are not offended though the teller of ridiculous stories—a talent which, though it be no very eminent one, is generally well received—should throw out those circumstances which would tend to diminish the ridicule of the rest, or add those which would heighten it. Nay, we can even allow him to make up a story altogether, but this seldom takes so well. ⟨Now* if we would make the story perfectly and completely ridiculous or melancholy or merry, we must leave out those jarring and dissimilar circumstances.⟩ There are also tellers of wonderful stories, and tellers of mournful, lamentable ones. These as well as the others are often obliged to add [to] or take away from their story, as they can seldom get one that will prove so very wonderful or so very lamentable that there is nothing in it that appears little, or at least of an ordinary nature. Now these are altogether disagreeable: we know that these stories are forged, and yet they tell them with a grave face and appear evidently to desire that we should believe them. There are even some who take pains to tell ill-natured stories, and turn a thing of a very harmless nature into a very black and shocking one: these deserve no quarter, though they are often well received. The wonder teller and the teller of lamentable stories are always despised. It is only the teller of ridiculous stories that can be at all tolerable in conversation: as we know his design is harmless, so we are readily inclined to grant him some licence.

The poet is exactly in the same condition. His design is to entertain, and he does not pretend that what he tells us is true; for which reason we are not offended if he makes some additions to the story he relates. But not only are ridiculous stories allowable in poetry, but also the wonderful and lamentable. The teller of wonderful or lamentable stories is disagreeable because he endeavours to pawn them upon us for true ones. But as this is not the case of the poet, we can receive not only the ridiculous ones, but the others also. The subjects are generally so distant that we are not offended at the poet if he embellishes his story with the addition of some circumstances. The taking of Troy, the foundation of the Roman Empire, or the life of Henry the Fourth of France[1] are not so much connected with us as to make us much concerned in what way they are represented. For we do not read Homer to be instructed in the events of the Trojan war, nor Virgil to know ⟨the origin of the Romans⟩,[2]

---

[1] Voltaire, *La Henriade*, in 10 cantos (1723).
[2] The MS has 'the particulars of the voyage of Æneas' cancelled.

nor Milton to be informed on the scriptural account of the Fall of Adam —though indeed most of the particulars be brought into it, yet none reads it to increase his faith. But as it is entertainment we look for from the poet as well as the story-teller, so we make them the same concessions: as we know that no story is so completely ridiculous as to tell well without some cobbling, so we know that no series of adventures are so entirely of a piece, either so wonderful and extraordinary, or so lamentable, or so absurd, that they could completely answer the design of a poet without some improvement. We therefore allow the tragic writer whose subject is the lamentable, the comic writer who has pitched on the ridiculous and absurd for his subject, and the epic poet who endeavours to interest us by a series of grand and extraordinary events, each to model his story (or even sometimes to invent one), so as to make it all suitable to this end. ⟨Dramatic* and epic poetry differ only in the connection of the scenes of action they exhibit: in the former the persons come on themselves, in the latter the connections are made in the person of the poet. He says 'such and such a person came in and said so and so, or did so and so, and then came another and said and did so and so'.⟩

From hence we may see that there is one requisite absolutely necessary both to epic and dramatic writing, that is, unity of interest. The greatest of critics have laboured to show in what it is that this requisite consists; but if we attend to it we will find that it is very easily comprehended, and what we meet with in every common story. It is no more than this: that every part of the story should tend to some one end, whatever that be. This we find in every nurse's tale. Every story of a king and queen, of the fairies, ghosts, and suchlike, have [sic] a regular beginning, a middle, and an end. There is one point which all the rest tend to bring about, and in which they are wound up and the story entirely concluded. This we find in them all, whether they be of a gay or grave, of a happy or joyous, or of a miserable nature. It may, indeed, be easier in them because they are shorter, but is certainly attainable by all. In the same manner as a story-teller would appear to have failed in his design of raising our laughter, or at least he could not answer it so well, if he should bring in any [thing] of a grave and serious nature, so it is necessary that the poet should accommodate all his circumstances so as that they tend to bring about the main event either directly or indirectly. A comic writer should make all the parts tend to excite our sense of ridicule, and at last conclude the work with the highest piece of ridicule which all the rest pointed at or tended some way to bring about.

The tragic writer must in the same manner make all the parts of the action of a lamentable nature, or some way tend to bring about the great catastrophe; and so of the epic writer. But it is to be observed that in comic writings the ridicule must consist in the characters represented: ridicule that is founded only on the ridiculousness of the circumstances into which the persons are brought, without regarding themselves, is the lowest species of wit, and such as is hardly tolerable in a common story. On the other hand, in tragedy or epic poetry the chief art does not consist in displaying the characters, but in showing in what manner the chief persons in whom we are chiefly concerned acted in lamentable or difficult circumstances, and how at last they were either, in the first, altogether oppressed by their misfortunes, or extricated themselves from them. The unity in comedy consists in the characters; whereas in tragedy or epic poetry it consists chiefly in managing the circumstances. But in no part should anything appear to have a contrary tendency to that of the whole piece. For this reason the scene [blank] on [blank] and the scene of the gravediggers in *Hamlet*, though very good scenes in their sort, had better been away, as they have no share in bringing about the main design of the piece, and are somewhat contrary to the temper of the rest of the scenes.

We may see from this that tragi-comedy, though the different parts be very well executed, and may be very interesting, is yet a monstrous production. Thus in the *Spanish Friar*[1] the tragical part is very good, and the comic part is admirable, so that the whole is no bad piece: but the parts had been much better taken separate; the effect of the one would not have contradicted that of the other.

There is another species of unity, viz. the unity of Time, which the more severe critics, though it is not necessary in the epic poetry, account indispensably requisite in dramatic writing, both tragedy and comedy. Now let us consider in what the difference betwixt tragedy and epic writing consists. It is no more than that in the one case the persons come on the stage and speak their parts, and in the other the poet tells us that after one had spoke so and so, another spoke after him. Homer tells us that a captain spoke to such a company in one way, left them, and spoke to another, and did such and such actions. Sophocles would, on the other hand, put these speeches in the mouths of the persons themselves, and represent the actions as then passing before us. But from this difference it must necessarily follow that the one must be vastly shorter

[1] By Dryden, 1681.

117

than the other. As the one is carried on by dialogue, the connection betwixt two parts can only be kept up by the changing of the persons; whereas in the other the poet can, in a few words, in his own person, keep up the connection. The actions of a year would take up a year to represent them; but a poet can dispatch them in two or three words.

Shakespeare and some other English writers have been chiefly guilty of omitting this; the French are generally very little. Racine never supposes more time to have been taken up in the actions than in the representations. Shakespeare, on the other hand, supposes often that three or four years have elapsed betwixt one scene and another. The reason generally given for the bad effect of such blanks, where no actions connecting them are represented, is that it prevents our deception. We cannot suppose that when we have been but half of an hour in the playhouse that two or three years has passed. But in reality we are never thus deceived.[1] We know that we are in the playhouse, that the persons before us are actors, and that the thing represented either happened before, or perhaps never happened at all. The pleasure we have in a dramatical performance no more rises from deception than that which [we] have in looking at pictures. No one ever imagined that he saw the sacrifice of Iphigenia; no more did any one imagine that he saw King Richard the Third. Everyone knows that at the one time he saw a picture and at the other Mr Garrick, or some other actor. 'Tis not, then, from the interruption of deception that the bad effect[s] of such transgressions of the unity of time proceed: 'tis rather from the uneasiness we feel in being kept in the dark with regard to what happened in so long a time. When, in the scene before us, there is supposed to have passed three or four years since the last was before us, we immediately become uneasy to know what has happened during that time. Many important events must have happened in that time [of] which we know nothing. We make a jump from one time to another, without knowing what connected them. The same jump is often made in epic poets; but then they take care to smooth it over by telling us in a few words what happened in that time. Was this small[2] connection omitted, the jump would be as uneasy in the epic poem as the dramatical performance. ⟨Le* Brun⟩ has represented the different actions of Mary of Medicis, [blank] the of [blank][3] and

---

[1] Cf. Johnson, *Preface to Shakespeare* (1765): 'The truth is, that the spectators are always in their senses, and know, from the first act to the last, that the stage is only a stage, and that the players are only players' (*Johnson on Shakespeare*, ed. Raleigh, 1908, p. 27).     [2] *small*: reading uncertain.
[3] This is the order of the blanks in the MS.

other painters have represented the different transactions of the heroic poem. This is surely a very pretty fancy, and may have a very good effect, but nothing equal to what the poem itself would have. The painting can only represent one moment or point of time, and the situation things were in at that time. Betwixt one moment and another there must have been a very considerable time, a great number of moments must have passed. The actions of all these are unknown and can only be conjectured. ⟨Several* painters have emulated the poets in giving a suite of actions, but these labour under a defect for want of connection. When we turn from one picture to look at another, we do not know the persons which act there till we have studied the piece, nor do we know what had happened intermediate and preparatory to this action.⟩ We are uneasy here just from the same cause as we are at an interruption of time in a dramatic performance. That it is not the preventing our deception which occasions it may appear from this, that we are not very uneasy at a small interruption: we can easily conceive what may have passed during the hour or two for which the action is suspended. We see also that these pieces, though they have not the effect they would have were it not for this defect, have yet a very considerable one, which would not be the case if the whole pleasure we take in dramatical works proceeded from the deception.

The same things may be said with regard to the Unity of Place, which some critics reckon indispensably necessary to the dramatical works. In an epic poem the connection of place is easily maintained, by the poet having it in his power to connect the different actions by a few intervening words. In the dramatic works the unity of place cannot be altogether maintained unless the action is such as that it be all supposed to be transacted in the same place, as well as at one time. Shakespeare in some of his plays breaks through this rule altogether: he makes one scene be in France, and the following one in England; one in London, and another at York, etc. In this case the distance is so great that we are anxious to know what has happened in the interval between them. The best way, surely, is to fix the action to one place if possible, as Racine and Sophocles have done; and if that is not possible, we should make the distance as little as possible, confining the action to the same house or thereabouts. But when this rule is not observed, we find the effect of the piece may still be very considerable, which, as we said before, shows that it is not deception which gives us the pleasure we find in these works, and, in fact, we never are deceived for one moment.

119

There is one thing, however, that must be always observed, otherwise the piece can never produce any great effect: it is the Propriety of Character. As comedy and tragedy are designed to produce very different effects, so the characters they place as the principal ones must be such as are suited to produce these contrary effects.

Kings and nobles are what make the best characters in a tragedy. ⟨The* misfortunes of the great, as they happen less frequently, affect us more. There is in human nature a servility which inclines us to adore our superiors, and an inhumanity which disposes us to contempt[1] and trample underfoot our inferiors.⟩ We are too much accustomed to the misfortunes of people below or equal with ourselves to be greatly affected by them. But the misfortunes of the great, both as they seem connected with the welfare of a multitude, and as[2] we are apt to pay great respect and attention to our superiors, however unworthy, are what chiefly affect us. Nay, such is the temper of men, that we are rather disposed to laugh at the misfortunes of our inferiors than take part in them.

'Tis for this same principle that persons of high rank make very bad actors in a comedy. Dukes and princes and men of high rank, though they be never so ridiculous in themselves, never appear the subject of laughter. The same prejudice which makes us be so highly interested in their misfortunes, makes us also imagine there is something respectable even in their follies. Persons of low life, either equal or inferior to ourselves, are the best characters for comedy. We can laugh heartily at the absurdity of a shoe-maker or a burgess, though we can hardly prevail on ourselves to weep at his misfortunes. Farces, where the characters are the lowest of any, make us laugh more than the finest comedy; and on the other [hand], we can hardly enter into the humour of a comedy of the highest sort, where dukes and nobles[3] are the objects of our laughter. ⟨We can laugh at Sancho Panza on his Island, because we know that he was no real but only a mock governor.⟩ We even carry this so far that we are rather apt to make sport of the misfortunes of our inferiors, than sympathize with them. The Italian comedy, by applying the misfortunes of the great personages of tragedy to persons in low life, and putting their speeches in their mouths, is so far from appearing

---

[1] *Sic*. Probably an error for 'contemn'.

[2] The MS here has 'they seem', apparently repeated by dittography from the previous line.

[3] The MS has 'princes' cancelled, as though the scribe still had in mind the phrase used earlier in the same paragraph.

lamentable that it is the most ridiculous of any, though no doubt persons in low life are as deeply affected with the passions of grief or sorrow or joy as those of greater fortunes.

⟨As it is the misfortunes or recovery of the chief persons in a tragedy that we are to be chiefly interested in, a villain can never be a fit person for the hero of such a piece. For this reason, though Iago makes a tolerably good actor in *Othello*, as the latter has evidently the superiority to him, in our opinion, yet Alonzo[1] in *The Revenge*, which is nothing more than *Othello* spoiled, is a very unfit character, as the hero (Alonzo) has such an inferiority of parts to Zanga, that we should rather take him to be the principal character.⟩

We observed before that the ridiculousness of comedy consists in the ridiculousness of the characters, and not of the circumstances. It will be necessary, therefore, that the characters should be changed. We cannot always be laughing at misers or fops; we must have a variety of characters, to make the pieces agreeable. But we will find that there is no such necessity in tragedy or epic poetry. The characters here are not the principal thing: the adventures or circumstances, and the behaviour of the different persons in these circumstances, is what chiefly interest us. We are uneasy when those worthy persons are in difficult or unhappy circumstances, and rejoice if they are extricated, and our grief is at its height when they are altogether overwhelmed. These circumstances may be varied a thousand ways: the grief or concern excited by *The Orphan*[2] and that by *Venice Preserved*[2] are very different.

Mr [blank][3], however, reckons this one of the essential beauties of an heroic poem. But when we consider that neither in Virgil nor Racine there is the variety of characters; there is no variety in the *Aeneid* at all; Racine's men are all of one sort, and his women also have all the same character: when we consider, too, that Virgil is in the opinion of many the first of epic poets, but by the universal consent he is the second: that Racine is universally acknowledged to be the second tragic writer, the French perhaps preferring Corneille and the English Sophocles: when we consider, I say, that the second—perhaps the first—of epic poets, and the second—perhaps the first—of tragic poets, have not the smallest share of this beauty, we will be apt to think it is not so very essential.

[1] The MS has 'Zara' cancelled. Young's *The Revenge* was first acted in 1719.

[2] Thos. Otway, *The Orphan*, 1680; *Venice Preserved*, 1682.

[3] Probably Addison is intended. Cf. *The Spectator*, No. 273, where, discussing characters in epic poetry, he praises Homer above Virgil, and Virgil above Milton, for variety of character.

Perhaps the great attention which these authors have paid to the propriety, decorum, and [blank][1] of their works, has hindered them from bringing in a variety of characters, through all which it is almost impossible to keep up the decorum and propriety of the pieces. In this point they are indeed greatly inferior to two other poets, Homer and Shakespeare. The first of these has a vast variety of characters, and the latter still greater. But then this vast variety has often led them into breaches of decency, propriety, and uniformity of interest. As Racine seems to have studied these last-mentioned perfections still more than Virgil, so he has a still less variety of character. And in the same manner Shakespeare, as the inconceivable variety of characters he has introduced far exceeds that of Homer's, so he has paid still less regard to decency and propriety. These different beauties of decorum and variety seem incompatible when in their greatest perfection, and we are not to condemn one who excels in the one as not being equally excellent in the other.

This decorum, we see, is very easily maintained in the lighter pieces of poetry such as Odes, Elegy, and Pastoral, where the length of the piece does not admit of any great variety of incidents. ⟨The* Elegy and all the other smaller compositions are the exhibitions only of a single event or action, or of one simple disposition in a person. They have not time nor connection sufficient to awaken great emotions.⟩ In all those pieces the affection or temper of mind they would excite should not be very violent. Great passions, as they are long of being raised in the persons themselves, so are they not to be raised in us but by a work of considerable length.[2] A temper of mind that differs very little from the common tranquillity of mind is what we can best enter into, by the perusal of a piece of a small length. A painting can only present us with the action at one point of time. For this reason it is that we are more pleased with those that represent a state not far different from that we are generally in, when we view the picture. When we take a view of the Cartoons of Raphael, it is not *Paul Preaching at Athens*, or *Elias Struck with Blindness*, that first attract our attention, but *Peter Receiving the Keys, Peter, Feed my Sheep*. This piece represents a state of mind in all the figures not much differing from that we are in. ⟨Poussin used to say that the tranquil pieces were what he liked best.⟩ Whereas the emotions in the others are so violent that it takes a considerable time before we

---

[1] Possibly 'uniformity' was intended.
[2] Cf. Aristotle, *Poetics*, VII, 8ff on 'magnitude'.

can work ourselves up so far as to enter into the spirit of the pieces.

In the same manner an Ode or an Elegy ⟨in which there is no odds but in the measure⟩, which differ little from the common state of mind, are what most please us. Such is that on the Church-yard, or Eton College, by Mr Gray. The best of Horace's (though inferior to Mr Gray's) are all of this sort. Pastorals, too, are subject to the same rule, for it matters not whether the sentiments represented to us be in the person of the poet, or in a dialogue. The pastoral poems of Mr Shen-stone, if he had put the account he gives of the effects love had on him-self into the mouth of a person in the dialogue, would have been pre-cisely similar to the Third Pastoral of Virgil. The only difference be-twixt an ode and the ordinary sort of pastorals is that in the one the temper of the poet's mind, and in the other of another person, are related.

# 22

HAVING now said all I think necessary concerning the two most simple methods of writing, the descriptive and historical, I might now proceed to the third method, viz, the didactic; but as the rules concerning it are very obvious, I shall here pass it over and proceed immediately to consider the oratorical style.

Eloquence, as I mentioned before, was divided by the ancients[1] into three sorts: 1st, the Demonstrative; 2nd, the Deliberative; 3rd, the Judicial. I shall begin[2] with the Demonstrative, as being most simple, and as the rules which regard it are almost all applicable to the other two species of eloquence; and also because those rules which are to be given concerning it have least dependence on what I shall advance hereafter with regard to the didactic, etc.

This sort of eloquence generally was directed to the commendation of some great man, which was given out to be the design of oratory, though as the name of Demonstrative or paren . . .[3] shows, the real design of the orator was to show his own eloquence. To maintain the glory of the person he commended was what he gave out to be his sole design in undertaking the work: but to raise his own glory was plainly the motive of his undertaking, as the glory of that person could not be very interesting either to the orator or his hearers, as they were generally persons who had lived some ages before.

In treating of this subject the following order shall be observed. In the first place I shall consider: I, the end proposed in these orations; II, the means by which this end may be brought about; III, the order in which those means are to be arranged; IV, the manner in which these are to be expressed; and V, lastly, what authors have most excelled for this species of writing.

First, as to the end proposed, it will not be difficult to determine

---

[1] Cf. Aristotle, *Rhetoric*, I, 3, 'deliberative, forensic, epideictic'.
[2] For what follows, cf. Quintilian, III, 7.
[3] Word unfinished, possibly 'panegyric' was intended.

what this is to be. The nature of the work plainly shows that it is to raise the glory and reputation of the person commended. For though the increase of his own fame may be the design of the orator, and generally is so, yet this is to be considered only as a secondary end. The glory of the person praised is the thing the orator is to have in view, and the other secondary end is to be brought about only by acquitting himself handsomely in the principal design.

Secondly, of the means by which this end may be accomplished. It is evident that there are but two ways in which a man may be commended: either, first, by describing his actions; or, second, by praising his character. The manner in which actions and characters are to be described has already been explained at some length, and need not be here repeated. What we are here to aim at is to point out the actions and particular parts of a character that are most proper to be described in a discourse of this sort. We may observe, then, that when a man's designs have for the most part proved unfortunate, when he has been baffled in his chief and favourite schemes, his actions are to be either passed over or but slightly touched, and the character or disposition of the man is chiefly to be insisted on. On the other hand, if he has experienced a great flow of prosperity, his actions are what we are chiefly to insist on. For as bad fortune is apt to give us a slow and contemptible notion of a man, though he be of a very different cast, so good fortune has a great tendency to attract our admiration and applause. But there is nothing which is more apt to raise our admiration and gain our applause than the hardships one has undergone with firmness and constancy, especially if they have at last been surmounted. We are told by Shakespeare that Othello gained the love of Desdemona more by the difficulties he had encountered than by all his assiduity.[1] We admire Ulysses more for the great mishaps he had to struggle with than if he had not been brought into such hazard. Uninterrupted prosperity does not convey such a high idea of a person who has experienced it, as if it had been intermixed with some strokes of adversity. The first seems more owing to chance, whereas the other demands all the attention and best endeavours of the sufferer. ⟨And* as a tract of adversity which ends well strikes us more than uninterrupted prosperity with admiration and respect, so a long course of prosperity is weakened in our esteem by an unlucky or ill-guided

---

[1] *Othello*, Act I, sc. iii, ll. 167-8:
> She lov'd me for the dangers I had pass'd,
> And I lov'd her that she did pity them.

conclusion. Thus Pompey's glory seems to be tarnished by the Battle of Pharsalia,[1] and that of Masinissa and Robert the Bruce. . . .⟩

⟨It is the steadfastness with which they have encountered danger and opposed themselves to hazard which has gained men the character of heroes. The heroes of romance are all carried through a series of disastrous adventures before they are brought to the happiness to which they are destined.⟩ Thus much with regard to the actions.

As to the character that is most proper to be given of a man we would extol, it is evident at first sight that it must be a virtuous one. Virtue adds to everything that is of itself commendable, whereas vice detracts from what would otherwise be praiseworthy. But all virtues are not equally proper to give us a high and exalted idea of him who is possessed of them, nor are all vices equally adapted to excite our contempt and dislike of the man who is guilty of them. Nay, the different virtues do not claim our admiration in the proportion they bear to one another in the scale of virtue, nor do all vices degrade in our opinion the person guilty of them, in the precise proportion we should expect from the degree in which they are generally placed. There are some virtues which excite or attract our respect and admiration, and others which we love and esteem. ⟨It* would appear that, as in external objects the mind is pleased with two kinds, the great and the beautiful, so also in these internal objects she discovers two kinds, which affect her with delight, the good and the amiable.⟩ There are in the same way some vices which we contemn and despise, and others which we abominate and detest; and (as we said) these opinions do not always keep pace with one another. Fortitude is generally more admired and respected than humanity, although this latter virtue is perhaps more loved and esteemed. And on the other hand, cowardice and want of resolution are more contemned and despised than cruelty and inhumanity; and though cruelty and inhumanity are more detested and abhorred, men generally are more desirous of being thought great than good, and are more afraid of being thought despicable than of being thought wicked. Divines have commonly ascribed this inclination, which prevails so much among men, to the depravity of human nature, and philosophers who have taken up the cause of our nature and endeavoured to clear her from this charge of depravity, have for the most part denied this to be the case. But it would be easy to shew, were this a proper place, that there is no part of our nature which more evidently appears

[1] Probably Smith has in mind Lucan's poem *De Bello Civili*.

to be contrived wisely and kindly, or tends more to promote our happiness.

The respectable virtues are those which are most suited to a commendatory discourse, where we would excite the admiration and wonder of the audience. For besides that (as we said) they are of themselves more commonly admired than the amiable ones, for those latter are often found connected with the contemptible vices. Thus good nature and humanity are frequently joined with timidity and want of resolution. And on the other hand, those vices which most demean and degrade one in the eyes of men, are the contemptible ones; for those which we would detest are as often found connected with the respectable virtues. Amplicatives and superlatives are the terms we commonly make use of to express our admiration and respect. But this is not the genuine and natural language of love. There is none of the human passions which, when it speaks as nature dictates, is less apt to address its objects in amplicative and magnifying expressions. The romance writers of the Middle Age, and others on love subjects, have indeed introduced those terms into their love language; but nature never expressed itself in that manner. Diminutives and such-like are the terms in which we speak of objects we love. We are most [ready] to fondle women and children whom we esteem of less capacity and worth than ourselves, and to those we never express ourselves in the superlative degree. 'Tis the respectable virtues which we find most generally made use of in panegyrics. In the panegyrics of the saints and martyrs (a species of writing very common in France) the patience, fortitude, and magnanimity with which they endured the torments and cruel treatment inflicted on them, is [sic] what they insist chiefly upon. The martyrs were those who in their own time drew most the attention of the people. Their virtues of patience, fortitude, etc. made them more admired than the saints themselves were for their humility and resignation and piety. And it is their praises which we see most extolled and discovered in the terms of the highest admiration. Such expressions do not at all suit with the other more amiable but not so respectable virtues. Flechier[1] has indeed made use of them in his panegyrics on those saints and their virtues of humility and resignation; but they suit as ill to them, and appear as ridiculous, as when Don Quixote applies them to his Lady Dulcinea del Toboso.

[1] Name inserted in the second hand. Esprit Flechier (1652-1710), French preacher and author, noted for sermons and funeral orations, especially the oration on Marshal Turenne (1676).

Thus much of the means, whether actions or character, by which a man may be praised. We may observe that, in general, the same rules are applicable to those discourses which are intended to praise or extol a nation, as are applicable to those which are wrote in praise of a single person; and this holds both of these already delivered, and those that are to follow.

We come now, in the third place, to consider in what order these means are to be arranged in the discourse which we have here pointed out. The character of a man is never very striking nor makes any deep impression: it is a dull and lifeless thing, taken merely by itself. It then only appears in perfection when it is called out into action. We are not then generally to begin our panegyric with a character of the man whose reputation we are to raise, but are rather to begin with an account of his more [blank] actions, commencing from his birth and tracing them on in the order in which they happened. With these as we go along we may intermix some of the more minute and private actions of the person. The smallest circumstances, the most minute transactions of a great man, are sought after with eagerness. We watch the sayings and catch the apophthegms of great men, with which we are infinitely pleased, and are fond of every opportunity of using them, although we everyday hear better from most of our intimate acquaintance, which we let slip unheeded. Having thus, as it were, conjoined the manners of describing a character made use of by Theophrastus and La Bruyère, we recapitulate (or tell over a second time) the character of the person, in the manner of the Abbé Retz. This is precisely the method which Xenophon has followed in his panegyric on Agesilaus.[1] He begins with his birth and gives us an account of the more memorable events of his life. He gives us also many particulars of his private life which tend to illustrate his character, and concludes the whole by drawing a character of him in the direct manner.

This may answer very well in most cases, but is not to be so strictly adhered to as not to be deserted when circumstances require it. If it should so happen that the most actions of a man's life had ended unhappily, it would be very improper to introduce our panegyric with an account of them, which would in effect be an account of his failings. We should rather in these circumstances give an account of his character, illustrating the several virtues with any facts that will admit of being introduced in that manner, concealing, or at most slightly touching on, those of a disastrous character.

[1] A minor work of Xenophon. Cf. *Scripta Minora*, *Agesilaus*, especially x and xi.

There are other circumstances also which make it expedient to alter this method. Thus Cicero, in the Manilian oration,[1] when his design was to recommend Pompey for the commander in the Mithridatic war, does not give an account of his actions in the order they happened; but after having enumerated the requisites in a general who should command in that expedition, shows that Pompey possessed all those necessary qualifications, which [he] confirms by suitable actions taken from the different stages of his life, without regard to the order of time. This may suffice concerning the arrangement.

It may be observed that there are some other circumstances which may afford matter for a panegyric, besides those above enumerated. Thus if the person be of a good family, noble ancestors, etc. ⟨or* virtuous children and good,⟩ these may be recorded, as well as his own qualifications.[2] For everything that is connected with rank, nobility, or grandeur receives tincture from them, and is looked on in that light by the generality of people.

Fourth: of the manner in which these are to be expressed. The panegyrist will not, as the historian, content himself with barely relating any fact or affirming a proposition, but will embellish the one with ornamental decorations and go about to prove the other by different methods. Thus Xenophon, in the afore-mentioned work, not only affirms that Agesilaus' conduct to Tissaphernes was the beginning and foundation of all his good actions, but also proves it by different methods.

[1] Cicero's *Pro Lege Manilia*, in which Cicero supported the successful proposal of Manilius that Pompey should be put in charge of the campaign against Mithridates (66 B.C.).

[2] Cf. Quintilian, III, 7 passim.

# 23

In the last lecture I gave you some account of the design of Demonstrative orations, the means by which this end may be attained, and the arrangement of those means. I shall make some observations on those authors who have chiefly excelled in this manner of writing. There have been but very few who have turned their thoughts this way. It is very late before this species of writing is at all cultivated; the subject is not one which would naturally interest very much either the speaker or his audience. Deliberative and Judicial eloquence would arrive much more early. Men would much sooner consider what was to be done, or consider the merit of those actions that have been done, than they would think either of commending men and actions, or of discommending them, and consequently would sooner apply themselves to the cultivation of the Deliberative and Judicial eloquence than of the Demonstrative. Their subjects are such as would be interesting both to speaker and hearers, whereas that of the latter could interest neither; for though the speaker gave out that his design was to commend some person or nation, yet the motive was the advancement of his own glory.

This species of eloquence took its rise from the old Hymns in honour of the gods and heroes, in the same manner as history arose from the ancient Ballads and Heroical Poems. The style of these two is very different, the one raising our opinion of the persons whom they celebrate only by recording their actions, whereas the other celebrate the persons they extol, which are gods or heroes, in the most high and exalted epithets. Thus Virgil, who proposes to celebrate the actions of Aeneas, does this only by recording them, and never exclaims on the danger or difficulty of the adventures which he had to encounter. But when he comes to the reception of Hercules by Evander, the speech he puts into the mouth of the former[1] in praise of that hero is in a very different strain.[2]

[1] *sic*: latter?
[2] *Aeneid*, VIII, ll. 293-302. But the words are not spoken by Evander; they are part of the songs of praise in honour of Hercules.

The poetical panegyrics were very long in use before the prose ones. It is always late before prose and its beauties come to be cultivated: poetry is always precedent, and is generally arrived to some tolerable perfection. It will no doubt seem at first sight very surprising that a species of writing so vastly more difficult should be in all countries prior to that in which men naturally express themselves. Thus in Greece poetry was arrived to its greatest perfection before the beauties of prose were at all studied. At Rome there had lived several poets of considerable merit before eloquence was cultivated in any tolerable degree. There were English poets of very great reputation before any tolerable prose had made its appearance. We have also several poetical works of the old Scots language, as *Hardyknute, Cherry and the Slae, Three Died in*[1] *Lochaber*, and *Wallace Wight*,[2] in the original Scots; but not one bit of tolerable prose. The Erse poetry, as appears from the translations lately published,[3] have[4] very great merit, but we never heard of any Erse prose. This indeed may appear very unnatural, that what is most difficult should be that in which the barbarous, least civilized nations, most excel in: but it will not be very difficult to account for it. The most barbarous and rude nations, after the labours of the day are over, have their hours of merriment and recreation and enjoyment with one another. Dancing and gambolling naturally make a part of these diversions, and this dancing must be attended with music. The savage nations on the coast of Africa, after they have sheltered themselves through the hot day in caves and grottoes from the scorching heat of the sun, come out in the evening and dance and sing together. Poetry is a necessary attendant on music, especially on vocal music, the most natural and simple of any. They naturally express some thoughts along with their music, and these must, of consequence, be formed into verse to suit with the music. Thus it is that poetry is cultivated in the most rude and barbarous nations, often to a considerable perfection; whereas they make no attempt towards the improvement of prose. 'Tis the introduction of commerce, or at least of the opulence that is commonly the attendant of commerce, that first brings on the improvement of prose. Opulence and commerce

[1] The reading 'Died in' is uncertain.
[2] *Hardyknute*, published 1719, a ballad imitation by Lady Wardlaw (1677-1727); *Cherry and the Slae*, published 1597, by Alexander Montgomerie (1556?-1610?); *Three Died in Lochaber*, I cannot identify; *Wallace Wight*, presumably Henry the Minstrel's *Wallace* (c. 1470-90).
[3] James Macpherson's *Fragments of Ancient Poetry* (1760), *Fingal* (1762), *Temora* (1763). [4] *Sic*. Should probably be 'has'.

commonly precede the improvement of arts and refinement of every sort. I do not mean that the improvement of arts and refinement of manners are the necessary consequences of commerce,—the Dutch and the Venetians bear testimony against me,—but only that [it] is a necessary requisite. Wherever the inhabitants of a city are rich and opulent, where they enjoy the necessaries and conveniences of life in ease and security, there the arts will be cultivated, and refinement of manners a never-failing attendant. For in all such states it must necessarily happen that there are many who are not obliged to labour for their livelihood, and have nothing to do but display themselves in what most suits their taste, and seek out for pleasure in all its shapes. In this state it is that prose begins to be cultivated. Prose is naturally the language of business, as poetry is of pleasure and amusement. Prose is the style in which all the common affairs of life, all business and agreements, are made. No one ever made a bargain in verse: pleasure is not what he there aims at. Poetry, on the other hand, is only adapted for pleasure and entertainment; the very nature of poetry, the numbers it is composed in (for there can be no poetry without numbers) declare the intention is to entertain. In the first stages of society, when men have their necessities on their hands, they keep their business and their pleasure altogether distinct; they never mix pleasure with their business, nor business with their pleasure. Prose is not ornamented, nor is verse applied to subjects of business. It is only when pleasure is the only thing sought after that prose comes to be studied. People who are rich and at their ease cannot give themselves the trouble of anything where they do not expect some pleasure. The common transactions of life, as deliberation and consultation on what they are to do, are of themselves too dry and unpleasant for them, without the ornaments of language and elegance of expression. 'Tis then Deliberative and Judicial eloquence are studied, and every ornament is sought out for them.

Till the Persian expedition arts were unknown in the greater part of Greece. The military art was the employment of the people, and as the education must be suited to the business, it was to this that the youth was trained. But lest this education should give their manners a rudeness and ferocity which it had a great tendency to produce, music was added to correct the bad effects of the former part of education. These two made the whole of the education of the youth, even in Athens, the most civilized of any. Philosophy and the arts were entirely neglected. In the colonies, indeed, philosophy, etc., were come to some perfection before

132

they were heard of in the mother country. Thales[1] had taught at Miletus, Pythagoras[2] in Italy, and Empedocles[3] in Sicily, before the time of the Persian expedition,[4] from which time commerce, that had been cultivated in the colonies, flourished in the continent, and brought wealth, arts, and refinement along with it. Gorgias of Mitylene[5] was the first who introduced eloquence into Greece. He is said to have astonished them with the elegance and force of the oration he delivered on his embassy from his country. From that time eloquence began to be cultivated, and was soon encouraged by the addition of wealth and opulence to the Grecian states ⟨which was made after the Persian expedition. This expedition likewise added to the improvement of eloquence, as the Athenian state ordered by a public decree that annual orations or panegyrics should be read on the persons who had signalized themselves in the defence of their country and died in battle.⟩

As arms and music made the chief part, indeed the whole, of the education of youth at that time, so to encourage those who excelled in those arts, games were instituted at which the prizes were adjudged to the victors in the different exercises, as running, wrestling, chariot races, etc., and to those who excelled in the other branch, music. The competition for the prize in music naturally introduced a competition amongst the poets, as their art was nearly connected with that science. The orators, seeing the success of the poets and the great encouragement which they met with, were tempted to try their art also. There was no prize, indeed, assigned to those who excelled in this science; but that could be no great discouragement, for the prizes that were assigned to the victors in the others were of no value in themselves, and only served as a mark of honour, which could be very well attained without that badge. The praises of the conquerors in these games also furnished them with an opportunity of displaying their talents. At these games Herodotus read his history and Isocrates his orations: (at least had them read by another, for his own voice was so bad that he never read himself).

The orators at this time, as they rivalled the poets, so they imitated them. The Hymns and Praises of the Gods was that sort which best suited these sort [sic] of orators. As they imitated the poets in their design, so they did in the subject—the praises of divinities, and heroes

---

[1] Thales, c. 624-c. 546 B.C.    [2] Pythagoras, fl. 540-510 B.C.
[3] Empedocles, c. 494-c. 434 B.C. Smith would appear to be wrong here.
[4] Persian Expedition, 480 B.C.
[5] i.e. Gorgias of Leontini, in Sicily, c. 480-c. 380 B.C. 'Mitylene' is an auditory slip.

who were so much obscured by antiquity as that they might pass for deities, were the subject of these hymns. The first of these orations were also on the same subject. Those of Gorgias, as we are told, and others of his time, were generally in praise of Theseus, Achilles, Meleager, or other such personages. As they imitated the subject, so did they the manner of the hymns. These writings were all in a very desultory and unconnected manner. They mind connection no more than it suits them, and bring in whatever they think can please the reader, not regarding the subject. All passions, especially admiration, express themselves in a very loose and broken manner, catching at whatever seems connected with the subject of the passion, which, as it seems important itself, so it makes everything which is connected with it seem so also. The higher the rapture, the more broken the expression. All the lyric poets are in this way desultory, and Pindar, the most rapturous of all, is the most unconnected, or at least appears to be so.

Isocrates is the first of these writers which has come down to us. His manner is said greatly to resemble that of Gorgias. He, as well as the old poets and lyric writers, is very unconnected, and introduces any subject that is the least connected with that in hand. Thus in his oration in praise of Helen,[1] he introduces the praises of Theseus, Paris, Achilles, etc. and not a sixth part is concerning Helen herself. He is fond of all sort of moral sayings, and coins figures or ornamental language—metaphors, similes, hyperboles, antitheses, etc. The beauty he chiefly studies is that of a sounding uniform cadence and equality of members in the sentence. These may all be seen in the introduction of the oration to Democles,[2] which also shows his design and temper, how he claimed a superiority over the other sophists and endeavoured to rival the poets in sweetness and numbers. Brutus,[3] who had the idea that all eloquence was to be directed to discover the truth of the matter in question, and lead us to a certain conclusion with regard to the debate, heartily despised this orator; whereas Cicero[3] greatly admired him, as he considered

---

[1] Isocrates, Loeb ed., vol. III, pp. 6off.

[2] 'Democles' would appear to be a conflation of 'Demonicus' and 'Nicocles'. Cf. Isocrates, vol. I (Loeb), To Demonicus (pp. 2-37), and To Nicocles (pp. 38-73). The reference seems to be to the former, where he says 'I put the philosophers right'; on the other hand, the poets do not appear to be mentioned here, whereas they *are* mentioned in the introduction to the *Nicocles*. Smith appears to have confused the two. Unless it be that he really said 'the orations to Demonicus and Nicocles'.

[3] Cf. Cicero, *Orator*, 40: 'Isocrates who is always praised by me [Cicero], though occasionally, Brutus, you demur in a quiet and scholarly way.' Smith's 'heartily despised' is surely an exaggeration.

134

only the beautiful, the pleasing, and what would entertain and please the audience, without regarding the argument. And indeed if we should read Isocrates for instruction in order, method, argument, or strength of reasoning, we should lose our labour. But if we expect entertainment and pleasure from an agreeable writer, we will not be disappointed.

The victory of the Grecians over the Persians has furnished us with three orations by very eminent hands on the subject of the Praise of the Athenians. One is by Lysias.[1] He is said chiefly to have excelled in judicial private cases, where he maintained the character of a plain man, not versed in the chicane of the Bar or Courts of Justice, and lost himself much when he attempted anything florid and extraordinary, such as this subject required. In this oration he appears to have endeavoured at all the beauties of language and ornament of expression, as well as moral sayings and reflections. He does not relate many of the actions of the Greeks, these being exhausted by former orators; but those which he does relate are not well adapted to the circumstances. These, as well as his reflections, are all trite and commonplace. He exaggerates everything, and often affirms what was far from being true. He is very fond not only of all sorts of figures, but even is full of exclamations and wonder.

The second is Plato's.[2] His style is more correct; his reflections and circumstances well chosen, and not commonplace, like those of the former. He has still fewer actions than Lysias, but in the choice he excels him, and where they hit on the same one his superiority is evident, as in the accounts of the Battles of Marathon and Salamis.[3] His style is not so extravagant, but is at the same time too verbose, which often conceals his other beauties.

Pericles, in the oration Thucydides gives us in the introduction to the Peloponnesian War,[4] is more correct, less exuberant and extravagant, than the former; strong and nervous, precise and pointed, and carries along not only a direct commendation of the Athenians, but an indirect discommendation of the Lacaedemonians, then their rivals. His beauties are so manifest that I shall not insist on them any longer.

[1] *Epitaphios*, Loeb ed., pp. 30ff.
[2] *Menexenus*, 236ff (Speech of Aspasia the Milesian).
[3] *Ibid.* 240, 241.          [4] Thucydides, I, 140-4.

135

# 24

Monday, 24 January 1763

Sine libro, *except what he read from Livy*.

HAVING in the two fore-going lectures made all the observations I think necessary on the first sort of eloquence, viz. the Demonstrative, I now come to the second sort, the Deliberative. But before I enter particularly upon it, it will be proper to make some observations on a species of writing more simple than either it or the Judicial. I mean the Didactic, in which the design of the writer is to lay down a proposition and prove this by the different arguments that lead to that conclusion. If there be one proposition necessary to be proved, there can be nothing more simple. The best method here, undoubtedly, is to lay down the proposition, and afterwards advance the several arguments that tend to prove it: which may be summed up, or brought to conclude, in the same terms as the proposition. It is proper to begin with laying down the proposition, as the arguments advanced will by that means make a greater impression on the mind, as it is evident at what they point, than if they were delivered without informing us what was to be the conclusion. But it will often happen that, in order to prove the capital proposition, it will be necessary to prove several subordinate ones. In this case we are first to lay down the proposition, and then shew in what manner the truth of it depends on that of some other propositions; and having proved this, sum up the whole as before.

⟨'Tis in this manner Lord Shaftesbury proceeds, in his *Inquiry*[1] *into the Nature*[2] *of Virtue*, and also in that[3] where he endeavours to prove that virtue is our greatest happiness. Whether his reasoning be sufficient or not, his method is perfect, and if the subordinate propositions are clearly proved, the principal ones must necessarily be true.⟩

We are to observe, however, that these subordinate propositions should not be above five at most. When they exceed this number, the

---

[1] Shaftesbury, *Characteristics*, vol. II, *Inquiry into the Nature of Virtue*.
[2] A blank in original is filled by 'Nature' in the second hand.
[3] Shaftesbury, *Characteristics*, vol. III, *Miscellaneous Reflections*, Misc. 4, ch. 1.

mind cannot easily comprehend them at one view, and the whole runs into confusion. Three, or thereabout, is a very proper number, and it is observed that this number is much more easily comprehended, and appears more complete than two or four. In the number three there is, as it were, a middle and two extremes; but in two or four there is no middle on which the attention can be so fixed as that each part seems somewhat connected with it. The rule is in this matter the same as in architecture: the mind cannot there comprehend a number at sight, without counting, above nine or ten. Three is the number of all others the most easily comprehended: we immediately perceive a middle and one on each side. ⟨Swift proposed a panegyric on the number three,[1] and this was one of the articles of its commendation. There is undoubtedly something in this number that makes it more agreeable than others. In architecture, there being a middle one to which we first turn our eyes is a sufficient reason, though it appears whimsical when applied to writing. There are more sermons and other discourses divided into this number of heads than into any other.⟩ In four there is no middle, and though in numbers of windows or columns it may be easily enough comprehended, yet it seems awkward, and in architecture there is one evident defect, as there is no regular place for the door. Five is easily comprehended, one in the middle and two on the sides, or three in the middle and one on each side. Six and seven are in the same manner not difficult to comprehend, and in the same manner nine, as it may be divided into three times three. But though in architecture we can comprehend this number with tolerable readiness, we cannot in writing reach so far. Columns and windows are things exactly similar, and are for that reason more easily comprehended, as when we know one or two we know them all. But the propositions which are brought as secondary to the primary one are often noways connected but as they all tend to the same point, and we have not only a number but also the nature of each proposition to remember. It may often happen that it will be necessary to prove fourteen or fifteen subordinate propositions, in order to confirm the principal one. In this case it is much better to form three or five propositions on which the truth of the principal one evidently depends, and under each of these propositions to arrange five or three of those which are necessary to confirm the primary one. The mind will much more easily comprehend the ten propositions in the one case, or

---

[1] *Tale of a Tub.* Swift lists it among the treatises 'by the same author', and later (p. 57, ed. Guthkelch and Smith) gives some details about the proposed Treatise.

the twenty in the other, than it will fifteen which immediately depend on the principal one, without any intermediate steps. In the same manner in architecture, the architect generally makes one part of the building some way distinguished from the rest, either throws the middle part further back, or advances it further forwards than the sides, that is, in case there be above three (or five) windows or other parts. By this means one may with tolerable ease remember at least fifteen or sixteen propositions; whereas in the other case the mind finds a considerable difficulty in going above half that length. There are, however, sermons, wrote about the time of the Civil Wars, which have not only fifteenthly or sixteenthly, but twentiethly, thirtiethly, or fortiethly.

In architecture we can not only comprehend a considerable number of parts by sub-divisions, but by sub-sub-divisions, and we can go still farther. Thus if a building was to contain eighty-one windows or columns, let these be thrown into three 27s, distinguished remarkably from one another, the two side ones being similar; let each of these be again divided into three 9s, and those into three 3s, and let each sub-division be remarkably distinguished from the rest by a different order of architecture, or some other variety; and one, though not of very quick apprehension, will, if placed at a proper distance, readily conceive the order and number of the several parts. But in writing it is otherwise: sub-sub-divisions, etc. are not at all easily remembered: they always run into confusion, and become too intricate for our memory to comprehend. For this reason, one who was to read Aristotle's *Ethics*, or indeed any other of his works, ten times over, would hardly have a distinct notion of the plan. The divisions, sub-divisions, and sub-sub-etc. divisions, are carried so far that they produce the very effect he intended to have avoided by them, viz. confusion.

These divisions and sub-divisions are very useful, not only in such didactic writings as have in view the proof of a single proposition, but even in those where the design is to deliver a system of any science, e.g. Natural Philosophy: the divisions assist the memory in tracing the connection of the several parts. In Judicial eloquence it is often indispensably necessary. Facts and points of law often occur which cannot be decided without the proof of several previous propositions, and in this case the divisions and sub-divisions are to be applied in the same manner as that above mentioned. But in Deliberative eloquence there is seldom any occasion for it. This is not to say that no order or method [is] to be observed; yes[1] there is, without doubt, but only that the arguments to be used in this case where we would persuade others to do or not to do something, to make peace or continue war, to fight or not to fight,[2] are either so evident and conclusive and make it so plainly appear to be honourable, attainable, and for the advantage of those we would persuade, that there is no occasion for ranging them in a set order. If they happen not to be entirely plain and conclusive, it is the business of the orators to make them appear so. Now, a long chain of metaphysical arguments, one deduced from another, do not promise to have this appearance, in the opinion of such people as an audience where these orations are delivered generally consists of. And although the arguments were really conclusive, yet the appearance of so much subtlety and laboured trains of argument would make it very much to be suspected that the arguments were not altogether solid and conclusive.

⟨Aristotle[3] makes no use of divisions and sub-divisions in any of his Deliberative orations, though he frequently does in his Judicial ones. Cicero, in those which are the best in the Deliberative, makes no divisions, and very sparingly in any of that sort.⟩

There are two methods in which a didactical writing, containing an account of some system, may be delivered. Either, first, we lay down one or a very few principles by which we explain the several rules or phenomena, connecting one with the other in a natural order; or else we begin with telling that we are to explain such and such things, and for each advance a principle either different or the same with those which went before. Virgil, in his *Georgics*, follows the latter method. His design is to give us a system of husbandry. In the First he gives us directions for the cultivation of corn; in the Second, of trees; in the Third, of cattle; in the Fourth, of the insects called the bees. If Virgil had begun with inquiring into the principle of vegetation, what was proper to augment it, and *ex contra*, in what proportion it was in different soils, and what nourishment the different plants required, and, putting all these together, had directed us what culture and what soil was proper for every different plant, this would have been following the first method, which is, without doubt, the most philosophical one. In the same way, in Natural Philosophy, or any other science of that sort, we may either, like Aristotle, go over the different branches in the order they happen to

---

[1] *yes*: reading uncertain.
[2] The words 'to make peace . . . to fight' are written in the margin of the page.
[3] *Sic*: Demosthenes?

[be] cast up to us, giving a principle, commonly a new one, for every phenomenon; or, in the manner of Sir Isaac Newton, we may lay down certain principles, primary[1] or proved, in the beginning, from whence we account for the several phenomena, connecting all together by the same chain. This latter, which we may call the Newtonian method, is undoubtedly the most philosophical, and in every science, whether of Morals or Natural Philosophy, etc., is vastly more ingenious, and for that reason more engaging, than the other. It gives us a pleasure to see the phenomena which we reckoned the most unaccountable, all deduced from some principle (commonly, a well-known one) and all united in one chain, far superior to what we feel from the unconnected method, where everything is accounted for by itself, without any reference to the others. We need [not][2] be surprised, then, that the Cartesian philosophy (for Descartes was in reality the first who attempted this method), though it does not perhaps contain a word of truth,—and to us who live in a more enlightened age and have more inquired into these matters, it appears very dubious,—should nevertheless have been so universally received by all the learned in Europe at that time. The great superiority of the method over that of Aristotle, the only one then known, and the little inquiry which was then made into those matters, made them greedily receive a work which we justly esteem one of the most entertaining romances that have ever been wrote.

The Didactical method, though undoubtedly best in all matters of science, is hardly ever applicable to rhetorical discourses. The people to which [sic] they are ordinarily directed have no pleasure in these abstruse deductions. The interest, and practicability, and honourableness of the thing recommended, is what alone will sway with them, and is seldom to be shown in a long deduction of arguments.

As there are two methods of proceeding in Didactical discourses, so there are two in Deliberative eloquence, which are no less different, and are adapted to very contrary circumstances. The first may be called the Socratic method, as it was that [of] which, if we may trust the dialogues of Xenophon and Plato, that philosopher generally made use. In this method we keep as far from the main point to be proved as possible, bringing on the audience by slow and imperceptible degrees to the thing to be proved, and by gaining their consent to some things whose tendency they cannot discover, we force them at last either to deny

---

[1] *primary*: reading uncertain.
[2] *not*: conjectural addition.

what they had before agreed to, or to grant the validity of the conclusion. This is the smoothest and most engaging manner.

The other is a harsh and unmannerly one, where we affirm the things we are to prove boldly at the beginning, and when any point is controverted, begin by proving that very thing; and so on. This we may call the Aristotelian method, as we know it was that which he used.

These two methods are adapted to the two contrary cases in which an orator may be circumstanced with regard to his audience. They may either have a favourable or an unfavourable opinion of that which he is to prove: that is, they may be prejudiced for, or they may be prejudiced against. In the second case we are to use the Socratic method; in the first, the Aristotelian. I do not mean by this that we are to suppose that in any case the orator and his audience are to hold a dialogue with each other, or that they are to go on by granting small demands, or by boldly denying what the other affirms: but only that, when the audience is favourable, we are to begin with the proposition and set it out roundly before them. As it must be most for our advantage in this case to show at the first we are of their opinion, the arguments we advance gain strength by this precaution. On the other hand, if they are prejudiced against the opinion to be advanced, we are not to shock them by rudely affirming what we are satisfied is disagreeable, but are to conceal our design, and, beginning at a distance, bring them slowly on to the main point, and having gained the more remote ones, we get the nearer ones of consequence. The first is seen exemplified in the oration of Titus Quinctius Capitolinus,[1] and the latter in that[2] of Appius Claudius Crassus, in Livy.

[1] Livy, VII, chs. 40-1.     [2] Livy, V, chs. 3-6.

# 25

HAVING in the foregoing lecture given you all the observations I think necessary with regard to Deliberative eloquence, I might now, according to the method I proposed, proceed to point out the proper method of choosing the arguments and the manner of arranging them, as well as the expression. But directions of this sort can seldom be of any advantage. The arguments that are to be used before a people cannot be very intricate. The proposition generally requires no proof at all, and when it does, the arguments are of themselves so evident as not to require any elaborate explanation. There must be in this case no nicety nor refinement, no metaphysical arguments: these would both be altogether superfluous in the circumstances an orator is generally in, and can very seldom be in any shape applicable. As the arguments are in themselves so simple, there can be no great nicety required in the arrangement. And in general, in every sort of eloquence, the choice of the arguments and the proper arrangement of them is the least difficult matter. The expression and style is what requires most skill, and is alone capable of any particular directions. We see accordingly that Cicero, Quintilian, and all the best authors who treat of Rhetorical Composition, treat of the invention of arguments, or topics, and the composition or arrangement of them, as very slight matters and of no great difficulty, and never seem to be in earnest unless when they give us directions concerning the ornaments of language and expression; and even this, in the manner they have handled it, does not appear to be of very great importance,[1] though it might without doubt be treated of so as to be both entertaining and instructive. I shall therefore omit these altogether, and come to the last thing proposed, that is, to give you some account of the authors who have excelled in this manner of writing. I shall follow the same plan, too, in Judicial eloquence, for after having explained the general nature and principles of that sort of eloquence, I shall proceed to give an account of the chief orators and the manners of different writers in this manner,

---

[1] MS reads 'maner the . . . important'.

both with respect to Greece and Rome, and the English writers. I shall, however, take up some longer time on the nature of Judicial eloquence, as here, in the proving of facts and points of law, a good deal of nice and delicate reasoning and argumentation may be introduced, which, as I said, the Deliberative hardly ever admits of, and for that reason is the simplest of all the three species of eloquence. I shall in this lecture give you some account of the manner of Demosthenes' Deliberative orations, and then of Cicero's.

Of sixteen[1] Deliberative orations which have come down to us under the name of Demosthenes, two are plainly the work of a different hand, probably of Hegesippus: they have a rusticity and coarseness of expression, with an affectation of force, which is very unlike the manner of an orator. These orations are that on [blank][2] and that [blank].[3]

Of the fourteen remaining ones, ten are those employed to excite the Athenians to war with Philip of Macedon, or to encourage them to prosecute it with vigour. The other four are on different subjects, but as their design is much the same as that of the *Philippics* I shall say nothing concerning them, confining my observations entirely to the *Philippics*, and take as an instance of the manner of Demosthenes that of them which is called the third (and is the second) Olynthian oration. Not that it is the most elegant or finest of the orations, which in my opinion is that $\pi\epsilon\rho\grave{\iota}$ $X\epsilon\rho\sigma\sigma\nu\acute{\eta}\sigma\sigma\upsilon$,[4] but as it will as well shew the peculiar manner of the author.

That we may the better understand his manner and the observations on it, it will be necessary briefly to consider the state the Athenian affairs were in at the time these orations were composed. The government of Athens was long before that time become altogether democratical. The Council of the Areopagus, which was composed of the nobility and chief men of the commonwealth, was altogether abolished, and that great check on the fury of the people removed. The Council of [blank][5] and the Prytaneum,[6] which made parts of the aristocratical government,

---

[1] Of the 16, 5 are now considered not to be by Demosthenes. The two which were regarded as spurious in antiquity are No. 7 ('On Halonnesus', which was ascribed to Hegesippus), and No. 17 ('On the Treaty with Alexander'). Referred to again in Lecture 26.  [2] Perhaps 'Halonnesus'.

[3] Perhaps 'On the Treaty with Alexander'.

[4] Properly called $\pi\epsilon\rho\grave{\iota}$ $\tau\hat{\omega}\nu$ $\grave{\epsilon}\nu$ $X\epsilon\rho\sigma\sigma\nu\acute{\eta}\sigma\omega$, 'On the events in the Chersonese'.

[5] Possibly 'of Five Hundred', i.e. *Boulë*.

[6] Smith uses the word as a collective term for the *Prytaneis*, or 'presidents', i.e. the members of that one of the ten sections of fifty each into which the *Boulë* was divided, whose turn it was to preside for one-tenth of the year.

were then laid aside, and no barrier remained against the unruly multitude. But still it was the nobility which directed the management of public affairs. The balance of wealth and rank on their side gave them also the balance of power. The lower rank were not conspicuous enough to have a chance for the regulation of affairs. The Battle of Platæa,[1] where by the advice of Pericles the soldiers first received pay from the public, gave the first beginning to the democratical government,[2] and the commerce which followed it strengthened that change. Commerce gave the lowest of the people an opportunity of raising themselves fortunes, and by that means power. They had by the government an equal chance for all magistracies with the greatest of the nobles, and by their wealth were enabled to have equal weight with the people. This it was which introduced the great change in the tempers of the people, and the means of gaining their favour. Before that time one who had a mind to gain the favour of the people and have influence with them, as riches were not to be got in the state, was generally obliged to make his end by planning out new expeditions and new wars by which a people might be enriched. Those who executed these schemes best were those who had most of their favour. There was therefore no one ever at the head of affairs who had not distinguished himself by military exploits. ⟨But afterwards we find this was little attended, for at the beginning of the Peloponnesian War we find Cleon at the head of the state, and in the end Theramenes and [blank],[3] neither of whom had ever been any way distinguished by military glory; and of the ten orators who in their turn directed the affairs of Athens, none unless Demosthenes had ever seen a battle.⟩

The Athenians were on this account the most enterprising and active people in all Greece, insomuch that the chief leaders and directors had as great difficulty in restraining them as afterwards in rousing them to war. Commerce and luxury entirely altered the state of affairs. They gave the lowest an opportunity of raising themselves to an equality with the nobles, and the nobles an easy way of reducing themselves to the state of the meanest citizen. In this state foreign wars was not the way most likely to give wealth to the people. Those, therefore, who desired to ingratiate themselves did not take that method. They found it easier

---

[1] 479 B.C. Army pay was introduced after the Persian wars, but it is uncertain whether Pericles was responsible. One ancient authority attributes it to Pericles, but there is probably confusion between soldiers' pay and jurymen's.

[2] MS inserts 'by the pay which was at that time appointed to the people', which has been cancelled.        [3] Perhaps 'Critias'.

to give them riches which they had no title to, from the plunder of their fellow-citizens, than from the spoils of their enemies.

The first thing they did was to procure them pay in war: which, though it might appear of no great consequence, yet had a great effect on the nature of the government. Commerce, as it introduced trade or manufacture into all the members of the State, made them unwilling to attend the courts. There were three courts, each of 500[1] men, where private causes were tried, and these three were joined in all public or criminal debates. These, being chosen by lot from the poorest as well as the richest, would be very unwilling to leave their work for an employment which brought them no profit. Pericles, therefore, to gain the favour of the public, brought it about that every judge who attended the court should get two oboli, about threepence, per diem. Nay, so far did this method go, that one Eubulus, or Eubulides,[2] made a law that every citizen should receive the same sum from the community in order to enable him to attend the theatre, that is, in our language, to pay for his ticket at the play. This was the foundation of all their disorders. Demosthenes opposed it without effect, and a law was afterwards made which made it capital in anyone to propose to repeal it. From this time the people became altogether idle and inactive; they received the same pay for sitting at home and doing nothing but attending the public diversions as they did for serving their country abroad, and the former was without question the easiest duty. Military glory had then no weight. The orators ruled the people, coaxing them with new schemes of additional wealth, and often over-ruled the most experienced commanders, turning[3] them, continuing them, or changing them, as they thought fit. Levies were then seldom voted, and where they were, as seldom made. The Athenians, from being the most enterprising people in Greece, were now become the most idle and inactive: they who had such a spirit for enterprise that they had frequently in their wars with Lacedæmon,

---

[1] The judges (*dikasts*) composing the popular tribunals numbered 6000; they were distributed into ten sections, so that each tribe was represented in each section. From these the courts or juries (*dikasteria*) were chosen by lot, varying in size from 201 upwards according to the nature of the case to be tried.

[2] The *theoric* fund, from which grants of two oboli each were made to poor citizens to enable them to attend the theatre and public shows was instituted long before the time of Eubulus (*not -ides*); he was in charge of the fund (*c.* 354-350). In 348 B.C. he got a measure passed that it should be a capital offence to propose that this fund be used for military purposes. After Chaeronea, Demosthenes succeeded in getting the system abolished.

[3] *turning*: reading uncertain.

Syracuse, and other states, risked their whole strength to the fortune of a battle; which sometimes ruined the state, at least for a time.

In this state were the Athenians when Philip of Macedon arose. This prince soon made himself formidable to them by his enterprising and political conduct. The States of Greece were all sensible of their danger, and wanted nothing to cause them declare war but a proper leader. The Lacedæmonians were ruined by the battle of Leuctra. The Thebans were powerful but universally hated. The Athenians alone remained fit for this post. They accordingly were pitched upon for the leaders of the league,[1] and immediately declared war. But though they declared war, they did not go to action. Levies when decreed were never made. Fleets and treasure were to be sent out, but never sailed; and nothing was done with any spirit or activity. They saw their danger, but as war did not promise any advancement of their fortunes, they could hardly be prevailed on to engage in it. Demosthenes took upon him to stir up the Athenians to a more vigorous conduct, and this is the subject of his Philippic orations. His manner is that of one who spoke to a favourable audience, for though the Athenians were sluggish and dilatory in undertaking the war, they saw well enough that it was for the good of the state; but as it promised them no private advantage, they would not be very eager to engage in it. For this reason he never insists very much on the reasonableness of the war, nor on the practicability of succeeding in it, for it was universally allowed that they were no match for their enemies. He dwells on the growing power of Philip, and the danger delay would expose them to, and prompts them to assert themselves and repeal the law of Eubulus. His expression and manner is such as becomes one of sense and dignity, with a sort of innate pride, and contempt for those who opposed him. This makes him frequently rather expostulate with him[2] on the folly of their conduct, than show them the practicability or advantages of more vigorous measures. In this strain he often condescends to downright scolding, and gives them very opprobrious and scurrilous language, but never in a manner improper for a man of dignity and authority. He does it in a manner natural to one who reproves those whom he is sorry to see acting amiss though they know the right, and hence he is always remarkably strong and passionate. ⟨He, however, never lays the blame on the people's want of courage or spirit, but on the false arguments and seductive counsel of the orators, who, bribed, as he said, by Philip, and from other private motives, dissuaded

[1] *league*: reading uncertain.    [2] *Sic*: an error for 'them'.

the people from what they well knew was their real interest. It is to be observed that in no former war, though these were often carried on with more wealthy nations than Macedon, yet [*sic*] this accusation was never so much as mentioned. The reason is not because the orators were then less liable to take such gratuities, but because what was contrary to the interest of the country could not then be of any weight, nor would be at all received.⟩

In the course of the affair with Philip it happened that the city of Olynthus, a port of some note on the coast of Macedon, was brought by presents and solicitations into the interest of Philip. The Athenians were very solicitous to bring them over to their interest. This they accordingly obtained. The Olynthians declared war on Philip. But when Demosthenes was using his best endeavours to prompt the Athenians to a vigorous defence of their allies, the other orators amused them with debates concerning what punishment they should inflict on Philip when they had got him into their power! 'Twas on this occasion Demosthenes spoke the Olynthian oration above-mentioned. We may observe that Sallust has copied the speech[1] in that he puts into the mouth of Cato, and has even gone so far as to translate the first sentence, which could not suit that cause.

[1] Sallust, *Catiline*, 52. The opening sentence resembles that of Demosthenes, *Olynthiac*, III.

147

# 26

IN the last lecture I endeavoured to give you some notion of the manner and spirit of the Deliberative orations of Demosthenes. Besides them, there have no Deliberative orations of any of the Greek orators come down to our time, unless we should reckon those two, περὶ Χαλονήσου[1] and περὶ τῶν μετ᾽ Ἀλεξάνδρου[2] συνθήκων, which are commonly ascribed to Demosthenes, but more probably were composed by Hegesippus. But whoever be the author of them, they are certainly not Demosthenes'; they are altogether silly and trivial, and are not of merit sufficient to deserve any consideration.

We shall therefore proceed [to] the Deliberative orations of Cicero, which are the chief ones that remain in the Latin language. These we shall find are of a very different genius from those of Demosthenes. They have a certain gravity and affectation of dignity which the latter want. It is commonly said the Latin is a grave and solemn language, and much more so than the Greek, which is said to be a merry and sprightly one. It were easy to shew that all languages, Greek and Latin not excepted, are equally ductile and equally accommodated to all different tempers. The style, indeed, of the Latin authors has much more of solemnity and affected dignity and ornament than that of the Greek authors. The difference betwixt style and language is often not attended to, and has not been observed by several authors, though they be in themselves very different, and to this it is owing that what is true only of the style of the writers has been ascribed to the nature and temper of the language itself.

That we may the better understand the particular temper and genius of Cicero's manner of writing, and the causes of it, it will be proper to make some observations on the state of the Roman commonwealth and the temper of the people at the time he wrote, which, though one of the most important parts of history, is generally too little insisted on by authors, and understood by very few.

[1] An error for Ἀλοννήσου.
[2] Should be πρὸς Ἀλέξανδρον.

Before this time the great distinctions of the people had been in a great measure abolished: all magistracies were now become attainable by the whole of the multitude. Those magistracies which were formerly the peculiar province of the Patricians were laid open to every one. The Senatorial dignity, the office of the Praetor, Censor, Aedile, etc. (which were called the Curule magistracies), were no longer confined to the Patricians. The factions of the State were formerly those of the Patricians and Plebeians. The differences and contentions which sprang up after the expulsion of the Kings all arose from the rivalship of those two bodies. But by these continued contentions, the magistracies, and all the power and profit, were by degrees opened to the people. From these immense riches and immense power and interest were often acquired by individuals, both of the Patrician and the nobler Plebeian families. There are many instances of immense fortunes raised by the oppression of those who were under the power and direction of the different officers. The pro-consul[1] Verres may serve as an instance of this; and there are many of as extraordinary and immense power obtained by those who, instead of oppressing, chose to ingratiate themselves with those whom they had under their subjection,—Marius, Cinna, etc. The authority of the Senate was now, indeed, little more than nominal: they could make no laws nor transact any business of importance without the consent and approbation of the people. Some few offices remained at their disposal: but their approbation to the decrees of the people was in most cases no more than a mere form. There had, indeed, been some attempts to reinstate the Patricians in their former authority. Sulla even made laws to this effect; but the alteration made by them was so great that they were allowed to subsist no longer than the power of him who introduced them. By this means the old parties of Patrician and Plebeian were at an end. It was now as much the interest of the chief men of the Plebeians to support the authority of the Senate and other dignified offices, as it had formerly been to curb them. The power or wealth they had acquired, or had a prospect of acquiring, by them, were sufficient motives for them to promote the authority of those officers, and the depression of those who were subject to them. This joint interest formed a division amongst the citizens, somewhat similar but considerably different from the old one. On the one side were the richer and more powerful of the citizens, whether Patricians or Plebeians, all who had either enjoyed the offices of power and profit, or those who had a prospect of reaping those advan-

[1] *Not* pro-consul but pro-praetor (of Sicily, 73-71 B.C.). See below, p. 151.

tages—that is, today, the people of fashion, all who would go under the denomination of Gentlemen. These are called Optimates, a word signi-fying no more than that they were, as we would say, the better sort, people of fashion. The other faction was those of the Plebeians who had not power nor riches to make them considerable, nor any hopes of arriving at those offices which would make it in their power to obtain them. These were the lowest, most despicable people imaginable, supported chiefly by the donations of the nobles. They were the rabble and mob, and the most wretched and miserable set of men imaginable. These would for their own safety oppose the oppression and extortion of the nobles, and attach themselves to those who, to gain power and weight in the commonwealth, courted the favour of that order. The method [used by][1] these men, who from their attach-ment to the populace were called Populares, was to propose laws for the equal division of lands and the distributing of corn at the public charge, or else by largesses and bounties bestowed out of their own private fortune. Of this sort were Clodius, Marius, and others.

The effects, therefore, of the communication of the magistracies and the laying them open to all the people, were very different at Rome from what they were at Athens. Neither the territory of the commonwealth nor the authority of the magistrates was so considerable as to put it in the power of those who filled the offices of state to acquire any extra-ordinary riches, and consequently gave them less opportunity of courting the favour of the multitude with success.[2] By this means the magis-tracies continued open to all those who had merit enough to deserve them and gained the favour of their fellow-citizens. The inequality of fortune was not so great as to make any distinction amongst the citizens. Five talents was reckoned a great estate for an Athenian citizen, for we find Demosthenes reproaching his rival Aeschines[3] with not having celebrated with sufficient magnificence some public show, 'for', says he, 'you cannot plead poverty in your defence, as you was then worth above five talents'. A hundred times that would have been but a very

---

[1] *used by*: conjectural addition.

[2] Smith does not make it clear, at first reading, that this sentence and the next two apply to *Athens* only, not to Rome.

[3] Demosthenes, *De Corona*, 312. Smith would appear to be inaccurate in (1) speaking of Aeschines as celebrating a public show; (2) making the sum five talents, Demosthenes says Aeschines had received a further two from another source.

modest fortune at Rome. And Demosthenes also mentions[1] that his brother-in-law would have been one of the richest men in Athens, as his father left him five talents. The poorest citizens might there by trade raise themselves fortunes equal to those of the most wealthy. As there was therefore no considerable distinction of fortune, so there was properly but one rank of citizens: the highest were citizens and no more, and the lowest had the same privilege. In Rome, on the other hand, the great power and immense wealth which were attendant on all the chief offices of the State soon destroyed that equality which the communication of the magistracies was meant to establish. The people was therefore divided into two factions, that of the Optimates and that of the Populares. The first comprehended all those who had either enjoyed, or had a reasonable expectation of enjoying, the magistracies, that is, the few remaining Patricians and all the noble Plebeian families, and those who had power or interest to advance themselves. In the other were all the Plebeians who were not noble nor had any expectations of raising themselves to offices by which they might attain power or riches. These (as I said) were a most wretched and destitute set of men: they depended for their very subsistence on the liberality of the candidates in their largesses at elections, which were indeed often prohibited, and could not afterwards be publicly avowed. But it was a vain attempt to hinder the people from accepting of such presents for their votes, or the candidates from endeavouring to carry their elections by that means. Or, secondly, [they depended] on the distributions of corn or other necessaries which were made by the public, either for no price or at a low one. There was here no middle rank betwixt those who had the greatest wealth and power, and those who were in the most abject poverty and dependence. The Knights in the earlier periods were a sort of middle betwixt the Plebeians and the Patricians, and somewhat restrained the extravagances of either. They were at this time horsemen, *Equites*, and were distinguished from the rest of the people by the manner of their service.

We may observe the knights in all countries were mere horsemen originally, but when military service was not so much used, they have become of a very different rank. A knight in this country is a very different person from a dragoon. In the same manner the Roman *Equites* were at first those who composed the cavalry. But after the

---

[1] Demophon, Demosthenes's brother-in-law, was one of his three fraudulent guardians. Smith rather overstates the case. Demosthenes's own father left him an estate worth nearly fourteen talents, not five.

victory of Marius over the Cimbri,[1] they were never employed in that service. They were soon after allowed to be elected into the Senate, and from that time became of the same party with the remaining Patricians and other nobles. As there was but one order at Athens, so there were properly only two orders at Rome, the great and the populace.

Besides this, the Athenians and the Romans treated their favourites in a very different manner. All appearance of pride, extraordinary authority, or presumption of any sort was looked [on] at Athens with a jealous eye. The people were offended with Alcibiades, their greatest favourite, for wearing a dress somewhat more splendid than was ordinarily worn by the citizens. But the luxury of Lucullus, or the splendour of Pompey, were not objects of jealousy to the Romans, Though the Athenians could not allow Alcibiades to go gaily dressed, the Romans beheld without suspicion Pompey attended by the flower of the young nobility, a great part of the Senate, and the chief men of the city.

⟨The people never at this time opposed the growing power of their favourites; all they did was looked on with the greatest ease. The only check they met with was from the opposition and contrary endeavours of the nobility, who in the same manner strove to get to the head of affairs.⟩

The nobleman of Rome would, then, find himself greatly superior to the far greater part of mankind. He would see, at Rome, a thousand who were his inferiors for one who was even his equal; and anywhere else there would be none who could compare with him in power or wealth. Finding himself thus superior to most about him, he would contract a great opinion of his own dignity. He would have an air of superiority in all his behaviour. As he spoke generally to his inferiors, he would talk in a manner becoming one in that station. Respect and deference would be what he thought his due as one of superior dignity, and his behaviour would aim at approving himself to be such. His discourse would be pompous and ornate, such as appeared to be the language of a superior sort of man.

At Athens, on the other hand, the citizens were all on equal footing: the greatest and the meanest were considered as being no way distinguished, and lived and talked together with the greatest familiarity. Difference of fortune or employment did not hinder the ease and familiarity of behaviour. It is observed that there is no politeness or compli-

---

[1] In 101 B.C., Marius and Catulus defeated the Cimbri and their allies at Vercelli, near Verona.

ments in the Dialogues of Plato, whereas those of Cicero abound with
them; particularly in his dialogue *De Oratore*, the noble men he introduces talk in the most polite manner and pay one another the greatest
respect, and commend in the most complimenting style. Plato, again,
introduces persons of the most unequal dignity or power in the State
talking with the greatest freedom and[1] familiarity, such as would appear
very odd to this day amongst people of such different stations: and
there is generally one person who roasts, teases, and exposes the others
without mercy, and often with a turn of humour which would not at
this day [be] altogether polite or even decent. In the one country the
people, at least the nobles, would converse and harangue with dignity,
pomp, and the air of those who speak with authority. The language of
the other would be that of freedom, ease, and familiarity. The one is
that where the speaker is supposed to be of superior dignity and authority to his hearers, and the other is that of one who talks to his equals.
Pomp and splendour suit the former well enough, but would appear
presumption in the other.

These considerations may serve to explain many of the differences
in the manners and style of Demosthenes and Cicero. The latter talks
with the dignity and authority of a superior, and the former with the ease
of an equal. Cicero, therefore, studies always to add whatever may give
this appearance to his style, even on the most trivial occasions; and the
other talks with ease and familiarity even when he is the most earnest
and vehement. ⟨Demosthenes abounds with all the common phrases
and idioms and proverbs; Cicero, on the other hand, avoids all idio-
matical turns or other expressions with the greatest care.⟩ Cicero abounds
with all those figures of speech which are thought to give dignity to
language; his style is always correct to the highest degree, with the
greatest propriety of expression and strictest observance of grammatical
propriety. This makes it evident that the author considers himself to be
of importance and dignity, for this exact and ornate style shows that
every word is premeditated, and that he has settled before he began the
sentence in what manner he was to conclude it. There are certain forms
of speech which are peculiar to common conversation, and plainly appear
to proceed from the carelessness of the speaker, who had not resolved
when he began his sentence in what manner he was to end it. These are
called ἀνακόλουθα i.e., unconnected, without consequence, where the one
part of the sentence is of a different grammatical construction from the

[1] 'and familiarity ... stations': inserted in the margin, in the first hand.

other. The Greek writers abound in this figure, but none more than Xenophon and Demosthenes. I shall mention an instance from each to explain the matter. In Xenophon, the sentence in Latin would run thus: *Hephæstus et Menon, quoniam sunt amici vostrum, remittite nobis.* The grammatical construction plainly would require here that he should have *Hephæstum* and *Menona*, etc. In the same manner we would say in easy conversation, 'Hephaestus and Menon, as they are your friends, send them back to us', or 'Send back, etc.'; or, 'John or James such-a-thing, I know not what is become of them', instead of 'I do not know', or 'I know not what is become, etc.' The one we would use in conversation or familiar letter-writing, and the latter in a formal discourse or in writing a history. This has been much used by Demosthenes and other Greeks; but Cicero and most Latin writers have entirely rejected it, as well as almost all modern authors, as it testifies a great degree of carelessness in the speaker. The instance in Demosthenes I do not remember, but there are two places in the same sentence where the foregoing member by the means of some words would require the subsequent to have been altogether of another form.

Again, Demosthenes' periods are for the most part short and concise, without any redundancy of expression: whereas Cicero always runs out into a long train of connected members, even on the most simple subject. And even when Demosthenes is obliged by the quantity of matter which crowds in upon him to form a long period, he never affects those ornaments of similarity, of cadence, and uniformity of length in the several members, which is so much studied by Cicero. This difference is very visible in their Deliberative orations, but still more in their Judicial ones.

Again, the familiarity and ease with which Demosthenes writes makes him often use illustrations or examples, as well as expressions, that appear rather low or ludicrous. This is remarkable in his comparisons, where he often compares things of the greatest importance to others of a very contrary nature. Thus he compares[1] the [blank][2] sending a fleet to [blank], after it had been plundered and destroyed, to a boxer who always clapt his hand to the place where he felt the smart of the last blow, without attending to parry off the approaching ones or *lay on* any himself. Cicero, on the other hand, compares the most trivial things, and that, too, when he is rallying, with the most serious; as for instance, he

[1] Perhaps 'Athenians' was intended.
[2] *First Philippic*, 40.

154

says that the conduct of Mithridates[1] in leaving his treasure in Pontus, which, by employing the troops in plunder, gave the king himself time to escape, was like that of Medea, who, to retard the pursuit of her father, tore her brother in pieces and strewed his limbs on the sea, that she, whilst her father was employed in taking them up, might have time to escape.

These differences in the style of these orators may probably arise from the different condition of the countries in which they lived. The tempers of the men would no doubt also have had their effects. The vanity and pride, if you will call it so, which Cicero was possessed of, may perhaps have made him more ornate and pompous than the temper of his audience would have required; and on the other hand the severity and downright plainness of Demosthenes may have made him more bare and careless than even the familiarity and equality of his countrymen would have required. To this, too, it may be owing, that Demosthenes is at no pains to repeat or expatiate on his subject; which Cicero, as we hinted, always studies. This much with regard to the expression and manner of writing.

As to the matter and the arrangement, these two great orators seem to have succeeded with equal good fortune. The matter and the arrangement of Demosthenes, as we said, is almost always the same, as his design is the same and his audience favourable. Those of Cicero are more various in all these respects, but his success in adapting himself to the several exigencies of the cause is no less conspicuous.

Such, then, are the different manners of Demosthenes and Cicero, both adapted to the state of their country; and, perhaps, had they been practised in the other countries, they would have been less successful. Brutus and [blank],[2] we are told, attempted this, which they called the meek eloquence, and blamed Cicero for the unpolished and bold method of his orations. But we do not read that their success was at all comparable to that of Cicero, or of Hortensius, and [blank][3]; the first of which, if we may believe Cicero,[4] was still more florid and ornate than he; and the other appears from the fragments preserved by Quintilian[5] to have been *very pretty*, and *very florid, just like Cicero*. This study of ornament and pomp was common, not only to all the Roman orators, but to the historians and the poets themselves. Thus Livy and Tacitus are much

---

[1] *Pro Lege Manilia*, 22.  
[2] Perhaps 'Calvus'.  
[3] Perhaps 'Caelius'.  
[4] *Brutus*, 325ff.  
[5] Quintilian, IV, 2, 123; XI, 1, 51; and elsewhere.

more ornate, etc. than Herodotus and Thucydides; Virgil[1] than Homer and Hesiod, Propertius than Theognis, etc.; [blank] and Lucretius, the most simple of all the Roman poets, is far more ornate than Hesiod. When this study is so general we may be well assured that it proceeded not from any peculiarity or humour of the writer, but from the nature and temper of the nation. 'Tis this ornate manner I would have you chiefly remark in Cicero. It appears, indeed, most in his Judicial orations. The one I shall translate is the fourth, Catilinan one. I translate it not because I in the least imagine there are any of you here who could not understand the original, but because it would be unfair to compare an original of Cicero with a translation of Demosthenes. The occasion was when Cato and [blank][2] counselled the Senate to put these unworthy and abominable cities[3] to death, and Caesar and [blank][4] counselled to spare their lives, as the Senate had not, after the Sempronian law, the power of condemning to capital punishment, but to confine them for life, alleging this to be a more savage and heavier punishment on courageous men. Cicero, then consul, was afraid to counsel death, lest the odium should fall on him alone, but yet inclined and offered to execute the commands of the Fathers to do it. Betwixt these he hovers, and his whole oration is one continued train of tergiversation; which, though a most weak and pusillanimous temper, and which afterwards caused him to be banished for that very action, which yet he was afraid to avoid, yet is managed in a most artificial, ornate, and elegant manner. And when in this case he is ornate, we may conceive what he was in other cases.

[1] The scribe has not been able to take down all the names rapidly. He pairs Propertius with Virgil against Homer and Hesiod, leaves a blank to balance Theognis, and a blank after 'Theognis, etc.' It seems better to move Propertius, and let Hesiod be balanced by Virgil (*Georgics*).     [2] Perhaps 'Silanus'.
[3] *Sic*: perhaps 'citizens' is intended.     [4] Perhaps 'Tiberius Nero'.

# 27

THE Deliberative orations of Demosthenes and Cicero are the only ones of that sort that have come down to us either in the Greek or Latin language, and as these are pretty much on the same occasions and designed to bring about the same ends, it would be unfair to form a judgment of the Deliberative eloquence of those two nations from so small and confined a specimen. It may not therefore be improper to take also into our consideration those Deliberative orations which the several Greek and Latin historians have inserted in their works. We are certain, it is true, that these orations are not genuine and those which were spoke on the occasions they are introduced. But at the same time they will serve to show what notion those writers had formed of Deliberative eloquence. They will also, perhaps, appear to be as perfect in their kinds as those either of Demosthenes or Cicero. The writers had more leisure to correct and polish them than those two great orators had, who often spoke them on sudden and unexpected occasions.

I shall first consider those which Thucydides has inserted in his history. I mentioned already, in treating of the historical writers, the particular end which that author had in view in composing his history, which was, to explain the causes which brought about the several important events that happened during the period. I observed also that it was chiefly the external causes which he calls in to this purpose. Now all his orations are excellently adapted to this idea of historical writing. There are three things which are principally concerned in bringing about the great events of a war (and as it is the history of a war which he writes, it is in such he is principally concerned), viz., the relative strength of the contending powers at the commencement of the war; the strength, fidelity, and good will of their several allies, and the circumstances in which the armies on both sides were placed; and the different incidents which influenced the success of each particular battle. The whole of his orations are employed either to persuade the people to enter upon the war, or to dissuade them from it; or they are the orations of the ambassa-

dors either asking an alliance, or defending the conduct of their countries, or settling the demands of the contending powers, either before
the war broke out or in order to bring about an accommodation; or they
are those of the generals at the head of their armies encouraging them
to battle.

Of about forty-five orations which there are inserted in Thucydides'
history, there are about twelve or thirteen which are represented as the
orations of those who were recommending war to their countrymen.
These evidently tend to make us acquainted with the comparative
strength, the valour, the designs and interests of the contending parties.
In these, and indeed in all his other orations, he has made chief use of
those arguments which in Deliberative orations are alone convincing and
conclusive. The arguments, as I mentioned before, which may be used
to persuade one to undertake any enterprise, are of three sorts: they
either show the utility and the honourableness of it; or, secondly, the
practicability; or, thirdly, they are such as take in both these considerations together, and show that the undertaking is both useful and practi-
cable to them in their present situation. These latter are those which are
conclusive and convincing, as they alone are suited to the particular
occasion on which they are delivered.

There is also a good number of orations of ambassadors, asking
alliance with particular states, etc. But the far greater part of his orations
are those of generals at the head of their armies. There are six or seven
orations, besides, which do not touch upon either of these subjects, but
then they are very well adapted to bring about the general end of his
history. The first is that which I formerly mentioned, of Pericles when
he draws the characters of the Athenians and Lacedaemonians. It is
evident that this will tend greatly to explain the events of the war, as
nothing gives greater light into any train of action than the characters of
the actors. The consultation of the Athenians concerning the punishment that should be inflicted by the Athenians on the [Mytilenians][1]
who had broke their alliance and were then reduced into subjection,
furnishes matter for four orations, two of which recommend the greatest
severity, and the other two a mitigation of their punishment. The reduc-
tion of Mytilene also affords the subject of two others on this head of
their punishment. The first day of the assembly Creon[2] advised the
putting of the whole inhabitants to the sword, which was accordingly
agreed to, and a boat dispatched with the orders. But the next day

[1] Thucydides, III, 36ff.     [2] *Sic*: an error for Cleon.

Democritus,[1] a man of a milder and more humane temper, called them together, and so changed the temper of the Athenians that they took the whole people again into their protection and alliance, or more properly subjection, in the same manner as they had been before.

The affairs of the Megareans, who had been attacked by the Lacedaemonians as refusing their commerce, has been the subject of several of his Deliberative orations: that[2] which Pericles is said to have delivered on this occasion may serve as an example of his particular manner and style in the Deliberative orations. In this oration, the point he insists most upon is the practicability of succeeding in a war against the Lacedaemonians. He passes over the utility and reasonableness of it, as he had explained them in the former orations on this head. He does not, however, consider those in the abstract, but has showed the justness of the cause that influenced them to declare war, and the great necessity of doing so, and in this he sets forth the great superiority the Athenians had over the Lacedaemonians. In this oration, as his design is to inform the reader of the situation of the Athenians at that time, and the motives for undertaking the war, but chiefly of their superiority over the Lacedaemonians at that time, so for the better understanding of these he thought it proper to divide his oration into these separate parts, and though he does [not][3] divide the discourse into a 1st, 2nd, and 3rd part, yet the transition from one subject to the other is distinctly marked. As the instruction of his reader is what he has chiefly in view, so he has no occasion to introduce any ornamental and what are called oratorical expressions, far less any exaggeratory or hyperbolical ones. Plain downright strong arguments are what best suited with his design, and are accordingly what is the material of all his orations. From this it proceeds that his orations are all so much alike. The character of the speaker has no influence, for as the instruction of the reader in the causes of the chief events is what he aims at here, as well as in the other parts of his book, the arguments which are deduced from these are what chiefly suit his design. ⟨An old man and a young, a passionate and a calm, talk in the same way. The [blank] and the [blank], the superstitious and solemn Cleon, and the loose, merry, and debauched Alcibiades, harangue in the same style.⟩

The whole of the orations, therefore, which are introduced in debates with regard to peace or war before the commencement of it, are of this

---

[1] *Sic*: an error for Diodotus.  [2] Thucydides, I, 140-4.
[3] *not*: conjectural addition.

same sort. There is no more variety in those where the ambassadors of one state ask the alliance of another. The arguments here all tend to show the advantage such an alliance would be of to the parties, and the disadvantage of rejecting it. And in the same manner his orations for generals all tend to the same end, to set forth the necessity of engaging, and the probability they had to conquer, from the nature and circumstances of their situation. ⟨The arguments he uses are in all cases such as would have most weight with his hearers, without considering what those were which would most naturally occur to one of such a particular temper, and would most strongly prompt him to such or such a scheme of conduct or particular action.⟩ By this means, though his orations have, properly speaking, no character at all, which they display, yet they tend greatly to illustrate the particular incidents. His orations on peace and war have none of those general expressions which are so common in other historians, no declamations on the glory of conquering or falling in the defence of liberty, nor other such like; nor his ambassadorial ones any of those high-flown expressions generally used on such occasions, as the glory and heroism of defending the oppressed, etc.; nor those of the generals any one general and commonplace expression on the magnanimity of exposing themselves to the hazard either of conquering or of falling on the field of honour, etc. By this means, though the orations on each subject are of the same kind, yet those regarding one debate on peace and war could not apply to any other, nor those of one alliance to the circumstances of any other in the whole book. And though he has above twenty orations of generals, yet none of them could be interchanged without [its] being easily perceived.

The Deliberative orations of Livy have a considerable resemblance to those of Thucydides and at the same time are very different. For this reason it will perhaps tend to give us the more distinct notion of both to make a comparison betwixt their different manners. The design of Livy seems to be much the same with that of Thucydides, to wit, to explain the causes of the several remarkable events whose history he relates. The causes, too, which he assigns, are in general the external ones. But though this be his chief plan, yet he does not adhere so much by it as not to give place to what appears to be entertaining and amusing to his readers. Thucydides never relates any fact but what is some way connected with the principal events of the history; nor does he introduce any speeches but such as tend to illustrate the causes or circumstances of some important event, or one nearly connected with them. In both of these respects he is widely different from Livy. That author never omits any event which promises to be interesting and affecting to his readers, however little connected with the chief events he is to relate. And as he never omits any event of this sort, so he commonly puts a speech into the mouth of the person chiefly affected, expressing his sentiments on that head. As an instance of this we may observe the account he gives of the discord betwixt Demetrius and Perseus, the sons of Philip of Macedon, the second[1] of that name. These, he tells us, came to such a pitch that the one at length told his father that his brother intended to murder him. The father then calls his sons before him to hear the cause, and we have a speech of his on this occasion, not after he had heard the cause as a judge, summing up the arguments and balancing them together, but before he had heard the cause, expressing how greatly he was affected by his situation, being the judge betwixt his sons and obliged to discover one guilty of an attempt of patricide, or one who had falsely accused his brother, etc. We have also the speeches of the brothers, where there is, indeed, some attempt to render a proof; but the far greater part is employed in expressing how greatly they were affected in being obliged to justify themselves each by accusing his brother, etc. But Philip at last concludes that he would not determine the cause by one hearing, but examine into all the actions of their lives and the general tenor of their behaviour. So that Livy has here bestowed three speeches[2] on an event which tends not in the least to illustrate the principal ones, nor had even any effect on the fate of the persons concerned.

There are two speeches, one in Thucydides and the other in Livy, which are on very similar circumstances and in many things resemble one another so much that Brissonius[3] affirms that Livy has copied his from Thucydides. The occasion of that in Thucydides[4] was the embassy of the Corcyreans to Athens, asking their alliance against the Corinthians, with whom the Athenians were then at war. The reasoning here is the strongest possible. They represent how that they were under a necessity of joining themselves to one or the other party. They were then the second maritime power, as Holland, Athens the first, as Britain, and Corinth the third, as France. They represent, therefore, that if the

---

[1] *Sic*: an error for 'fifth'.

[2] Livy, XL, chs. 5-15; the speech of the father is in ch. 8.

[3] Barnabé Brisson, French statesman and scholar. His Notes on Livy were used in Modius's edition of Livy (1588). Modius speaks of the 'eruditissimus praeses, B. Brissonius, cuius volumen *De Formulis* consultet qui sapiet.' Cf. *Biographie Universelle*, V, p. 620.     [4] Thucydides, I, 32-6.

Athenians accepted of their alliance, they would, without doubt, [be] superior to their foes; but if they rejected it, and obliged them to join the Corinthians, they would then be equal, if not superior, to them: and other arguments no less convincing.

The case of the Capuans, and the speech[1] of their ambassadors, is exactly similar to this. The Samnites were to them as the Corinthians to the people of Corcyra. The arguments in both are so similar that it is very probable Livy borrowed those of greatest strength from Thucydides. But besides these there are many which tend only to show how much the ambassadors and the people of Capua were interested in it, and how much they themselves were affected by it, but tend little to make it appear reasonable to the Romans. The arguments used through the whole of this oration are such as rather show the great affections and desires of the speaker, than tend to convince the audience. They are very strong to the speaker, but not of great weight with the hearer. As his speeches are those of persons deeply and passionately interested in the cause, they have consequently no set division, no transition distinctly marked from one part of the subject to another. But though they are not thus regularly divided, yet the sentences follow one another in a natural order, each one suggesting that which follows it; whereas in Thucydides there is no connection particularly observed in the several sentences, although the whole be distinctly divided. The one is the natural language of one deeply interested in the subject he spoke on; the other that of a calm, sedate man who valued nothing but strong and solid arguments.

The Deliberative orations of Tacitus are considerably different either from those of Thucydides or of Livy. They are, however, very consistent with that idea of historical writing which Tacitus entertained and which we have already explained. He is at no pains in any of them to unfold the causes of events in his orations. They are altogether designed to interest and affect the reader. The arguments, therefore, which he brings into them, are such as would have been very strong with the speaker, but would have no effect with the audience. Thus in the speech[2] which Germanicus makes to the soldiers to bring them from the sedition, there is not one argument which would induce them to quit it. All that he says tends only to show his own desire that they should leave it, and the great effects which it had on him. We will see that Tacitus carries this to a much greater length than Livy, if we compare this speech with one in

[1] Livy, VII, 30ff.      [2] Tacitus, *Annales*, I, 42-3.

the 2nd book of Livy,[1] which he puts in the mouth of Valerius Corvus, addressed to the soldiers who had revolted and obliged Titus Quinctius to take the command. In this speech the sedition was far from being of such consequence as that of the legions under Germanicus, yet there is greatly more argument and reasoning than in that which Tacitus gives Germanicus.

Livy, we may observe here, though he uses a great many arguments in his Deliberative orations which could be of no weight with the audience, carefully avoids them in the Judicial ones, of which he has several. It would be altogether absurd to introduce one defending himself basely by telling us how sorry he was to die, etc. etc. As Livy is a sort of medium betwixt Tacitus and Thucydides, so is Xenophon betwixt Thucydides and Livy. In his Judicial orations he introduces a great deal more of strong argument than Livy, and more convincing reasoning; but at the same time he has a great deal more of the affecting and interesting arguments which display the character of the speaker than is to be met with in Livy. The oration[2] which he says he delivered himself to the soldiers when they demanded the plunder of [blank][3] may serve to show all these particulars. It will also serve as an instance of that simplicity and innocence of manner which is so conspicuous in all his works.

[1] Livy, VII, 40. Smith, or the scribe, errs in saying Bk II.
[2] *Anabasis*, VII, 1, §§ 25-31.     [3] 'Byzantium' was probably meant.

# 28

HAVING now said all I think necessary to observe concerning Demonstrative and Deliberative eloquence, I come to the third and last species of eloquence, viz. the Judicial, which is employed either in the defence of some particular person, or the support of some particular right or claim as vested in some certain person, or in the contrary of these. That is, it is either Judicial or Civil. In treating of this kind, I shall consider firstly, what matters may be the subject of a Judicial oration; secondly, what arguments may be used in these discourses; thirdly, in what order they are to be placed; fourthly, how they are to be expressed; and fifthly, what writers have chiefly excelled in this manner of writing, with some observations on the distinguishing marks and characteristics of each.

First, we are to consider what may be the subject of Judicial oration. This may be either a matter of fact which is affirmed by the one party and denied by the other, or the question may respect a certain point of law. This latter again divides into two, for the question may be either whether such a point be law or not, or whether the circumstances of the fact are such as that they bring it within the verge of that law. So that all Judicial questions may be comprehended under some or other of these three heads:—Either, 1st, the question may be concerning the reality of a fact which is alleged by one party and denied by the other; or, 2nd, concerning the existence of a certain point of law; or, 3rd, concerning the extent of that law, that is, whether the circumstances of the fact are such that they bring it within the verge of the law. These three heads we will find exactly corresponding to the division given by the ancient writers on this subject. They said all questions were either *de re*, which corresponds to the 1st of our divisions; or concerning the circumstances and particularities of the fact, which they said was *de re finita*: or, after the affair was fixed, it might be disputed whether or not it was agreeable to law or not. Thus much concerning the subject of Judicial orations.

We come now to the second thing proposed, viz. what arguments may be used on these heads, in a Judicial oration. We shall consider this first with regard to the case where the question is concerning a matter of fact. Now arguments on a matter of fact may be drawn or proved in two ways: either, first, from its causes; or, second, from its effects. Now as it is the actions of men which commonly are to be examined into, the causes that must be advanced for the proof of any of that sort of events are those which generally tend to bring about human actions. Now the proof of any event from the causes that are imagined to have produced it is generally not very satisfactory, as there seldom can be causes shown which infallibly will produce such-and-such an event. But in no case is the proof of facts from the causes more uncertain than in that of human actions. The causes of human actions are motives, and so far is certain, that none ever acts without a motive. But then, it is not sufficient proof that one committed any action that he had a motive to do so. There are many things that may occasion the contrary. If the action be not suitable to the character of the person, the motive will not influence him to commit the action it prompts him to. Besides, though one had a motive to such-and-such an action, and though it was altogether suitable to his character, it is still requisite that he should have an opportunity, other-wise the action could not have been committed. In proving, therefore, an action to have happened, by proving that its causes subsisted, we must not only prove that one had a motive to commit such an action, but also that it was one that suited his character, and that he had an oppor-tunity also. But even when all this is done, it does by no means amount to proof of the action. The character of man is a thing so fluctuating that no proof which depends on it can be altogether conclusive. There may many circumstances interfere which will entirely alter the designs and disposition of the person for that time, and prevent the execution of an action, even when there is strong motive for it, the disposition and character agreeable to the action, and the fairest opportunity offered. In ... oration to prove that[1] ... murdered ... it is said *hereditatem sperabat et magnam* ... each of which arguments taken singly have[2] a considerable weight; but when considered in the gross, the showing that he had a motive, and that the action was suitable to his character, may serve to show that he might possibly have had an intention to have com-mitted the action; and where the motive, character, and opportunity

---

[1] Several 'blanks' in MS. The phrase 'hereditatem sperabat' does not appear in Cicero's speeches. The scribe may have erred. A possible allusion is to Oppianicus's murders, narrated in Cicero's *Pro Cluentio*, 19-40.      [2] *Sic*: has.

all coincide, there is a proof that the person may have possibly have committed it, but cannot amount to a proof that the fact was actually committed. But though these cannot make out clearly an affirmative proof, yet they will be very suffi[cient] to prove that an action was not committed. The want of opportunity alone is sufficient to prove that the action was not committed. The want of a motive is also a very strong proof, but not so conclusive as the other, since sometimes men act altogether unreasonably, and not out [of] any strong motive. The actions being contrary to the character of the person is a great proof of the contrary; but neither is it altogether certain, as there are many occasions on which one will deviate from the ordinary tenor of his conduct. Cicero, in his defence of Roscius,[1] endeavours to show that he had no motive to kill his father, that it was altogether unsuitable to his character, etc. . . . It is this sort of argument which the rhetoricians chiefly insist upon, and are at greatest pains to divide and sub-divide. Thus with regard to the motive, they say we do an action either to increase, or procure, or preserve something good, or to destroy,[2] divide, shun, or get free from, something evil, etc. They insist in the same manner on the character, and consider the age, the sex, the family, etc. and even the very name of the person. In the same manner they divide the consideration of the opportunity into that of [blank] time and place, and so [on]. This may serve to account why the later orators have insisted almost solely on this sort of arguments, as they alone are fully treated of by the rhetoricians, on whose directions they seem to have modelled their orations. This may suffice concerning the arguments which are used to prove a fact from its causes.

⟨Even Cicero himself insists greatly on these arguments, and seems sometimes to strain them rather too far in the case of Milo,[3] in which he would show that he had no reason to kill Clodius, though this man was continually seeking his life.⟩

The proof of an event from its effects is sometimes altogether certain. Thus if one has been seen committing the fact, and the witnesses testify it, there is no other proof necessary. But there are many cases where the effects either of the action itself or of the intention to do it, are not altogether conclusive at first sight, though they may be very strong presumptions. Thus in the old cause which is commonly quoted, the man

---

[1] *Pro Roscio Amerino*, Cicero's defence of Roscius from the charge of murdering his father (81 B.C.).

[2] *destroy*: reading uncertain.  [3] *Pro Milone, passim.*

who had been seen some days before the murder of a certain person walking about very pensive and melancholy, as if he was meditating some horrid or dreadful action, and was amissing all the night that the murder was committed and could give no account of himself, might very probably be presumed, from these effects, of the intention of killing, or to have had some hand in it, but could not be absolutely concluded to have been guilty of it. But when these effects of the intention are joined with those of the action itself, the proof is still stronger, as in the case where one who bore another an ill-will was found near his dead body, with his hands bloody, and a great appearance of terror, he would appear to be very probably the murderer, especially if the arguments from the cause of the action are joined with them. But though these arguments give a great probability of the commission of the action by the person in whom they are found, yet the want of them does by no means prove the innocence of the person. If one should be found whose hands were altogether clear of blood, and no appearance of concern after the murder nor anxiety before it, we could not conclude from this that he was innocent. For there are some people such consummate dissemblers that they can go about the most horrid actions without the least emotion and anxiety, either before or after the perpetration.

The rhetoricians divide all these topics into many orders and classes. (These will be found in Quintilian by those who incline to read them. For my part I'll be at no further trouble about them at present.)[1]

⟨It is in the proper ordering and disposal of this sort of arguments that the great art of an orator often consists. These when placed separately have often no great impression, but if they be placed in a natural order, one leading to the other, their effect is greatly increased. The best method to answer this is to throw them into a sort of a narration, filling up in the manner most suitable to the design of the speaker what intervals there may otherwise be. By this means, though he can bring proof of very few particulars, yet the connection there is makes them easily comprehended and consequently agreeable, so that when the adversary tries to contradict any of these particulars it is pulling down a fabric with which we are greatly pleased and are very unwilling to give up.⟩

We shall now make some observations concerning the topics or

---

[1] Smith's impatience with the sub-divisions of the rhetoric-writers is worth noting. John Holmes, in his *Art of Rhetoric made Easy* (1755), lists some 250 'tropes, figures, and turns'!

foundations of arguments that may be brought to prove anything to be law or not. Now when the law is plainly expressed in the statute there can be no question on this head. The only two methods in which anything can be shown to be law, are either to show how, by abstract reasoning, it follows from some statute, or how it has been supported as law by former practice and similar adjudged causes or precedents. This last, which is so much in use amongst modern lawyers, was not at all used by the ancients, either Greeks or Romans. The rhetoricians amongst all their topics make not the least mention of precedents. They have indeed one order of topics which they entitle *De Similibus et Dissimilibus*. In this they mention all the different sorts of similitude except that of precedents. They are such as the persons having done the like actions before, or other persons in similar circumstances—and which are evidently altogether different from prēcedents (or precēdents). As, therefore, there is such a remarkable difference betwixt the modern and the ancient practice in this respect, it may not be improper to make a digression in order to explain it.

In the early periods the same persons generally exercise the duties of judge, general, and legislator: at least the two former are very commonly conjoined. The first thing which makes men submit themselves to the authority of others is the difficulty they feel in accommodating their matters either by their own judgement or by that of their opponents, and find it most advisable to submit it to some impartial person. By this means some persons of eminent worth came to be settled as judges and umpires. When men, especially in a barbarous state, are accustomed to submit themselves in some points, they naturally do it in others. The same persons therefore who judged them in peace, led them also to battle. In this two-fold capacity of judge and general, the first kings and consuls of Rome, and other magistrates, would reckon the judicial part of their office a burthen, rather than that by which they were to obtain honour and glory; that was only to be got by military exploits. They therefore were very bold in passing sentence. They would pay very little regard to the conduct of their predecessors, as this was the least important part of their office. This part was therefore for their ease separated from the other and given to another sort of magistrates. These, as the Judicial was their only office, would be at much greater pains to gain honour and reputation by it. ⟨Having* less power they would be more timid.⟩ They would be at pains to strengthen their conduct by the authority of their predecessors. When, therefore, there

168

were a few judges appointed, these would be at great pains to vindicate and support their conduct by all possible means. Whatever, therefore, had been practised by other judges would obtain authority with them, and be received in time as law. This is the case in England. The sentences of former cases are greatly regarded, and form what is called the Common Law, which is found to be much more equitable than that which is founded on Statute only, for the same reason as what is founded on practice and experience must be better adapted to particular cases than that which is derived from theory only.

These judges, when few in number, will be much more anxious to proceed according to equity than where there is a great number. The blame then is not so easily laid upon any particular person; they are in very little fear of censure; and are out of danger of suffering much by wrong proceedings. ⟨Besides* that a great number of judges naturally confirm each other, prejudice and inflame each other's passions.⟩ We see accordingly that the sentences of the judges in England are greatly more equitable than those of the Parliament of Paris or other Courts which are severed from censure by their number. The House of Commons, when they acted in a Judicial capacity, have not always proceeded with the greatest wisdom, although their proceedings are kept upon record as well as those of the other Courts, and without doubt in imitation of them. ⟨In* censuring any of their own members or in any other such case, they have not distinguished themselves by their justice.⟩ The House of Lords have indeed proceeded in a very equitable manner, but this is not to be attributed to their number, but to [blank].

The case was the same with regard to the Areopagus and the Council of Five Hundred at Athens. Their number was too great to restrict them from arbitrary and summary proceedings. They would here pay as little regard to the proceedings of former judges as those did who at the same time possessed the office of general along with that of judge. The Praetor at Rome, indeed, often borrowed from the decrees; but then nothing could be quoted as law to him but what was found in his edict, which was put up at the beginning of each year, and in which he declared in what manner he was to regulate his conduct. (This was the custom till the time of the Edictum Perpetuum.)[1] He would have taken it as a great affront to his judgement to have been told that such an one before had

---

[1] Smith is thinking of the work of Salvius Julianus, who, in Hadrian's time, reduced the mass of existing *edicta* to order; the resulting corpus was given by the Emperor the force of law throughout the Roman Empire.

done so-and-so. And no part of the former edicts could be quoted but what was transcribed into his, and in his name it was always to be quoted. There was therefore no room for precedents in any Judicial pleadings amongst the Greeks or Romans, though nothing can be more common than it is now. And it may be looked upon as one of the most happy parts of the British Constitution, though introduced merely by chance and to ease the men in power, that the office of judging causes is committed into the hands of a few persons whose sole employment it is to determine them.

⟨The* separation of the province of distributing justice between man and man from that of conducting affairs and leading armies, is the great advantage which modern times have over ancient, and the foundation of that greater security which we now enjoy, both with regard to liberty, property, and life. It was introduced only by chance to ease the supreme magistrate of the most laborious and least glorious part of his power, and has never taken place until the increase of refinement and the growth of society have multiplied business immensely.⟩

It is evident that, in quoting precedents, the more directly they agree with the case in hand in all its circumstances, it will be so much the better; for where it differs in many or in any important parts, it will require a good deal of abstract reasoning to show the similitude and bring them to the same case.

The other way to prove anything to be law is to show that it follows from some Statute law by abstract reasoning. The other is always preferred to this, where it can be made use of, as the abstract reasoning renders it less easily comprehended. To show that anything is or is not comprehended within any point of law, there are two methods. We may either show, first, that the law could not have its desired effect unless it was extended thus far; or, second, that the law by the manner in which it is expressed must comprehend it. The first method is but very seldom applicable, and in most cases not conclusive, as the precise intention of the law is not always evident; and, besides, it requires a great deal of abstract reasoning. In the other manner, we must (to show the meaning of the law) give a definition of the meaning of the several parts, and show the extent of each. (We all know how the rhetoricians made their definitions by genus, species, and differentia.) This is very difficult in all things of a very general nature, and cannot be applied on many occasions. The best way of defining generally is to enumerate the several qualities of the thing to be defined. But in this case it is most advisable not to go about to define every part of the law and show the whole extent of it, but to show by some part of it, which we are to explain clearly, that the thing in question is comprehended by it, and leave the rest to others— as I do the rhetorical divisions of these heads.[1]

[1] Cf. p. 167. *n. 1. supra.*

# 29

IN the last lecture I gave ye [*sic*] an account of the several things which may be the subject of a Judicial oration, and also of the several topics from which arguments for the proof of those several questions may be drawn. The next thing which writers on this subject generally treat of is the method of a Judicial oration.

They tell us that every regular oration should consist of five parts. There are, it is true, two chief parts, the laying-down the proposition, and the proof. But in the connecting these two properly together and setting them out in the brightest light, the oration, they say, naturally divides into five parts. The *first* of these is the Exordium, in which the orator explains briefly the purpose of his discourse and what he intends to accuse the adversary of, or to acquit his client of. The *second* part is, according to them, the Narration. The orator in this relates not only those facts which he is afterwards to prove, but puts the whole story into a connected narration, supplying those parts of himself in the manner most[1] suitable design which he cannot prove.[2] The reason they give for this is that the several parts, being thus connected, gain a considerable strength by the appearance of probability and connection, so that it is difficult afterwards to wrest our belief from them. And by this means, though we can prove but a very small part of the facts, yet those which we have proved give the others, by the close connection they have with them, a great appearance of truth, and the whole story has the appearance, at least, of considerable probability. In the practice of the modern Courts of Judicature the narration is never introduced; the pleader barely relates the things he is to prove, without giving us a detail of the whole transaction, and it is only where there is very little attention and great ignorance that this can have much weight. The inattention and confusion which prevailed in the ancient courts is such as we have no

---

[1] *most*: reading uncertain.
[2] The scribe has become confused: the meaning is clearly 'supplying of himself those parts which he cannot prove, in the manner most suitable to his design'.

conception of, and the ignorance and folly of judges as great as can well be imagined. By this means a well-told story would have a great influence upon them. The courts were then in very little better order than the mob in the pit of an ill-regulated play-house, and easily turned to either side. We see in one of Demosthenes' orations, viz. that upon [blank],[1] when his adversary Aeschines had accused him of calling him the friend of Philip and Alexander, he said he did no such thing. He called him indeed the slave of Philip, who had been bribed by his gold, but had never given him the name of his friend. 'And this', he says, 'was the name he undoubtedly best deserved. We shall appeal', he says, 'to these judges. What think ye, my countrymen? Is this man to be called the friend or the slave of Philip?' The judges, we find, called out 'the slave! the slave!', for he goes on, 'Ye see what is their opinion.' Some persons which he had placed among them and had encouraged to that purpose, called out as he wanted them, and the rest seconded them without hesitation. These orators, then, managed the Courts of Judicature in the same manner as the managers of a play-house do the pit. They place some of their friends in different parts of the pit, and as they clap or hiss the performers the rest join in. And so the orators then got some person who began the cry, which the rest for the most part accompanied. This was the case at Athens. The courts at Rome were much more regular and in better order, and to this in a great measure we may attribute the stability of their Commonwealth. The Athenian state did not continue in its glory for above seventy years, viz. from the Battle of Plataea,[2] from which we may date the commencement of democracy, till the taking of the city and the settling of the Tyrants under Lysander.[3] The Roman State, again, continued in its grandeur for above 500 years, viz. from the expulsion of the Tarquins till the ruin of the Republic under Julius Caesar.[4]

But even in these courts the orators made a very great use of those narrations, and in cases where the facts they could prove were but very few and often little tending to the main point. Thus in the oration for Milo, Cicero gives us a very particular and minute detail of the whole transaction, how they met and fought, etc. etc. He would have us to believe that not Milo, but Clodius, had lain in wait for his adversary, though it was well known at Rome at that time that their meeting was

---

[1] Probably the Crown, see *De Corona*, 51-2.
[2] Battle of Plataea, 479 B.C., when the Greeks defeated the Persians.
[3] 404 B.C.
[4] Expulsion of the Tarquins, 510 B.C.; death of Caesar, 44 B.C.

entirely accidental. He proves, indeed, pretty plainly, that Milo had not
lain in wait for Clodius, as he stayed in the Senate till the ordinary time,
that he went home, changed his shoes and put off his cloak, etc., but
proves no more: the rest depends entirely on its connection with these
circumstances. In the same manner, in his oration for Cluentius,[1] which
I believe is the finest, as well as it is the longest, of all his orations, he
endeavours to prove that it was not Cluentius but his accuser [Oppiani-
cus][2] who had bribed the judges. He does not pretend to deny that they
had been bribed, as there had been several banished on that account by
a court in which several of the judges then sitting had been present, but
he gives the bribery to a different person. Cluentius had been acquitted
and [Oppianicus][2] condemned. The most probable account of the
bribery in this case was that they had been bribed by the person
acquitted. But he endeavours to prove, in a very pretty manner, that the
bribe had been given by the other. The only fact he proves in support
of this is that [Oppianicus][2] had given one [Staienus][2] 640,000 sestertii,
perhaps for a very different cause than the bribing of the judges. This,
he says, must have certainly been to bribe the judges, as it made 40,000
to each of them: else what would have been the design of the odd
40,000? The whole story is told in a very pleasant and entertaining
manner, and had such an effect on the judges that Cluentius was
acquitted, in all appearance contrary to justice. And we see that Cicero
glories more, on this occasion, of [sic] his address in the fooling of the
judges, than on any other.[3] ⟨We may observe also with regard to this
oration that Cicero gains the favour of his judges, in the exordium or
preface, to his client, and prejudices them against his opponent, by
telling before them the great and uncontrovertible crimes he had been
guilty of.⟩

The regularity and order of procedure of the courts, however, made
the lives and property of the subjects pretty safe in most cases, whereas
at Athens the disorder (as we said) was such that it was just heads or tails
whether the sentence was given for or against one. We see from the

[1] The circumstances were these: In 74 B.C. Aulus Cluentius Habitus accused his
step-father, Statius Albius Oppianicus, of attempting to procure his death by poison.
Oppianicus was condemned, and it was believed that Cluentius had bribed the judges.
In 66 B.C. Cluentius was accused by young Oppianicus, son of Statius Albius, who had
since died, of three acts of poisoning. Cicero's defence of him is the oration *Pro
Cluentio*.
[2] There is a blank in the MS.
[3] Quintilian (II, 17, 21) reports Cicero's boast. 'Cicero boasted that, in the case of
Cluentius, he had thrown dust in the eyes of the jury.'

accounts given of the condemnation of Socrates that it was not any crime he was convicted of, for all the judges inclined to acquit him, but that his behaving somewhat haughtily and not making the acknowledgments he required, which brought him under a capital punishment. This uncertainty and variableness of the courts at Athens was so great that none almost cared to stand their trial. When Alcibiades had performed the most gallant exploits at Syracuse, and learned that he was accused at home of impiety, he would not stand his trial, but fled to Lacedaemon (which was in effect the cause of the ruin of the State). When they asked him why he would not trust his life in the hands of his countrymen, he told them that he would trust them with anything but that, and with it he would not trust his own mother, lest she should put in the black bean instead of the white one.[1]

This, however, is not now in use, as the Courts of Judicature are brought into a different form: so that I shall not insist on the proper manner of executing it.

The other three parts are the Confirmation, the Refutation, and the Peroration. The Confirmation consists in the proving of all or certain of the facts alleged, and this is done by going through the arguments drawn from the several topics I mentioned in the last lecture; and the Refutation, or the confuting of the adversaries' arguments, is to be gone through in the same manner. The later orators adhered most strictly to the rules laid down by the rhetoricians. We see that even Cicero himself was scrupulously exact in this point, so that in many, indeed most, of his orations, he goes through all of those topics. It would probably have been reckoned a defect to have omitted any one, and not to have led[2] an argument from the topic *De Causa, Effectu, Tempore*, etc. This may serve to show us the low state of philosophy at that time. Whatever branch of philosophy has been most cultivated and has made the greatest progress will necessarily be most agreeable in the prosecution. This, therefore, will be the fashionable science, and a knowledge in it will give a man the character of a deep philosopher and a man of great knowledge. If Natural Philosophy, or Ethics, or Rhetoric, be the most perfect science at that time, then it will be the fashionable one. Rhetoric and Logic or Dialectic were those undoubtedly which had made the greatest progress amongst the ancients, and indeed, if we except a little of Morals, were the only ones which had been tolerably cultivated. These, there-

[1] Reported by Plutarch, *Regum et Imperatorum Apophthegmata; Moralia*, 186 E; Loeb ed., *Moralia*, III, p. 100.       [2] *led*: reading uncertain.

fore, were the fashionable sciences, and every fashionable man would be desirous of being thought well skilled in them. Cicero therefore attempts, and has succeeded in the attempt, to display in all his writings a complete knowledge of these sciences. He adheres, however, so strictly to their rules, that had it not been looked on as a mark of ignorance not to be acquainted with every particular, nothing else could have induced him to it. In his oration in defence of Milo he has arguments drawn from all the three topics with regard to the cause; that is, that he had no motive to kill Clodius; that it was unsuitable to his character; and that he had no opportunity. These, one would have thought, could not take place in this case, and yet he goes through them all. He endeavours to show that he had no motive, though they had been squabbling and fighting every day—he had even declared his intention to kill him; that it was unsuitable to his character, although he had killed twenty men before; and that he had no opportunity, although we know he did kill him.

Although, however, a science that is come to considerable perfection be generally the fashionable one, yet it takes some time to establish it in that character. Antiquity is necessary to give anything a very high reputation as a matter of deep knowledge. One who reads a number of modern books, although they be very excellent, will not get thereby the character of a learned man: the acquaintance of the ancients will alone procure him the name. We see accordingly that Cicero, when Dialectic and Rhetoric were come to be sciences of considerable standing, is at great pains to display his knowledge in all their rules. Demosthenes, who lived at a time when they had no long standing in Greece, has no such affectation, but proceeds in the way which seemed most suitable to his subject.

The Peroration contains a short summary of the whole arguments advanced in the preceding part of the discourse, placed in such a way as naturally to lead to the conclusion proposed. To this the Roman orators generally added some arguments which might move the judge to decide in one way rather than in another, by either showing the enormity of the crime, if the person accused be his opponent, and setting it out in the most shocking manner; or, if he is a defendant, by mitigating the action and showing the severity of the punishment. This latter the Greeks never admitted of: the other is the natural conclusion of every discourse.

We have a great number of Greek orations still remaining. We have several of Lysias, a good number of Isæus, some of Antiphon, one of

Lycurgus, of [blank],[1] and also several of Aeschines, besides about forty-five of Demosthenes.[2] We need not take examples of the peculiar manner of each of these, as they are now but obscurely understood, at least the more ancient ones.

The Judicial orations of the Greeks may be considered of two sorts:—1st, those which they called public; and 2nd, the private ones. In the causes which regarded only the private affairs of an individual, it was not allowed for anyone to plead the cause but the party concerned. The patrons or clients of Rome were never established in Greece in any shape. The only cases wherein anyone but the person concerned was allowed to plead was where the party could not through sickness or other incapacity appear at the judgment of a cause, and when he who under-took it was a near relation of the persons, whose cause he plead [*sic*]: both these circumstances were necessary. The orator in this case, there-fore, did not pronounce the oration himself, but composed one to be delivered by the party concerned and adapted to his character and station. In the public ones, in which the community was some way concerned, the orator spoke in his own person. I shall give you examples of both of these manners from Isaeus, [blank][3] and Demosthenes, betwixt whom and Cicero I shall make a comparison.

Lysias[4] is the most ancient of all the orators whose works have come to our hands. He wrote private orations to be delivered by the persons concerned, and in these he studied to adapt them to the character of a simple good-natured man, not at all versed in the subtlety and chicane of the law. Isaeus was the disciple of Lysias, and the master of Demos-thenes. He seems to have had neither the fire of the latter nor the simplicity of the latter.[5] The character he studied in his orations, which were on private causes, as well as those of Lysias, was that of a plain, sensible, honest man, and to this his orations are very well adapted. He is said, however, to have resembled Lysias so much that many could not distinguish betwixt the style of the one and the other. Dionysius of Halicarnassus,[6] however, shews us several differences, and by what we can now judge of their style and language, it seems to have been still greater than he makes it. The exordium of their orations is much the

---

[1] Andocides and Dinarchus are the two most obvious omissions.

[2] In Smith's day about 16 were considered spurious; now, about 32 (of the total of 61).                                                    [3] Perhaps 'Lysias'.

[4] Antiphon is the most ancient of the orators whose works are extant.

[5] *Sic*: 'former' was probably meant.

[6] Dionysius of Halicarnassus, *De Antiquis Oratoribus: de Lysia, de Isaeo.*

same. They in it barely give us an account of the thing they are to prove, without any incentive arguments to either side. But their narrations are very different. There is [this]¹ so far alike in both, that they do not wrest or torture any matter of fact to make it suit their purpose, but deliver it as it really happened. But as Lysias studied the character of a simple man, so his narration is altogether suitable to that character. He introduces it barely² by telling the judges that they could understand it better on hearing the whole story. In the course of the narration he observes no order, but delivers the several facts in the same order as they occurred, and seems to tell the story as much to refresh his own memory as to inform his judges; and for the same reason he narrates not only those which are necessary to the cause, but those which are no ways connected with it. And as they are delivered in this disorderly method, so it would be unnatural for him to recapitulate them, and therefore in the conclusion he only draws an inference from the whole. Isaeus, on the other hand, in the character of a plain and sensible man, appears to have considered and weighed maturely his subject before he ventures to speak on it, and for this reason they are all classed in proper order and are excellently adapted to the subject he has in hand. He introduces his narration not only by telling that they will understand the cause the better if they heard the story, but specifies the particular points he intends it should illustrate, and introduces such facts only as tend to this end. And as they are delivered in this orderly manner, so he sums them up exactly and in order at the end. We may take as an example of his method his oration concerning³ the succession of Apollodorus. N.B. regard to dead and keeping up house. Pub. Off.

¹ *this*: conjectural addition.     ² *barely*: reading uncertain.
³ On the estate of Apollodorus, Speech 7; Loeb ed., pp. 245ff.

# 30

Friday, 18 February 1763

In the last lecture I mentioned to you that all the orations of the Greeks may be considered as of two sorts, viz. either the public or the private ones. The first,[1] though composed by orators who made that their profession, were nevertheless spoke by the persons themselves, and of consequence were adapted to the character of those persons. They are therefore generally adapted to the character of a plain or simple countryman who was not in the least acquainted with the niceties of the law. Of this sort I gave you an example from Isaeus. The character he endeavours to maintain is that of a plain, sensible man. Lysias, again, endeavours to appear in the character of a man of the greatest simplicity, such as we might expect in a countryman not acquainted with the more refined matters. The private orations of Demosthenes very much resemble those of Isaeus, as to the character kept up in them. He has not, however, the orderly arrangement of Isaeus in the several parts of his oration, but has in that point more of the manner of Lysias. And if you can conceive the plainness and sense [of Lysias][2] joined with the simplicity and elegance of Isaeus, you will have a complete notion of the private Judicial orations of Demosthenes.

Of public orations we have no such great number. There is one of Lycurgus,[3] and three of Aeschines,[4] and of all those of Demosthenes[3] that remain there are but three or four which appear to have been spoken by himself, if we except the Philippics, which are more properly Deliberative orations. Of these orations there are two in which Demosthenes and Aeschines accuse each other, as well as those wherein they make their defence. Those are περὶ [τοῦ] στεφάνου and περὶ [τῆς] παραπρεσβείας, which are two of the most perfect and noblest of any of

---

[1] *Sic.* Probably 'latter' was intended.
[2] conjectural addition.
[3] Lycurgus, *Against Leocrates*, in Loeb. ed., *Minor Attic Orators*, vol. II, pp. 14-133. Aeschines, *Against Timarchus*; *On the False Embassy*; *Against Ctesiphon*, Loeb pp. 4-511. Demosthenes, Speeches 18-24, of which that *Against Meidias* was not delivered. Smith's figure of three or four is too low.
[4] MS 'Aeschylus'; in margin, *Lege Aeschines semper*. The mistake is repeated often.

the Greek orations. That particularly of Demosthenes is the most instructive and most elegant of any wrote by him. In it he accuses Aeschines by name of great misconduct in the embassy he had been sent upon. In that περὶ [τοῦ] στεφάνου Aeschines directs his accusation against one Ctesiphon, who had proposed that a crown should be decreed to Demosthenes, but as the design of it is to prove that Demosthenes was unworthy of it, the greatest part of the oration is taken up with him. Neither of these orations produced what they were intended for. But that of Aeschines was still less successful than that of Demosthenes. It was a maxim at Athens that if one had not the fifth part of his judges on his side, who were very ignorant and generally easily influenced, he was to be accounted guilty of calumny, and suffer the punishment the accused would if he had been found guilty. Demosthenes, though he seems to have accused Aeschines unjustly, had nevertheless one-fifth of the judges, which Aeschines had not, and was accordingly banished.[1]

The manner of these two orators is considerably different. Aeschines has a certain gaiety and liveliness throughout all his works which we do not find in the other, who, though he has a great deal more of splendour than the former orators, has not near so much as Aeschines, and still less than Cicero. That disposition for mirth often takes away from the force of his orations in other points, and indeed is not at all fitted for raising any of those passions which are chiefly to be excited by oratory, viz. compassion and indignation. This we see is the case in many passages which were proper to have been described in the serious manner, in which he frequently introduces touches of humour which entirely prevent all that effect, and prevent either indignation or compassion from being excited, as nothing can be more contrary to those passions: but though they do not at all suit with grave parts, are admirably adapted to a genteel and easy railing, which appears to have been his peculiar excellence. His humour is always agreeable and polite, and such as we can attend to with great pleasure. Whereas Demosthenes, whenever he attempts to rally, runs into downright scurrility and abuse, and abuse such as we could never attend to with patience, as nothing can be more disagreeable than this coarse sort of raillery, were it not that the earnestness and sincerity of the orator is hereby displayed.

[1] The sentence is misleading. Ctesiphon, on trial, was acquitted by more than four-fifths of the votes. Since Aeschines, the prosecutor, had therefore less than one-fifth of the votes, he incurred (a) a fine; (b) partial disfranchisement (he could not bring a similar suit in future). He was not 'banished'; he was so mortified that he voluntarily left Athens. For the facts, see Goodwin's ed. of De Corona, p. 331.

As gaiety and levity appear in Aeschines' works, so does a certain austere severity and rigidity in those of Demosthenes. As it is very well adapted to feed and excite the more violent passions, so it indisposes him to humour and ridicule, and we see accordingly that when the best oportunities offered of rallying his adversary, he hardly ever takes advantage of them, though Aeschines never fails to turn them to the best account. This last-mentioned orator is so agreeable in this gay and entertaining temper, that even those parts which are in most cases the driest and dullest of any, as the division of the subject of his oration, are made as entertaining as we can well conceive anything of that sort would admit of. Thus in the division of that part of his oration[1] where he intends to show the misconduct of Demosthenes in his general conduct, he tells the judges that Demosthenes and his life might be divided into four periods, from one time to another, and so on; and that when he came to this part of his oration, Demosthenes was to ask him in which of these he was to accuse him of bad conduct, and that if he did not answer him he was to drag him to the forum and compel [him] to determine which it was, or else to give up his accusation. 'When he does this', says he, 'I will tell him that it is not against any of these particularly that my accusation is directed, but that I accuse him in them all together, and in them all equally'. This manner, though rather somewhat pert, is at the same time very entertaining, and would probably fix the division he was to follow in the minds of the judges.

But though Demosthenes may be inferior to his rival in some of those more trivial points, he has greatly the advantage over him in the more important and weighty parts of his orations. The severe and passionate temper which appears in his works is admirably adapted to the graver and serious parts, which alone are capable of raising the passions of compassion and indignation: which latter particularly all his orations tend greatly to excite. His Judicial orations in most points indeed resemble his Deliberative ones, excepting that we find in the latter more eloquence and passion than is the case with all other authors. For as the subject of Deliberative orations is politics or something nearly allied to it, the object of this must be the concerns [sic] of a whole people, at a debate concerning peace or war, etc. which, though very important, will never affect the passions so highly as the distress of a single person or indignation against the crimes of an individual. When Aeschines enters upon these subjects, he often misses the effect by the

[1] *Against Ctesiphon*, 54-6.

interruption of some stroke of raillery, as that[1] where he represents
Demosthenes hopping into the market place, through grief that he had
received none of the money which was distributed amongst the Thebans.
And when he sets himself purposely to affect the passions in a high
degree, he generally runs into bombast, as we see in the exclamation
[blank] ⟨and several other passages.⟩ Those actors who enter least into
their parts are observed to use more grimace and gesticulation than
those who are greatly affected by what they act, for whatever is affected
is found always to be overdone. This is the case with Aeschines; his
temper was not adapted to gravity, or anyway greatly affected by those
things which would stir up the passions of more earnest men; so that
whenever he attempts anything of this sort he always outdoes. In all
such more interesting events, Aeschines has generally little more than
common-place remarks, and such incidents as happen on every such-like
occasion. Thus in the description he gives[2] of the taking of Thebes, one
of the most important events that happened about that time, he dwells
greatly on the carrying the old men into captivity, the rape of the virgins
and matrons, and other such like, which happen on the taking of every
city: whereas Demosthenes, in describing the taking of Elatea[3] and the
confusion this occasioned all Athens, though the event was of much
less moment and the danger which threatened Athens was still at a
distance,—yet, I say, he points out the several circumstances of the
confusion, the crowd which gathered at the Forum, how everyone looked
on the others in expectation that they had discovered some expedient
which had escaped him, etc. etc. and in such an interesting manner and
with circumstances so peculiar to the event, that it is highly interesting
and striking, etc.

However, as no one is altogether perfect, it is greatly to be suspected
that Demosthenes has not divided his orations in the most happy order,
a talent which Aeschines and Cicero have possessed in a very high
degree. There is in all his orations a confusion in the order of the
argument and the different parts it consists of, which will appear to
anyone on the slightest attention. Dionysius of Halicarnassus, a critic
of great penetration, but whose observations appear sometimes to be
rather nice and refined than solid, would persuade us that this confusion
is merely apparent, and that the order he has chosen is the most happy
he could possibly have hit upon. But as far as I can see there is not only

[1] *Against Ctesiphon*, 149.
[2] *Against Ctesiphon*, 157ff.    [3] *De Corona*, 169ff.

an apparent but a real confusion. Thus in the oration περὶ [τῆς] παραπρεσβείας he begins his oration with telling the people that there were five things[1] which a people had to expect from an ambassador, and these he repeats in order. One should expect from this that he was to begin with the 1st, and having discussed it, proceed to the 2nd; from that to the 3rd; and so on. But of this we find nothing through the whole. He begins at the first to give us a narration of the whole story as it happened, and though we might perhaps reduce all that he has thrown together in that oration to one or other of these, yet they are not all classed in that order, but told in the very order they happened; and from the whole it appears most probable that this division was added after the oration was wrote, and that when he began it he had no thought of dividing it; but finding before he got to the conclusion that it would be difficult to observe at what the several parts pointed, he has afterwards prefixed the division, to point out what the hearers were chiefly to consider in the oration.

Aeschines, on the other hand, is very happy in his divisions, and, as I said before, attains in them a perfection very seldom met with, as he renders them even entertaining, and to these divisions he adheres very strictly. The best apology we can make for Demosthenes in this defect, is that his eagerness, vehemence, and passion have hurried him on, both in speaking and writing, to deliver the several parts of his oration in the manner they affected him most, without considering in what manner they would give the hearer or reader the clearest notion of what he delivers. ⟨And we see this accordingly is most remarkably the case in those orations which he himself delivered, and in which he was most interested.⟩

The characters of these two orators were, we are informed, very agreeable to that which we would be apt to form from the consideration of their writings. Aeschines, who was bred a player, an employment as creditable at that time as it is discreditable now,[2] had all the mirth, gaiety, and levity which we find in most of his profession. This temper made his company be greatly sought after by all the young people of

[1] Demosthenes, *De Falsa Legatione*, 4.
[2] Smith, with the Principal and two other professors of the University, took part in an effort by the Senatus to prevent a theatre from being established in Glasgow. The agitation was still active when Smith resigned his Chair, 1764. In that year the mob, instigated by a preacher, set fire to the new theatre. Cf. Rae, *Life*, pp. 79-81. Smith's views had undergone a change by the time he wrote *Wealth of Nations*, Bk. v, ch. 1, art. 111.

his time, as he himself tells us,[1] and Demosthenes throws [this] up to
him as being no way to his honour.[2] He seems also to have had a good
deal of the mimic about him[3] and there are some passages in the oration
above-mentioned which are evidently intended to mimic Demosthenes,
and must have been delivered with his tone and gesture. This talent
of mimicry recommended him to the favour and patronage of Philip,
who, we are told, was extremely delighted with all sorts of mimics and
buffoons.

Demosthenes, on the other hand, was of an austere and rigid disposition, which made him not be affected with anything which was not
of importance; but at the same time his vehemence made him enter into
everything which was of any moment with the greatest warmth, and
prosecute those who seemed to deserve his indignation. This temper
made [him] not much entertained with common conversation, as there
are but few things of importance generally canvassed in it, and at the
same time not be much desired as a companion, as men of this character
can neither be much entertained by others or be very entertaining. He
therefore lived for the most part shut up in his own house, seeing, and
being seen by, very few. He spent much of his time in the study of the
Stoic and Platonic philosophy, to the latter of which he seems to have
been most addicted. He has in most of his passionate and animated
passages many of the sentiments of those philosophers, particularly in
that where he introduced the famous oath mentioned in Longinus.[4]
And there [are] many passages which resemble Plato so much even in
the expression that I have been often tempted to believe that he had
copied them from him. I should have given you a translation of these
two orations[5] were it not that they are both of them very long and
could not be abridged without losing greatly in their merit. I would,
however, recommend them greatly to your perusal, as they are not
only excellent in their way, but also as they give us a very good
abridgement of the history of Greece for a period of considerable
length.

There are several other Greek orators whose works are still remaining, but as they are but little read and are generally in private causes,

---

[1] *Against Ctesiphon,* 216; *Against Timarchus,* 135.
[2] Demosthenes says nothing about this. Aeschines states that Demosthenes made
it a reproach against him.
[3] For Aeschines as actor, cf. *De Corona,* 180, 262; *De Falsa Legatione,* 246-7.
[4] Longinus, *On the Sublime,* 14, 2, quoting Demosthenes, *De Corona,* 208.
[5] i.e. *De Corona* and *De Falsa Legatione.*

which are commonly not the most entertaining, I shall pass them over altogether, and proceed to make some observations on Cicero, and the differences betwixt his manner and that of Demosthenes.[1]

I have already pointed out some of the differences betwixt those two great orators, which appear to me to proceed chiefly from the different conditions and genius of their two nations. I shall now observe more particularly those which proceed from the differences of character and circumstances of the men themselves.

There is no character in antiquity with which we are better acquainted than that of Cicero, which is evidently displayed in all his works, and in particular must receive great light from his epistles. But we may perhaps discover more of the real spirit and turn of his writings by considering his natural temper, his education, and the genius of the times he lived in, than from the observations of his critics. But although these men have a very extraordinary knack at mistaking his meaning, yet they have not been able to err so greatly with respect to his character, so clearly does it shine out (as the sun now does) through all his writings. He seems to have by nature had, along with a great degree of sensibility and natural parts, a considerable share of vanity and ostentation. Sensibility is without doubt a most amiable character, and one which is of all others most engaging. We may, therefore, with justice make some allowance if it be joined with some failing. Now there are no two tempers of mind which are so often combined as levity in a certain proportion and a great degree of sensibility. The same temper which disposes one to partake in the joys or misfortunes of others, or to be much affected with one's own, is naturally connected with a disposition that makes one both easily buoyed up by the smallest circumstances of the pleasant kind and depressed with those which are in the least distressing, and at the same time prompts them to communicate their feelings with others, no less at the one time than at the other. One who is of a joyous temper turns everything that happens to him into an object of pleasure, and dwells on the most minute circumstances, and is no less inclined to communicate it to others. If it happens that he has nothing which immediately calls for any exertion of this happy temper, his happy condition becomes an object of his joy, he looks on himself and his condition with a certain complacence, and his joy becomes the object of his joy.

[1] See Quintilian, x, 1, 105ff. for a similar comparison; and also Longinus, *On the Sublime*, 12, 4. Smith probably knew also Fénelon's comparison; cf. *A Letter to the French Academy* (Glasgow, Foulis, 1750), pp. 182-3.

P

FRIDAY 18 FEBRUARY

The same disposition which makes him communicate his joy at other times and expatiate on the agreeableness of certain things around, makes him now dwell upon himself and be continually talking about the happiness of his circumstances and the joy of his own mind. A morose or melancholy man, on the other hand, takes everything in the worst light, and finds something in it which depresses him, and when nothing occurs which can give him any real distress, his own unhappiness becomes his vexation. He continually dwells on the misery of his own disposition, which thus turns everything to his misery. He talks of himself no less than the joyous man, and as the one dwells on the happiness of his condition, so he insists on the misery of his.

A man of great sensibility, in the same manner, who enters much into the happiness or distress either of himself or others, is no less inclined to display these sensations to others, and in this way will frequently talk of himself, and frequently with a good deal of vanity and ostentation. We see that the women, who are generally thought to have a good deal more of levity and vanity in their temper, are at the same time acknowledged to have more sensibility and compassion in their temper than the men. The French nation, who have more levity and vanity than most others, are reckoned to be the most humane and charitable of any.

Cicero seems in the same way to have been possessed of a very high degree of sensibility, and to have been very easily depressed or elated by the misfortunes or prosperity of his friends or of himself ⟨as his letters to them evidently show, where he enters entirely into their misfortunes, etc.⟩ Which levity of temper, though it might indispose him for public business and render him somewhat unsettled in his behaviour, would nevertheless be of no small advantage to him as a speaker. ⟨Men of the greatest calmness and prudence are not generally the most sensible and compassionate.⟩ It would also make him a very agreeable and pleasant companion, and dispose him frequently to mirth and joviality. We are told accordingly that his apophthegms or sayings were no less esteemed than his orations. Volumes of them were handed about in his lifetime, and his servant Tiro published seven volumes[1] of them after his death. We may reasonably suppose that one of this temper would be very susceptible of all the different passions, but of none more than of

[1] Cicero's apophthegmata published by Tiro are mentioned by Quintilian, VI, 3, 5, and Macrobius, *Saturnalia*, II, I, 12. Quintilian says there were only three books. For their being handed about in Cicero's lifetime, see his letter, *Ad Familiares*, IX, 16, 4.

pity and compassion, which accordingly appears to have been that which chiefly affected him.

Cicero lived at a time when learning had been introduced into Rome, and was indeed but just then introduced. It was in very high reputation, and as novelty generally enhances the value of a thing, it was perhaps more highly esteemed than it deserved, and than it was afterwards when they became better acquainted with it. Rhetoric and Dialectic were the sciences which had then arrived to the greatest perfection, and were the most fashionable study amongst all the polite men of Rome. Their Dialectic was pretty much the same with that of Aristotle, though somewhat altered and improved by the Stoics, who cultivated it more than the Peripatetics. Their Rhetoric was that of Hermagoras,[1] which I have already touched upon. To these studies Cicero applied himself with great assiduity till the age of twenty-five. He tells that he disputed under the inspection of some of the most renowned masters several hours every day. After this, having appeared in two or three causes, one of which was that of Roscius[2] of Ameria, and gained no little reputation as a speaker, he went over into Greece, where he stayed about two years. This time he employed in attending the harangues and discourses of the most celebrated orators and philosophers of the time, under whose direction he wrote and delivered harangues and orations of all sorts. The eloquence then in fashion in Greece had deviated a good deal from the simplicity and easiness of Demosthenes, but still retained a great deal of familiarity and homeliness, which was unknown in the pleadings at Rome, for the reasons I have already pointed out. When he returned from his travels[3] he found a more florid and splendid style to be fashionable at Rome than what he had met with at Athens or the other parts of Greece, and Hortensius, the most celebrated orator of his time, was more florid and used more of the splendour and grandeur then esteemed than any other. We would naturally expect of a man of this temper, this education, and in these circumstances, the very conduct that Cicero has followed in his works. We should expect that he would aim at that splendour and dignity of expression which was then fashionable, though contrary to the familiar method which was esteemed in Greece. We may expect that he will be at considerable pains to display his knowledge in those sciences

---

[1] Cf. Cicero, *Brutus*, 263, 271, *De Inventione*, 1, 8, 12, 16, 97. Cicero thought him of little help in acquiring a polished style, but full of precepts useful for providing arguments for any kind of debate.

[2] *Pro Roscio Amerino*, which won the acquittal of Sextus Roscius.

[3] 76 B.C. Hortensius and Cotta were the other leading advocates at Rome.

which were then in highest repute; that we will find in [his] orations the whole of those parts which were reckoned proper to the form of a regular oration—a regular exordium, narration wherever the subject will admit of it, a proof, a confutation, and peroration, all regularly marked out. We might expect also that he would even sometimes adhere to the rhetorical divisions and topics where they appeared to be very unsuitable to the cause in hand, as we saw in his oration for Milo. We may expect also that one of this cast, as his temper naturally leads him to compassion, will be more inclined to undertake a defence than to accuse, which we see was the case; and when he has been necessitated to accuse, he will insist rather on the misfortunes of the injured than on the guilt of the offender, as we see he does in his orations *In Verrem*, where he dwells chiefly on the misfortune of some of the oppressed Syracusans, etc., touching but little on the crimes of the Praetor. We may expect, too, that he would have some part of his oration where he would purposely endeavour to move the compassion of the judges towards the injured persons. This he generally places in places immediately before the peroration, which is much preferable to one placed nearer the beginning, for compassion even when strongest is but a short-lived passion, so that the whole influence of it would be lost if it was placed near the beginning, before the time came where it was to produce its effect.

[Blank] observes that Cicero generally draws the attention of the reader from the cause to himself, and though we admire the orator, we do not reap great instruction with regard to the cause. This observation, so far as it is just, proceeds from the digressions which Cicero introduces in many parts of his orations to raise the passions of his audience, though sometimes they do not tend to explain the cause.

Demosthenes was very different from this, both in natural temper and the genius of the country. He was of an austere temper which was not easily moved but by things of a very important nature, and in all cases his indignation rose much higher than his compassion. His earnestness makes him hurry on from one thing to another without attending to any particular order. Logic or Dialectic was not then, nor was it or Rhetoric ever, in such high reputation as they were afterwards at Rome, and accordingly we find no traces of their divisions in his orations. He frequently has no exordium, at least none distinctly marked from the narration; and the other parts are in like manner blended together. The florid and splendid does not appear in his works: a more easy and familiar one was more esteemed in his time. The passion which animates him in all his orations is indignation, and this, as it is a more lasting passion than compassion, he often begins with and continues through a whole oration. The free and easy manner of the Greeks would not admit of any such peroration designed to move the passions as those we meet with in Cicero, and it is not accordingly to be met with in any of the Greek orators. Upon the whole Cicero is more apt to draw our pity and love, and Demosthenes to raise our indignation. The one is strong and commanding, the other persuasive and moving. The character Quintilian gives of Cicero entirely corresponds with this. . . .

Of all the immense number of orators who are numerated in Quintilian, none have come down to us excepting Cicero. With regard to those who preceded him and were his contemporaries, we surely may regret the loss; but as to those who came after him, they are perhaps as well buried in oblivion as if they had remained to perplex us. We see that even Cicero introduces in his orations several digressions which tended merely to amuse the judges, without in the least explaining the cause. This became the universal and ordinary practice after his time, insomuch that there were fixt places where these digressions were introduced. There was one betwixt the narration and the proof, of which I can see no design unless it was to make the judge forget what they were to prove. There was another betwixt the proof and the confutation, and another betwixt that and the peroration, for which I can see no purpose but the same as the former. The whole of their oration was also filled with figures, as they called them, no less useless than these digressions. We may see how far this was come so soon after Cicero's time as that of Tiberius, by this story of one [Albucius].[1] He, when pleading against one [Arruntius], offered to refer it to his oath, which he accepted. 'But', says he, 'you must swear by the ashes of your father, which are unburied, etc.' and so on, laying all sorts of crimes to his charge. The man accepted the conditions, but [Albucius] refused to allow him to swear, saying that it was only a figure. But when the man insisted on his standing to his word, he told them if that was the case there would be an end of all figures. [Arruntius] told him he believed men could live without them, and still insisted on the oath being put to him, which the judges agreed to. But [Albucius] was so enraged at his figures being thus laid hold on,

[1] The story is told most fully in Seneca the Elder, *Controversiae*, VII, praef. 6-8; referred to in Quintilian, IX, 2, 95, and in Suetonius, *De Grammaticis et Rhetoribus*, 30.

that he swore he should never appear at the bar for the future. He kept his word, and we are told he used to brag that he had more hearers at his house listening to his declamations on feigned causes than others had at their pleadings on real ones. In a short time their orations came to be nothing but a string of digressions and figures of this sort, one after another, so that we need not wonder at what Quintilian informs us of,[1] that there were many orations delivered for which the pleader was highly commended, when at the same time no one could tell on which side of the cause he was. We need not, therefore, regret much the loss of these latter orations.

I shall now give ye some account of the state of the Judicial eloquence of England, which is very different from that either of Greece or of Rome. This difference is generally ascribed to the small progress which has been made in the cultivation of language and style in this country, compared with that which it had arrived to in the Old World. But [though] this may be true in some degree, yet I imagine there are other causes which must make them essentially different. The eloquence which is now in greatest esteem is a plain, distinct, and perspicuous style, without any of the floridity or other ornamental parts of the Old Eloquence. This and other differences must necessarily arise from the nature of the country and the particular turn of the people. The Courts were then much in the same manner as the Jury is now. They were men unskilled in the law, whose office continued but for a very short time, and were often in a great part chosen for the trial of that particular cause, and not from any particular set of men, but only by ballot and rotation from the whole body of the people, and of them there was always no inconsiderable number. The Judges in England, on the other hand, are single men who have been bred to the law, and have generally, or at least are supposed to have, a thorough knowledge of the law, and are much versed in all the different circumstances of cases, of which they have attended many before, either as judges or pleaders, and are supposed to be acquainted with all the different arguments that may be advanced on it. This therefore cuts them out from a great part of the substance of the old orations. There can here be no room for a narration, the only design of which is, by interweaving those facts for which proof can be brought with those for which no proof can be brought, that these latter may gain credit by their connection with the others. But as nothing is now of any weight for which direct proof is not brought, this sort of

[1] I have not found this reference.

narration could serve no end. The pleader, therefore, can do no more than tell over what facts he is to prove, which may often be very unconnected. The only case, indeed, when he can give a complete narration of the whole transaction, is when he has [a] witness who has been present through the whole, which can happen but very rarely. ⟨And if he should assert anything for a fact, as the old orators frequently did, for which he can bring no proof, he would be severely reprimanded.⟩ The pleader has here no opportunity of smoothing over any argument which would make against him, as the judge will perceive it and pay no regard to what he advances in this manner. Nor can he conceal any weak side by placing it betwixt two on which he depends for the proof of it, as this would be soon perceived. All these were particularly directed by the ancient rhetoricians. The inattention and ignorance of the judges was the sole foundation of it: as this is not now to be expected, they can be of no service. The pleader must be much more close than those of ancient R[ome] and G[reece], and we find that those pleaders are most esteemed who point out the subject in the clearest and distinctest manner, and endeavour to give the judge a fair idea of the cause.

The great popular assembly is a great object which strikes the speaker at first with awe and dread, but as they begin to be moved by the cause, and the speaker himself to be interested in it, they then animate him and embolden him. The confusion which he will perceive amongst them will give him courage and rouse his passions. A single judge is but a single man, and he, attended with a pitiful jury, can neither strike much awe nor animate the passions. Florid speakers are not at all in esteem. One who was to storm and thunder before five or six persons would be taken for a fool or a madman, though the same behaviour before a great assembly of people would appear very proper and suitable to the occasion. It might perhaps seem that the House of Lords, which consists of a considerable number, might give an opportunity of being more animated and passionate. But in most private causes there are not above thirty of them together. For State trials, indeed, they are all met, but then the great order and decorum which is kept up then gives no opportunity for expatiating. In all the State Trials which have been published, those speeches were most commended which proceeded in the most natural and plain order, and if ever one brings in anything that may appear designed to move the passions, it must be only by-the-bye, a hint and no more. The order and decorum of behaviour which is now in fashion will not admit of any the least extravagances. The behaviour

191

which is reckoned polite in England is a calm, composed, unpassionate serenity,[1] noways ruffled by passion. Foreigners observe that there is no nation in the world which use so little gesticulation in their conversation as the English. A Frenchman, in telling a story that was not of the least consequence to him or to anyone else, will use a thousand gestures and contortions of his face, whereas a well-bred Englishman will tell you one in which his life and fortune are concerned, without altering a muscle in his face. Montain,[2] in some [one] of his essays, tells us that he had seen the same opera acted before both an English and an Italian audience: the difference of their behaviour, he says, was very remarkable. At the time when the one would be dying away in ecstasies of pleasure, the other would not appear to be the least moved. This is attributed by that judicious Frenchman to their want of sensibility and ignorance of music. But in this he seems to be mistaken, for if there is any art thoroughly understood in England, it is music.[3] The lower sort often evidence a great accuracy of judgement in it, and the better sort often display a thorough and most masterly knowledge of it. The real cause is the different idea of politeness.

The Spaniard's notion of politeness is a majestic, proud, and over-bearing philosophic gravity. The Frenchman, again, places it in an easy gaiety, affableness, and sensibility. Politeness, again, in England, consists in composure, calm and unruffled behaviour. The most polite persons are those only who go to the opera, and any emotions would there be reckoned altogether indecent. And we see that, when the same persons go out of [sic] frolic to a bear-garden or such like ungentlemanly entertainment, they preserve the same composure as before at the Opera, while the rabble about express all the various passions by their gesture and behaviour.

We are not then to expect that anything passionate or exaggerated will be admitted in the House of Lords. Nothing will be received there which is not, or at least appears not to be, a plain, just, and exact account. The pleadings, for this reason, of the most celebrated speakers, appear to us to be little more than the heads of a discourse, as we are

---

[1] *serenity*: reading uncertain.

[2] *Sic*: Montesquieu; the passage is in *L'Esprit des Lois*, Bk. XIV, ch. 2. 'J'ai vu les opéras d'Angleterre et d'Italie; ce sont les mêmes pièces, et les mêmes acteurs; mais la même musique produit des effets si differens sur les deux nations, l'une si calme et l'autre si transportée, que cela paroît inconcevable' (*Oeuvres*, II, p. 36, London 1769). Montesquieu seems to say nothing about the ignorance of music.

[3] Smith also objects in his Lectures on Jurisprudence to this criticism of the English as not musical.

here accustomed with a more loose way of pleading. If, however, under this appearance of plainness and candidness, the pleader can artfully interweave something which favours his side, the effect may often be very great.

The Lords in their speeches to one another always observe the same rules of decorum, and if anything of passion be hinted at, it must be a hint only. We see that those who have made great figures as speakers in the House of Commons, where a very loose manner and often a great deal of ribaldry and abuse is admitted of, lost this character when transferred to the Upper House. For though they were sensible that the manner they had been accustomed to was not at all proper there, yet it was not in their power to lay it aside all at once. Many of the speeches of the State Trials must have had a great deal of their effect from the delivery and emphasis with which the different heads—for little more can be admitted of—were delivered. That of Atterbury,[1] which is spoken of with rapture by all who heard it, appears to us confused and un-animated, though it certainly produced a wonderful effect on the hearers.

Floridity and splendour has always been disliked. Mr Robert Walpole's speech on [blank] was, for its being somewhat of this sort, called by way of derision an 'oration'.

I shall only observe further on this head that the idea of English eloquence hinted at here is very probably a just one, as the two most admired orators, Lord Mansfield and Sir Wm. Pym,[2] spoke exactly in the same manner, though very distant in their time. The former, how-ever, is to us more agreeable on account of the language, and is without doubt greatly more perspicuous and orderly.

[1] Atterbury was generally supposed to have written the speech made by Dr Sacheverell at his trial. The text is in *Epistolary Correspondence*, etc. of Atterbury, vol. III, pp. 456ff (1784).

[2] *Sic*. Probably an error for 'John' Pym.

# Appendix

DESCRIPTION OF THE MANUSCRIPT OF ADAM SMITH'S LECTURES ON
RHETORIC

*by* T. I. RAE

The manuscript is in two volumes, each measuring 120 × 195 mm., bound in a contemporary binding of quarter leather and marbled paper; on the spine of each volume has been written in ink the words 'Notes of Dr. Smith's Rhetorick Lectures' with the volume number. The first volume contains 202 ff., the second, 256 ff., excluding the end papers which contain no writing. The first 16 ff. volume i are written on small paper of fairly good quality (103 × 165 mm.) and the next 42 ff. on larger but thinner paper (113 × 183 mm.); the remainder of the volume, and all of volume ii (except ff. 69-76, 90-1) is written on a uniform-sized paper (120 × 195 mm.) with the watermark 'L.V. Gerrevink' and a crown supported by a shield.

In the first volume are 14 lectures, delivered between 19 November and 24 December 1762, numbered from 2 to 14; two lectures numbered 4 occur on ff. 37 and 49. The second volume contains 15 lectures delivered between 26 December 1762 and 18 February 1763.

The writing of the text is mainly on one side of the paper only, the other side being used for notes and comments; some of these are in the hand of the writer of the text, others in what appears to be another hand or, possibly, the same hand at a later date. The writing, the gaps in the text, and the existence of certain comments, seem to suggest that these are the original notes written at speed in the lecture room, and not a fair copy. The difference in the sizes of the paper, on which the text is written continuously, indicates that the student wrote on loose pieces of paper folded up into gatherings, which were later bound up into the two volumes. Each gathering generally consists of 4 leaves, and was numbered by the writer before being bound.

Collation: $1-13^4$, $14^2$, $15-51^4$ [vol. i]; $52-73^4$, $74^4$ (a bifolium added after 1), $75-93^4$, $94^6$, $95-114^4$ [vol. ii].

# INDEX

noblemen, 152; complimentary manners, 153; order of Courts better than at Athens, 173; greater stability of Roman republic, 173; long-continued grandeur, 173
Rosa, Salvator: addition of human interest to landscapes, 66, 67
Rousseau, J. J.: difficulty over 'generalised' words, 8

Sallust: description of Catiline, 74, 76; preface of common-place morality, 86; *Jugurthan War*, 87; treatment of Catiline conspiracy, 87; defective and commonplace in descriptions, 105; aptness of expressions and variety of speeches, 106; copies one of Demosthenes' Olynthian orations, 147
Sanazzaro: wearisome parody of ancient Latin poets, 42
Sancho Panza: speaks in figures, 30; why we can laugh at him, 120
Saxe, Count Hermann Maurice de: character, 75
Scarron: *Virgil Travesti*, 41, 42
School philosophy: displeased Shaftesbury, 53
Scott, W. R.: *Adam Smith as Student and Professor*, quoted on Rhetoric lectures, xx
Sempronian Law: took away Senate's power of capital punishment, 156
Shaftesbury, Ashley Cooper, Earl of: style obscure, 5, 6; superflouus words, 34; admired for non-colloquial style, 38; character and style, 52–7; Theocles (in *The Moralists*) a more polite Socrates, 55; humour in *Characteristics: A Rhapsody*, 56; method in *Inquiry into Nature of Virtue*, 136
Shakespeare, William: confusion of metaphors, 27; Hamlet's soliloquies parodied, 42; indirect description in *King Lear*, 60; descriptions more animated than Spenser's, 63; often uses contradictory epithets, 73; grave-diggers break unity of *Hamlet*, 117; breaks unity of time, 118; of place, 119; vast variety of characters, 122; breaches of decorum and propriety, 122; *Othello*, 125
Shenstone, William: his pastorals, 123
Sheridan, Thomas: lectures under auspices of Select Society, xxxv
Smith, Adam: Cannan's edition of *Lectures on Jurisprudence*, xii; new Manuscripts of Jurisprudence, and Rhetoric and Belles Lettres, xii; previous accounts of Rhetoric lectures, xiii; contribution to first Edinburgh Review, xiv–xv; summary of contents of Rhetoric lectures, xvii–xix; object of, xvii; Smith's characteristics revealed, xix; speaks without notes sometimes,

xix; absent-mindedness, xix–xx; influence of, xxi–xxiii
Socrates: ridiculous in Aristophanes' *Clouds*, 40; imitated by Shaftesbury's Theocles, 55; points out his transitions, 55; his method, 140, 141; contrast with Aristotelian, 141; when to be used, 141; condemned not because guilty but for haughtiness to judges, 175
Somerville, Dr Thomas: on Stevenson's lectures, xxvi; on change in pulpit oratory, xxxiii
Sopists: use of descriptions by the later, 60
Sophocles: observes unity of place, 119
Spaniards: notion of politeness, 192
Spenser, Edmund: his descriptions direct and less animated than Shakespeare's, 63
Stevenson, John, Professor of Logic: teaches Belles Lettres and Criticism, xxv–xxix; theses written for his class, xxvii
style: to be suited to author and circumstances, 30, 31; contrast of orator or didactic writer and historian, 31; historian's rare use of exclamation in his own person, 32; the plain and the simple, 32, 33; Swift's and Temple's, 34, 35; beauty of style, 36; affected by character of author, 35, 36; differences between spoken and written, 38; requirement of a good writer, 38; the perfection of, 51; what agreeable in, 51, 52; composition, 58 seq.; narration of facts, 60; style makes disagreeable agreeable, 60, 61; description, 61; new objects not agreeable by newness, 61; indirect description best, 63; though more difficult, 64; rules for description, 67, 71; unity of emotional effect, 67; human interest required, 67; 'nice' details to be given, 67; not to be long, 68; description of objects, 69; order of simultaneous objects, 70; of objects in time-sequence, 70; of contrived objects, of man-made objects, 70; minute detail necessary in objects from nature, 71; internal objects best described by effects, 71; rules for descriptions, 71, 72; direct description of complex objects, characters, actions, 74; indirect description of character, 76; comparative merits of methods of character-writing, 77, 78; descriptions of complex actions, 80; Livy's method, 81; deep grief best told simply, 82; narrative and rhetorical styles distinguished, 84; history essentially actions of men, 85; contrasts rhetorician and historian, 96; dissertations, 97; reflections in history-writing, 98; varied repetition in oratory, 113; repetition disagreeable in poetry, 114; licence to story-tellers, 114, 115; in what unity of